SUCCESSFUL COLD-CLIMATE GARDENING

Cold-Climate Gardening

*How to Extend Your Growing Season
by at Least 30 Days*

BY LEWIS HILL

Illustrations by Kathleen Kolb

A Garden Way Publishing Book

Storey Communications, Inc.
Pownal, Vermont 05261

Cover photograph by Walter Chandoha
Cover design and production by Wanda Harper
The drawings on pages 96 and 116 are by Judy Eliason
Typesetting by Yankee Typesetters, Inc., Concord, New Hampshire
Printed in the United States by Murray Printing Company,
    Westford, Massachusetts
First printing, December 1986

Library of Congress Cataloging-in-Publication Data

Hill, Lewis, 1924–
    Cold-climate gardening.

    "A Garden Way Publishing book."
    Originally published: Successful cold-climate
gardening. Brattleboro, Vt. : S. Greene Press, 1981.
    Includes index.
    1. Gardening—Northeastern States.   2. Gardening—
Northwestern States.   3. Gardening—Canada.   I. Title.

SB453.H654   1987   635'.097   86–45712

ISBN 0–88266–441–7 (pbk.)
ISBN 0–88266–449–2

To OUR STIMULATING FRIENDS AND
NEIGHBORS WHO INSPIRED THIS PROJECT—
BOTH YEAR-ROUND RESIDENTS AND
THOSE WHO "SUMMER" IN THE NORTH.

TABLE OF CONTENTS

Introduction   ix

PART I   *Gardening in the North*

1. The Challenges of Climate and Weather   3
2. Getting the Most Out of the Growing Season   16
3. How to Lengthen the Growing Season   39

PART II   *Growing Food in the North*

4. Growing Vegetables   77
5. Tree Fruits   121
6. The Berry Patch   150
7. Grapes for the North   177
8. Growing Nuts in the North   185
9. Perennial Foods and Herbs   193
10. Grains   205

PART III   *Landscaping in the North*

11. Planning and Planting   215
12. Shade Trees and Evergreens   226
13. Ornamental Shrubs   246
14. Growing Flowers in the North   262
15. Hedges for the North   275
16. Lawns   285
17. Ground Covers and Vines   292

Appendix   301

Recommended Reading   301
Publishers of Garden Books   302
Seed Companies   303
Oriental Vegetables for Winter Gardens   303
Old-Time Seed Varieties   303
Nurseries   304
Sources of Fruit Tree Scions for Grafting   304
Evergreen Seedlings Nurseries   304
Greenhouse and Solar Materials   305

Index   305

INTRODUCTION

"I've just planted a dozen peach trees," one of my northern neighbors told me on a sunny spring morning.

"I wish you had talked to me first," I said sadly.

"Well," he said. "I would have, but I was afraid you'd talk me out of it. The catalog said they were hardy way up in Canada, but I wrote to the company anyway, to be sure, and they said the trees definitely would grow here. Tell you what, in two or three years I'll invite you over for some fresh peach ice cream."

Five years later there has been no further mention of trees, fruit, and no invitation for ice cream.

This episode made me realize how difficult it is to be realistic with northern gardeners. Too many times they don't want the harsh facts, only encouragement. Each year we get calls and visits from excited people who want to grow acres of grapes, apricots, Red Delicious apples, Carpathian walnuts, or landscape their homes with climbing roses, dogwood, or forsythia. The last thing they want to hear is any reason for not doing it. In spite of my pessimistic forecast, many go ahead and invest a lot of money, work, and time in this kind of planting. They often lose everything and still feel that the crop failed because of something they did wrong. I'm not sure why it is so difficult for many of us to accept the limitations of our climate and to work within those limits.

Northerners are accustomed to wisecracks about the climate. Summer here is reputed to occur on a Tuesday. An average year consists of eight months of winter plus four of poor sledding. Yankees are suspected of freezing up their old folks and burying them in a snowbank in October, then thawing them out in May.

Newcomers to our area often remark that we talk far too much about the weather, but after they have lived here for a few months, they do the same. We talk about weather because it figures heavily in our day-to-day lives. Schools and meetings are frequently canceled when storms make traveling dangerous or impossible. Our plans from November through April are usually made conditional upon blizzards, ice storms, or the unpredictable arrival of the mud season.

We not only talk about our weather a lot, but we frequently grumble about it. An unexpectedly heavy overnight snowfall can smash down limbs and greenhouses. Forty-degree-below-zero (F) temperatures may freeze the water pipes and kill our favorite trees; and we frequently cover the tomato plants to protect them from a late August frost. One New England farmer told me he calculated that 99.44 percent of his time and energy was spent getting ready for winter, getting over winter, or struggling against it. He is the same man who said that some days it's hard to rejoice over a south wind because just as often as not it is only the north wind coming back.

In spite of the climate, we've chosen to live here, just as you have. The North is healthy and invigorating. We frequently meet families new to the area who have forsaken longer growing seasons and milder winters because they, also, prefer the cool, crisp air, the clean white snow, the brilliant green grass and leaves, the deep blue skies and lakes, and the bright autumn colors.

No scorpions, rattlesnakes, or black widow spiders lurk among our cabbages, nor are there water moccasins or alligators in our clear running streams. A summer heat wave or a drought seldom burns our lawns or stops our garden from growing. Tornados, hurricanes, or floods almost never force us to flee; and fortunately many of the worst weeds and insects choose not to share our climate.

Some of our friends in the South occasionally joke about our attempts to garden on the fringe of the Arctic Circle, but their sympathy is unnecessary. Over the past two centuries Northerners have discovered how to grow a wide variety of useful plants successfully, even if our climate does at times resemble a giant icebox.

This book has been written to share with you some of the things we have learned about coping with our unusual climate. I hope you will use it in conjunction with some of the gardening literature listed in the appendix, because this book is not intended to be a complete course in growing the various crops described here. Rather, I've tried to show how to adapt their culture to the unusual growing conditions of the North.

Because of the wide variation in climatic conditions in the

northern United States and Canada, the experiences reported here may not always agree with those in your particular locale. I hope the information offered will be useful, however, in your northern growing, and that much of it can be adapted to where you live.

PART ONE

Gardening in the North

CHAPTER ONE

THE CHALLENGES OF CLIMATE AND WEATHER

Whenever I hear someone complain about the difficulties of gardening in the North, I think of dozens of our northern friends who produce vegetables, fruits, and berries as beautiful and nutritious as those grown anywhere. They have fine lawns, lush flower beds, vines, hedges, flowering shrubs, shade trees, and some grow small patches of grain.

I remember asking one extraordinary gardener the secret of his success. He shrugged modestly and implied that he didn't do anything special. I've never heard him complain about our short growing seasons, cold winters, abundant weeds, poor soil, ravenous woodchucks and deer, or the hard work involved.

Years ago I felt that he and any successful northern grower had some special growing secrets that they were unwilling to share. The old-time gardeners certainly had a lot of odd superstitions. My ancestors felt there was little hope for a bountiful harvest unless the seeds of the root crop plants were planted during the period of the waning moon. Seeds of plants that produced food above the ground should be planted only during the growing moon. Cucumbers were an exception. They must be planted before sunrise on the morning of June the second. Beans should never be planted on a cloudy day, or the plants would be covered with rust all summer.

That wasn't all. If by chance you shot a crow or blackbird while protecting your plantings, or destroyed their nests, the survivors, by the dozens, would proceed to wreck the entire garden in revenge. One gardener told me that plants watered even a few minutes after sunset would surely wilt and never recover.

Some people will always seek a magic elixir, a sign in the heavens, a spray, fertilizer, or a chanting ritual to guarantee a bountiful harvest, but in reality successful gardening does not depend on any secrets. Superior gardens and grounds are the result of careful and

The *snow* and *cold* temperatures of the North provide challenging situations for northern gardeners.

sometimes frequent attention to many details. Although gardeners everywhere need some skills, we in the North have discovered we must attend to many garden chores in a special way, since our climate is less forgiving and we are allowed fewer mistakes.

The term "northern climates" covers lots of territory and many different kinds of weather conditions, from Maine to Washington State, and from Newfoundland to the Yukon. Most of the region has adequate rainfall, but it may not always come in sufficient amounts during the critical growing season. Heavy dews during the cool nights of late summer are immensely beneficial in many sections.

Northern New England, the Adirondacks, and eastern Canada, except for the coastal regions and deep valleys, tend to have long, cold winters and extremely short growing seasons, as well as an abundance of wind and fog in the low areas from midsummer until fall. The Upper Midwest has a winter that is very cold but somewhat shorter, and considerable thawing and freezing cycles in late winter and early spring that are hard on plant life. Summers are hot, windy, and often dry.

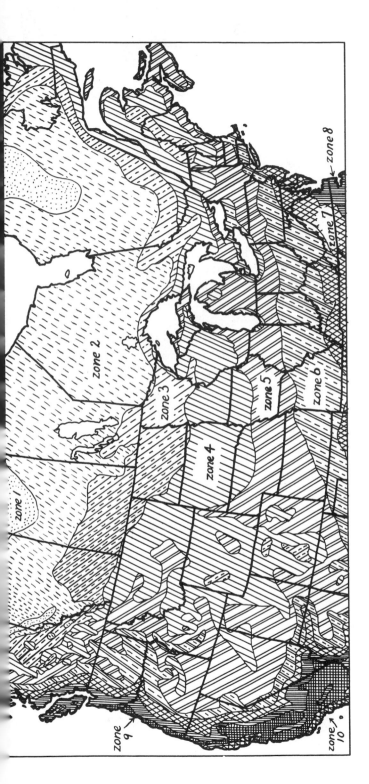

PLANTING ZONES OF NORTHERN UNITED STATES AND CANADA

The planting zones of the United States and Canada are determined by the minimum temperatures and the length of the growing season, or the number of days between the last frost in the spring and the first frost in the fall. These are the approximate average minimum temperatures in degrees Fahrenheit for each zone:

Zone *1*:	Below −50	Zone *5*:	−20 to −10	Zone *8*:	10 to 20
Zone *2*:	−50 to −40	Zone *6*:	−10 to 0	Zone *9*:	20 to 30
Zone *3*:	−40 to −30	Zone *7*:	0 to 10	Zone *10*:	30 to 40
Zone *4*:	−30 to −20				

The northern prairie states and Canadian provinces have long, cold winters and almost continuous wind. The ground sometimes freezes to great depths, causing frost heaves and drying out of shrubs and young trees. Sudden winds that are either very warm or very cold may come close together, and summers are often hot and dry with violent storms.

Sudden, changeable weather is characteristic of the North, especially in spring and fall. One old Yankee claimed that he counted eighty-seven different kinds of weather on a single April day. Paradoxically, however, weather can also be static, when global air patterns stall. We've known it to be clear and cold for a month, or sunny and hot for a long period. Sometimes it may rain, or snow, every day for six weeks or more. Northern gardeners are baffled when asked what an average year is like, because no one remembers ever having seen one.

If you have ever gardened in the North, you're aware that the short growing season and cold winter temperatures cause most growing problems. Many fruits and some vegetables need nearly 140 frost-free days to ripen properly, yet certain northern areas can count on less than half that number. Therefore, simple chores such as planting a vegetable garden become major decisions as gardeners weigh alternatives. Should we take a chance on planting our beans and corn early, although they might be caught in a late spring frost? Or should we wait awhile to plant and then find that they won't ripen before a likely fall frost? Sometimes we guess right, sometimes we don't.

Please don't be discouraged by my descriptions of the problems we all encounter as we hoe and prune in northern climates. As you will discover in later chapters, there are many ways to cope successfully with each challenge.

SPRING FROST INJURY

Spring fever sometimes causes both new and veteran gardeners to rush the season. After a few hot days in April have melted most of the snow, some early birds have returned from the South, the house windows can finally be opened, and long underwear is packed away. Although we know better, intoxicated by signs of spring we become so impatient to get growing that we till and

fertilize the garden and begin to plant the "cold weather" crops—
peas, lettuce, spinach, and radishes.

Having taken the first steps, because the soil seems warm and the
air is balmy, we plant the corn and beans and set out a few cauliflower and broccoli plants. Finally, in a burst of gardening frenzy,
we go all the way and put into the ground the tomatoes, peppers,
eggplants, cucumbers, squash, pumpkins, and even the marigolds
and asters. It's exhilarating to get things done so early!

One pleasant spring day, however, the wind suddenly changes
and warm south breezes are replaced by a steady, cooler, dry flow of
air directly from the North Pole. As evening comes and the wind
stops, we put on our jackets and shut the windows. After checking
the thermometer, and finding it is still 45° F, we go to bed, assuming that all is safe, since it is 13 degrees above freezing.

After midnight, while we are snug in bed, the mercury plunges
into the mid-twenties. In the morning we find not only our precious
transplants wiped out, but also the sprouting beans, corn, and
potatoes. We're left with almost nothing, and must start all over
again.

Spring holds many surprises in our area. The gamblers sometimes win, because some years there may not be a single frost after
mid-April. Other years, however, scattered hard frosts occur
throughout June. Although we worry about damage to tender vegetable and annual flower plants, the frost can injure perennials and
fruits as well. Spring cold snaps sometimes knock asparagus sprouts
back to the ground so that they must start over, and kill the new
growth on flowering trees, shrubs, grapevines, and evergreens.
Fortunately, unless a tree or shrub is especially tender, even
though it suffers a setback, it usually recovers. Some may need a
light pruning, however, to correct later growth that may have
started in the wrong direction because of injury to the original
sprout.

Late spring frosts can also cause severe injury to blooms on fruit
and berry-producing plants. This problem is in no way confined
to the North, however. Growers from Canada to the Gulf think up
ways to protect strawberries, grapes, and fruit trees from possible
frost at blooming time.

A hard frost will always injure buds and blooms, but even a light
frost can damage the fragile pistil through which the pollen moves

after the bees have deposited it in the blossom. Orchardists and berry growers hope to have lots of bees working when the flowers open, so each blossom will be pollinated as fast as possible in case a late frost occurs. Light frosts seldom damage those blooms that have already been pollinated.

FALL FROSTS

Although you will, no doubt, try to grow plants that need a longer season than your region usually supplies (wherever you garden), early fall frosts are an especially troublesome problem when you garden in the North.

In zones 3 and 4 it is practical to grow only the earliest ripening vegetables and tree fruits. So, regretfully, we leave to gardeners with longer seasons the white sweet corn, lima beans, watermelons, peanuts, quinces, and Granny Smith apples. We scan catalogs for seeds that promise high quality plants that ripen early, but sometimes we must sacrifice size, color, or some other desirable factor to get an early variety.

In an attempt to get earlier-ripening vegetables, we start seedlings inside, put up elaborate windbreaks and shelters, and sometimes save our own seeds. We use small greenhouses, hot caps, hotbeds, and cold frames; and when the temperature dips, we dutifully cover up the plants, hoping to beat Jack Frost. Sometimes he wins, and sometimes we do, but we usually end up with enough to fill our freezer, pantry, and root cellar.

Like late spring frosts, fall frosts are also unpredictable, and temperatures can drop suddenly with little warning; but there's a difference. Because the soil is warmer in the fall, the ground heat often helps to protect a crop from the first fall frosts if you understand how to use it.

Fall frosts can usually be counted on to stop the growth of tomatoes, cucumbers, corn, potatoes, peppers, eggplants, fall-bearing raspberries, and grapes, unless they are protected. Light frosts completely kill squash and pumpkin vines, although the mature squash and pumpkin can stand a great deal of cold.

There are bright spots. Most winter apples are unharmed by a few light frosts. Cabbage, cauliflower, and broccoli are quite cold-resistant, and the flavor of Brussels sprouts and the highbush cranberry are improved by frost.

Fall frosts are also hazardous to some trees and shrubs. They injure the woody growth of those that grow too late in the season. Native, acclimated plants stop growing in midsummer and "harden up" before the cold arrives, but grapes, peaches, apricots, blueberries, nectarines, many plums, cherries, tea roses, and some evergreens keep growing. If plants and trees are imported from a slightly warmer zone, they may need special protection.

Probably autumn frosts are more responsible than cold winters for the death of tender plants in the North. Many catalogs list Carpathian walnuts, certain grapes, peaches, apricots, and other trees and shrubs with the notation, "Hardy to 30 degrees below zero." This claim is no doubt true in areas where the growing season is long enough to allow the plants to harden their wood properly before cold weather. But if the new growth on a tree or shrub is still green, lush, and full of moisture, it can't survive even a light, early frost. Dieback on the outer parts of branches is a common sign of early frost injury, and many semihardy trees and shrubs need heavy pruning in the spring to make them look healthy again.

EXTREMELY COLD TEMPERATURES

Although early fall frosts kill many tender trees and shrubs or cause injury to their new growth, cold winter temperatures are also responsible for the failure of some plants to survive in the North. Many fruits and ornamentals begin to suffer when temperatures fall below 20° F. Some plants, however, sustain less injury when winter temperatures stay low for most of the season than when they fluctuate and there is little snow cover during mild winters.

Prolonged cold spells can sometimes be more damaging than a brief period of very low temperatures, as frost penetrates deeper into bark and wood cells. Occasionally trees even snap in a loud explosion. More winter injury results if high winds are forcing chill into the plants. Extreme cold can affect any part of the plant—its bark, new growth, roots, or flower buds. Different plants have various tolerances and weaknesses, but trees and plants brought from warmer areas are particularly susceptible to cold.

Extremely low temperatures can be especially injurious to new growth that was improperly hardened, even if it survived the early fall frosts. Tea roses, hawthorns, peaches, pears, grapes, plums, blueberries, and blackberries often have a great deal of twig and cane injury, although their roots may survive. Many varieties of fruit trees are not hardy themselves, but they may be grafted on roots that are hardy. When this is the case, although branches and perhaps the entire tree may be killed by winter cold, the wild roots survive and send up a new tree that, unless regrafted, will probably produce only inferior fruit.

Some plants are more vulnerable than others to winter root injury. The dwarf apple trees that are grafted on tender English apple varieties called Malling often suffer winter damage and survive only if the roots are mulched heavily with hay, leaves, evergreen boughs, or snow. Northern gardeners also often have trouble growing shrubs and small trees in planters or large pots above ground, because the roots cannot withstand prolonged exposure to low air temperatures. We find we must grow annual rather than perennial plants in the raised bed terraces designed by modern architects.

SUNSCALD

"Sunscald" is another common tree injury. During the lengthening days of March and April bright spring sunlight may shine warmly on brown bark, which quickly absorbs the heat. The temperature of the bark becomes many degrees higher than that of the surrounding air. If the sun slips behind a cloud or hill, the temperature drops suddenly, and the quick change often ruptures the moisture in the cambium cells. The bark splits in long, ugly cracks that eventually expand into an open wound.

FLOWER BUD DAMAGE

Some flowering shrubs, the popular forsythia, for example, are perfectly hardy in most of the North, yet they seldom bloom well in zone 3 and many parts of zone 4 because low temperatures damage their flower buds. In years when heavy snows come early, forsythia lovers rejoice to find a few blooms near the bottom of the shrub where insulating snows have protected the tender buds.

Some fruit and berry plants suffer in the same way, from frost damage to their buds. Growers of nuts, peaches, and strawberries worry about it, knowing that many crop failures result when a colder than normal winter damages the fruit buds. Strawberry growers have long realized that it is almost a requirement for them to cover their plants if they are to get a good crop. Although the plants themselves are slightly more hardy, the forming buds inside the crown of the plant are so tender that, unless they are well covered, very few of them will bloom and bear fruit. Scientists work steadily to cope with this problem and are now developing both strawberry and peach varieties with more hardy buds.

WIND

Because the chill factor affects plants as much as people and automobiles, wind makes a big difference. It may be more troublesome to gardeners in summer than in winter. Cold northern and westerly winds blowing across your garden can keep it from warming up fast in spring. Cool winds in late summer can stop corn, tomatoes, peppers, squash, and other heat-loving plants from growing.

During northern winters when there is little snow, the ground may freeze very deep, far below the root level of newly planted or shallow-rooted evergreens. In early spring, as sun and warm air induce transpiration from the needles, the frozen roots are unable to replace the evaporating moisture. Not only the top, but sometimes the entire bush turns brown. If the injury has been extensive, it may take most of the summer before "windburn" damage disappears; and if the buds are killed, the tree may never recover. Many imported trees are sensitive to windburn. Taxus (yews) and junipers are especially vulnerable, but the native red spruce and Canadian hemlock also suffer injury if they are in exposed windy places and away from the protection of woods or buildings.

MIDWINTER THAWS

Most years gardeners in the Northeast don't need to worry about midwinter thaws that melt off their snow cover, exposing the roots to the next cold snap. Midwestern and western prairie growers often have this problem, however. About Groundhog Day in February midwinter temperatures may suddenly become rather warm, and if snow is sparse, the ground may thaw and remain bare for several days. Native trees and plants seem to take it in their stride, but those not as well adapted may have problems. Trees with shallow roots, the dwarf fruit trees, for example, might have their roots heaved partially out of the ground. They soon will dry out and freeze. Perennials and shallow-planted bulbs may also be affected. Plants and trees imported from areas where spring ordinarily starts in February often begin to grow if the warm spell continues for several days, with disastrous results when it turns cold again.

Those trees and plants that have been set out recently usually suffer the most. For this reason, all new, bare-rooted plants should be set out only in the spring in the North. If you move your own trees or shrubs, do it in the spring also. Only balled and burlapped evergreens, or deciduous trees and shrubs in containers or large pots should be planted at any other time. Plants need several months to get their new roots growing and well-anchored in the ground before winter comes.

COOL GROWING SEASONS

Although frosts get the brunt of the blame for gardening difficulties in the North, a cool growing season also makes it hard to ripen certain vegetables. Our heavy sweaters hang near at hand throughout the summer, because days seldom get very warm and nights are often chilly, especially in August when the weather should be warm if corn and many other crops are to ripen. Cabbage, greens, potatoes, and peas flourish, even in cool summers, but gardeners devise ingenious methods to increase heat around tomatoes, peppers, eggplants, melons, pumpkins, and winter squash. Grapes, elderberries, and late varieties of apples may have their growth slowed so much during a cool summer that the fruits will not ripen fully. Where we live beans grown for drying are often not fully mature before the first frost, either.

Air currents, rather than lack of sun, are the villains, and the north wind is the chief troublemaker. The same wind that blows off the polar icecap, giving us those brilliant, unpolluted blue skies and clear summer days we love, also brings the cool temperatures that delay the growth of heat-loving plants.

MORNING FOG

"The morning sun warms fastest and best," goes the old saying. Even before our energy consciousness was raised, people in cool climates traditionally built their houses to face southeast to catch the first rays of the winter sun. Greenhouses are usually designed with the same orientation. From the earliest days, New England farms that sloped to the south and east were deemed more choice and consistently sold for higher prices.

Although the valleys are usually warmer than the mountain tops, many collect fog, as motorists and airplane pilots will testify. The heaviest and most persistent fogs occur near rivers and lakes, where humidity is high. Fog is most prevalent in late summer and fall, when days are still warm and the nights are cool. Many days fog persists until the morning sunshine "burns" it away, sometimes not long before noon.

Fog can be valuable when it wards off early fall frosts, but if it keeps the land cool and damp all morning, it greatly lessens the amount of sunshine the plants get during the day. This can be a problem as the days get shorter and the growing season nears its end, before fruit, corn, and other vegetables have ripened fully.

SNOW AND ICE DAMAGE

Deep snow offers a welcome protection from the cold, and it delights winter sports enthusiasts, camera buffs, and those of us who depend on it to insulate the floorboards of our homes. We like it as insulation for our plantings, but we recognize that it can cause problems for us gardeners. Even where snow doesn't drift, it may measure several feet deep, and drifting snow often piles up to even greater depths. The snow by itself creates tremendous weight, which can break tender limbs, and if a midwinter rain forms a solid icy crust over the snow, serious damage may result to plants and trees.

By the time the weather begins to warm up in the spring, the icy crust may be covered with still more snow, which will then

Both *hedges* and *specimen evergreens* should be pruned in narrow forms with pointed or rounding tops to protect them from heavy snow loads.

settle down slowly, taking branches and small plants with it. The weight of the settling snow sometimes tears sizable limbs from shade and fruit trees, flowering shrubs, and evergreen hedges.

Ice storms often cause tremendous limb breakage on large as well as small trees. Late spring snowstorms, also, sometimes drop several inches of heavy, wet snow on trees and shrubs after their leaves are fully grown. Branches sag and sometimes break from the weight. Usually little can be done to prevent this kind of catastrophe. We can only attempt to repair the damage.

Lawns, groundcovers, and perennial gardens sometimes suffer from heavy layers of ice or snow. Golf course managers in the North are continually troubled by winter injury and disease problems caused by snow and ice, especially on the closely mown putting greens, where grass root growth is often shallow.

Although gardening is a challenge almost everywhere in the North, as I mentioned, it is being done successfully; and as we glean knowledge from the experiences of others, it is becoming easier.

Research and plant breeding are constantly going on and increasing tremendously the number of varieties of fruits and vegetables, shrubs, trees, and flowers that can be grown here.

Gardeners transplanted to the North are usually delighted to find that the cool temperatures allow many plants to grow all summer. Heavy dews, cool nights, and short days in mid-August keep plants growing and lawns green. Many ornamentals, grasses, evergreens, and flowering shrubs grow better in the North than in the South, as do many varieties of vegetables, fruits, and berries.

Many taste best only when they've been nurtured in a cool climate. Rhubarb, peas, members of the cabbage family, chard, lettuce, spinach, carrots, beets, parsnips, turnips, and asparagus grow to perfection. Currants, gooseberries, elderberries, raspberries, and many varieties of apples are also right at home in the North.

Many perennial flowering plants thrive as well. Delphiniums, lupins, peonies, daylilies, and a raft of others seem to live longer, grow huskier, and bloom better in a cool climate. Biennials like pansies, Sweet William, foxglove, and hollyhocks often bloom for several years instead of only one as they do further south.

Several shallow-rooted plants and shrubs also do better where winters stay cold all season, because there is usually not the intermittent thawing and freezing that heaves roots out of the ground. We can usually count on a blanket of snow that makes it possible to grow tender, low-growing plants such as the alpines, which would be winter-killed further south.

We sometimes feel sorry for ourselves, having to cope with such a miserably short growing season, but we find that many gardeners in more southerly areas don't take advantage of their lengthy growing season. They seem to lose interest in vegetable gardening before the long summer is over. It may be that the challenges we face, and the short season, inspire us to more intense and creative activity.

Each fall when our friends proudly show off their bulging freezers, overflowing root cellars, shelves of colorful canning jars, jelly cupboards, and wine closets, it reaffirms for us the saying of an old successful Yankee: "Ain't nothing wrong with the climate. All you got to do is make the most of it."

CHAPTER TWO

GETTING THE MOST OUT OF THE GROWING SEASON

Although the early settlers in New England had no experience in dealing with a climate so unlike that of Great Britain, they quickly learned a great deal from the native peoples, many of whom were master horticulturists. Although some historians would have us believe the two factions warred constantly, so great was the exchange of ideas between them that only a short time after the colonists staked out their homesteads they were planting corn, beans, tobacco, squash, potatoes, and making maple syrup, while many "Indians" were growing apple trees and pressing cider, European style.

The colonists succeeded in feeding their families only because they adapted their cultural methods to the new climate, and they didn't try to grow things they found were unsuited to the New World. Sometimes we see newcomers in our area determined to grow peach trees, apricots, walnuts, peanuts, lima beans, and other things that grow well on Long Island or in Virginia. They prune, mulch, fertilize, and cultivate their gardens just as they did farther south, and are surprised and frustrated when their crops fail.

They conclude, eventually, as the colonists did and as I did, that to garden successfully in the North we must not only choose acclimated varieties of plants, but place them in the proper location to make full use of sun and possibly wind barriers as well. We must also encourage the plants to grow rapidly and lengthen the season in various ways. Pruning, mulching, and fertilizing practices are somewhat different from those elsewhere, since our growing season lasts only ten to fourteen weeks.

CHOOSE VARIETIES CAREFULLY

Land and hard work, as well as hard cash, are wasted each year when northern gardeners plant seeds, shrubs, plants, and trees that are completely unsuited for the area. Many hardware stores, farm supply houses, and garden centers get their seeds and nursery stock through suppliers who send the same assortments to Aroostook County, Maine, and southern Pennsylvania. The fact that a product is being sold in an area is no guarantee that it is suitable. I've found white sweet corn, beefsteak tomatoes, lima beans, soybeans, peach trees, dogwood trees, azaleas, climbing roses, and many similar items for sale in stores and garden centers in the Northeast Kingdom, Vermont's icebox country, with no hint on the label that it would be a neat trick to grow any of them successfully here.

Seed and nursery catalogs are not always reliable sources for items suitable for northern gardens either. The label: "Days to maturity are . . . " may mean, as in the case of tomatoes, days from transplanting time rather than days from planting seed. It may also indicate days with good growing conditions. Since this means, for most heat-loving plants, *warm* days, some of your favorites may have to be omitted. In frost-prone areas it's difficult to grow successfully peppers, eggplants, melons, pumpkins, and winter squash, for example. Only the earliest tomatoes, corn, and cabbage usually ripen, also, unless the summer season is exceptionally warm.

Fortunately, there are plenty of superb vegetables, fruits, and berries we can grow well and possibly barter with friends who can grow things we cannot. We may also locate a warm spot in the ell of the house, behind the barn, or another more charitable location to grow the toughies, if we insist.

Since many years of experimentation have gone into finding what grows best in each climate, it would be foolish not to take advantage of that knowledge by checking extension service leaflets and talking with other gardeners in the area, both the experienced old-timers and the new homesteaders, who are often extremely well informed. Visiting their vegetable patches and orchards at harvest time and listening carefully can save money, futile work, and frustration over lost crops.

LOCATING THE GARDEN

Residents in the hills and mountains of the North are aware of wide temperature variations in different regions. Some people live in very cold locations, and their houses are difficult to heat. Others, only a few miles away, are snug and comfortable. The snow may melt in early April in some sheltered places, but it can be used for maple sugar parties in late May in others.

Hilltops are ideal for spectacular views and sunsets, but they are usually bad places to garden. Northern winds keep the plants and soil cool, and the limited number of growing weeks are curtailed even more when summer days are too cold for plant growth. Hilltop locations also are hit with storms and high winds that may flatten cornstalks, blow fruit from the trees, and make pollination difficult in the garden.

Don't be too hasty about moving your garden into a valley, how-

HOW TERRAIN AFFECTS
AIR AND SOIL TEMPERATURE

A. Frost pocket collects cold air sliding down from hill.
B. Fairly sheltered area is protected by trees from settling, cold air.
C. Frost pocket created by trees.
D. Well-drained area sloping toward the sun.
E. Cold, windy hilltop.
F. Northwestern slope exposed to cold winds and little direct sunlight.

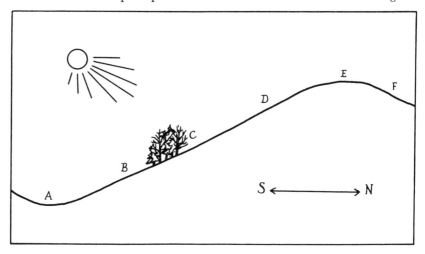

ever. Just as warm, still water rises to the top of a pool, air also separates rapidly, especially at night when it's not windy. The warm air rises, and the cold air settles into the valleys. In our hilly region, neighbors frequently compare temperatures and find they vary from ten to twenty degrees within a three-mile radius.

We used to take early morning rides on small Honda trail bikes, and the sharp contrast between the different areas of quiet air was striking. Sometimes we were dressed far too warm at the high levels, but suddenly we'd become cold as we entered a cold spot where the road dipped suddenly. On a windy day the situation was reversed, and we were cold on the upper, open areas.

Since neither the windy hilltop nor the frosty valley is ideal as a gardening spot, if you have a choice, probably the best location for your garden, trees, and shrubs is partway up a sunny hillside that gently slopes toward the south or southeast, protected from the wind, yet in a spot where the cold air can drop to the valley below. If there is a lake or a large river in the valley, the location would be even more hospitable.

It is difficult to overemphasize the importance of sun to northern plant life. Although New Jersey citizens often successfully raise flowers and vegetables in a small backyard surrounded by trees and buildings, northerners find it difficult to grow plants in similar conditions.

Because northern air currents are usually so cooling, growing areas should be placed with optimum exposure to the sun. A garden tipped slightly toward the southeast catches the sun's beneficial rays much better than one tipped in any other direction, or even one that is flat. Scientists have calculated that certain degrees of slope are equal in heat-collecting value to flat land many miles further south.

In contrast to areas nearer the equator, where the sun's arc stays nearly constant throughout the year, the North experiences a wide variation in the angle of sunlight. Sometimes when people tell me they have a sunny location for their fruit tree, they are speaking of a late June day when the sun rises in the northeast and sets in the northwest. Later in the summer, when the sun makes a much lower arc, the tree or plant may be shaded by trees and not get nearly enough sun to thrive.

When you're looking around for a future growing area, choose one where trees, shrubs, or buildings do not cut out part of the day's sun at any time of the growing season. Be on the lookout, also, for small growing trees that may become a problem when they're older. You might even inquire about your neighbors' building plans if their land is nearby. You can grow a limited number of flowers and shrubs in light shade, but all berries, fruits, and vegetables thrive only in full sun in the North, no matter what your garden guidebooks may advise.

You may wonder about all the directions telling you to plant orchards and berries on the northern slope so they won't bloom too early in the spring and get caught in a frost. Such instructions may be valid wherever growing seasons are long; but where we live, our plants need all the sun they can get, as early in the day as they can get it. Northern slopes are more suitable for late spring skiing or for growing forest trees, Christmas trees, or grass.

If your garden or fruit trees and berries will be placed on a hilltop or hillside, choose a spot with good air drainage. Obviously it is to your advantage that cold air follow its natural inclination and drop to a lower level.

Never stop the flow of draining air, if you have a choice. Sometimes gardeners who live on a slope may decide to place hedges or buildings below their plantings to beautify their property, for privacy, or for some other reason. These barriers effectively block the flow of cold air away from the planting areas and create a pocket of cold air precisely where you want it least, directly over the garden. Sometimes wild trees, bushes, or tall grass and weeds grow up and create the same effect. It is not necessary that the entire slope be clear, but a corridor directly below your growing area should be wide enough for the easy passage of huge amounts of cold air to the valley below.

Lakes and large rivers are great modifiers of climate. Because they hold heat they prevent temperatures from becoming extreme during the months of the year they are not frozen. Areas around the Great Lakes, the Finger Lakes of New York, Lake Champlain, as well as the Hudson, St. Lawrence, and Missouri rivers are usually good growing spots because they are frost-free much longer than those only a few miles away from the water. Small lakes, ponds,

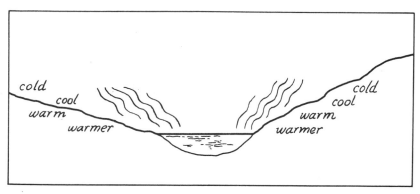

Lakes, rivers, and ponds radiate collected summer heat and keep surrounding area frost-free later in the fall.

and rivers help to modify the climate somewhat, but their influence is useful for a shorter distance, naturally.

Most of us are stuck with a less than perfect location, and it is comforting for us to know that lots of good gardening is done where conditions are not ideal. Beautiful vegetables, fruits, berries, and flowers are being grown on hilltops, flat areas, and even in the bottom of frost-prone valleys.

MICROCLIMATES

All regions have microclimates, that is, small areas within each zone that vary widely from the general climate. They are created by land slopes, bodies of water, or wind currents. Temperatures there may be ten to twenty degrees warmer or colder, and the growing season may be weeks longer or shorter than it is only a few miles away in any direction.

A friend of ours had the good sense to build his new house in one of these warm pockets, and he improved on it even more by digging a small pond and planting several windbreaks. Consequently, his home rates at least a zone warmer than his neighbors' only a mile away. A visit to his garden makes us feel we've taken a trip to southern New England. He grows and ripens Bartlett pears, Delicious apples, and several kinds of grapes. Chrysanthemums, mallows, forsythia, Weigela, and cannas bloom around his home in apparent defiance of all rules governing northern weather.

Gardeners in microclimates or miniclimates, as they are some-times called, must adjust their gardening practices to the imme-diate area rather than to the zone map. People buying property in the North should seek out the region that best suits their growing needs.

WINDBREAKS AND SNOW TRAPS

Our gardening area is on the top of a windy hill—not the ideal location, but because it's where we live we must make the best of it. We have created artificial heat pockets by planting windbreaks to slow down the cold north and west winds that bring us late spring freezes, keep the soil from warming up, and make the corn stop growing in late summer. Our hedges, by stopping cold winter winds and drifting snow, not only make life more pleasant for sensitive trees and plants, but also help keep our house and other buildings warm. Windbreaks are particularly useful, also, in the North Central Prairie States, where the wind seems to blow con-tinually.

Evergreens make the best windbreaks. Firs and pines are the fastest-growing, but spruces and arborvitae hold their branches to the ground better as they get older, so are a better choice. Plant them 6 or 8 feet apart on the north and west side of the area you want to shelter, and shear them back once or twice when they are young to make them grow thicker. A tight hedgerow 30 feet high will reduce wind velocity as much as 50 percent for a distance of 300 feet on the protected side, and as far as 200 feet on the windy side. If snow piling up in the sheltered area is likely to create a problem by injuring fruit trees or bushes, you may plant a second windbreak 50 to 100 feet outside the first one to trap drifting snow between the two hedgerows.

ACCELERATED GROWTH

In addition to planting proper varieties in a favorable location, northern gardeners have two ways to cope with the short growing season. One is to lengthen it artificially by starting seeds in the house or greenhouse, and using hot caps, plastic tents, and other shelters to fend off spring and fall frosts. These and similar methods, which are discussed in Chapter 3, can add precious days or weeks to the growing season, allowing vegetables and fruits to mature and produce for a longer period.

The second way of coping with our extraordinarily short season has been used since people began farming in the North. Each generation has added improvements, and now, in the Golden Age of homesteading, "Accelerated Growth" has become almost a science.

For as long as I can remember it has been a tradition in our area to plant the vegetable garden on Memorial Day, and many of our friends with summer homes travel north for that weekend to plant their seeds. Although this date works out well some years, when May is cold or wet it may be too early to plant safely; and when the weather is good, it is beneficial to get the garden in a week or two earlier.

Although the growing season may be shorter the further north you are, the periods of sunlight are somewhat longer than in the South during June and early July. To take advantage of the long days and increased sunlight, we must plant our seeds as early in the season as possible. Summer visitors who wait to plant until the Fourth of July miss the best growing days in the North, and can grow only very short-season crops.

There is no advantage in planting early, however, if the seeds don't sprout and keep growing. In order to have them sprout fast and grow speedily, all the things a plant likes for optimum growth must be available from planting time on—light, heat, fertilizer, and moisture.

Because soaked seeds sprout several days earlier than those planted dry, like most gardeners we soak the large seeds—peas, corn, and beans, and hard-coated seeds like New Zealand spinach— in water that has been slightly warmed. We soak them overnight, but seldom longer or they may come apart.

We use lots of manure and rotted compost on the garden soil, tilling it in the fall so it will be absorbed by spring; and we check the pH of the soil annually to make sure that fertilizer will be available to the plants as soon as they need it.

Because our soil is heavy, we occasionally mix a truckload of screened sand with it to lighten it. The sand helps it to dry out and warm up faster in the spring, and the improved texture allows better root movement and, therefore, faster plant growth. Many northern gardeners, like ourselves, with heavy, mucky soils, find that sand must be added more than once, because in a few years it gradually disappears in the heavy soil. We also till the soil several times on a warm day before planting, to mix air with it and help it warm up faster.

There are other ways to help speed up the growth of your plants. Lay a flat sheet of clear plastic over an area in the garden for a couple of sunny days before planting to build up heat in the soil, creating a greenhouse effect. Water the garden directly after planting, if the season is dry, to help the small seeds sprout sooner and to keep the soaked pea and corn seeds from drying out. Frequent waterings may be helpful, and are sometimes necessary if June is unusually dry.

The contrast between a sluggish and an "accelerated" garden is impressive. Plants that have received special attention, instead of barely surviving throughout the long June days, grow rapidly, and may be harvested days, sometimes weeks, earlier.

Although most growers believe that it's best to garden in the North using a combination of artificial, protective shelters and accelerated growth techniques, some people feel that unless you are growing for the market, the accelerated method is good enough. They don't care to bother with expensive plastic tents and covers if they can grow everything they need without them.

Another benefit of accelerated growth, some gardeners feel, is that it keeps the garden season confined to an enjoyable length of time. They have no desire to weed for six months, and by the time September comes around they are tired of canning and freezing, and ready to live out of their freezer, pantry, and root cellar.

Accelerated growth practices can be used not only for vegetable gardens, but also for annual flowering plants, and young shrubs, shade trees, fruits and berries. The growth rate of these, also, can be doubled or tripled by careful planting and attention to fertilizer, weed control, and moisture during the growing season.

MULCH

Organic gardeners have a high regard for mulch. When I first started to use it, I applied it only over the roots of fruit trees,

berry plants, rhubarb, asparagus, and other perennial plants that
live over the winter. The results were excellent. So, when I heard
that other gardeners used it on their vegetables, I decided to try
that as well. If it conserved moisture, protected the soil from washing and blowing away, and kept the vegetables clean—how could
I go wrong!

I found that although mulch on the garden has many advantages, it must be used differently in the North than in southern
Connecticut, where Ruth Stout had become the "First Lady of
Mulch." She covered her garden plot with hay and introduced the
"no tilling" method. In spring she simply pushed the hay to one
side, planted her seeds, and added more hay as the seedlings grew.
No hoeing or cultivation was necessary, because the hay shaded the
area between the rows, so weeds couldn't get started. An abundance
of earthworms, plus the rotten hay, kept the soil loose and full of
humus.

Gardeners in northern New England who have tried the Stout
method don't usually get such good results. Small seeds often rot in
the cold earth before they sprout, and when they do start, their
growth is slow compared to that in unmulched gardens. Soil must
be thoroughly warmed in order for seeds to start well. In the
North, mulch shades the earth and keeps it too cool in the spring.
Although peas grow if they are planted as soon as the ground
thaws, most seeds succeed only if the soil is well-tilled and warm.

Heat-loving plants, such as tomatoes, peppers, melons, and
grapes don't do well if they are mulched where summers are cool.
By placing a layer of mulch around them as well as pumpkins,
squash, eggplants, and similar plants early in the season, you prevent the soil from warming up at all.

Mulch has an important place in northern gardens, however. Peas,
carrots, beets, lettuce, cabbage, broccoli, Brussels sprouts, potatoes,
cauliflower, chard, spinach, radishes, and turnips all thrive when
they are planted in rows with mulch spread between them. The
time of application makes a difference, however. Instead of using
the Stout method of year-round mulch, we apply it only after the
seedlings are well started. When they are poking out of the ground
an inch or two and the soil is warm, after a rain, we spread a thin
layer which does all the things mulch is supposed to do: suppress
the weeds, retain moisture, and keep the vegetables clean. Even

corn thrives under mulch if it is applied in midsummer after the plants are a foot or more tall.

In late summer mulch can create a bad effect if it has been spread around tender, frost-prone plants. It insulates the ground, trapping the heat beneath it, so the plants may freeze more easily during the first frost. We observed an example of this phenomenon by examining a patch of beans, half of which were mulched and half not. In the first light frost of fall the unmulched beans were protected by radiation of heat from the soil that had collected it all summer, and they did not freeze. The mulch on the other half of the bean patch, however, served as a heat retainer, and the beans froze into lifeless, wizened strings.

COMPOST-MAKING IN THE NORTH

Northern gardeners working with shallow soils recognized the importance of humus long before the word "organic" was common, and used manure or peat moss to condition their soil. Since these materials are now either expensive or not always available in large amounts, many people are making part or all of their humus directly from garden wastes, home garbage, leaves, grass, and a raft of other products, including human hair.

Books on the subject list dozens of complicated ways to make compost, and garden firms sell earthworms, activators, and special kits to speed up the process. Northern gardeners have discovered that these aids are usually unnecessary because, in our moist summers, compost decomposes easily and quickly by itself.

A mystique has grown up around compost-making that sometimes makes the uninitiated think it's a complicated business. Actually, the process involves simply making a sort of "manure" from organic matter. If you were to pile hay, garbage, dry leaves, or sawdust in a pile, it would eventually rot, but it might take years. Moisture, heat, and bacteria are all needed for the materials to decompose, so we speed up the process by increasing the presence of all three. We add additional water if rains don't supply enough; add manure which furnishes nitrogen to feed the bacteria and heat for fermentation; and soil to supply bacteria and act as a cooling agent when it overheats.

Most compost-makers like to have three piles under way at the

Garden wastes and other green material *decompose* quickly into *rich compost* when alternately layered with manure and soil and kept moist.

same time: one currently being made, the second in the process of rotting, and the third being used. If the compost is to be spread all at once instead of sporadically, only two piles are necessary.

Build the pile in layers. First, pile to a depth of one foot or less, a layer of "green" material—hay, grass, cornstalks, cabbage leaves, garbage, rotten apples, cider waste, shredded bark, or any similar material that's available. Seaweed is excellent, if you live on the coast. Then spread a thin layer of farm manure, dried manure, or compost about two inches thick. Add a thin layer of soil. Proceed to build up another layer of the green material and continue to layer the pile in this manner. As it rots, it will settle.

Cover it with soil for the winter, raking it flat and sightly concave so that rain and melting snow will soak in. It will quickly turn to a rich, dark humus full of bacteria and earthworms, ready to make things grow.

Where we live animals are a problem, and we must bury meat, bones, and any other garbage that may be tempting deep in the pile so that skunks, foxes, and dogs don't dig it out.

If you garden in a village or suburb where backyard, open compost piles are illegal or frowned upon, you can make compost in large, covered boxes, tubs, or garbage cans. Although a well-made, soil-covered pile seldom smells, keep in mind the neighbors and your guests, and give it a little extra care if strange odors start to appear. Usually more water and additional soil will cool it down sufficiently, and the smell will soon disappear.

Some northerners, unable to get to the heaps near their garden in the deep snows of winter, collect garbage in large plastic cans, store it in a garage or barn, and add it to the pile in the spring.

If possible, we like to spread our compost on the garden in the fall. If it is tilled into the soil immediately after it is spread, very little fertility is lost. The rains will not wash away the nutrients, nor will the wind and sun dry them out. They will be well incorporated into the soil before planting time the following spring.

MANURE AND OTHER FERTILIZERS

When land was cheap and plentiful, home gardens were often large, with the rows spaced far apart. Modern gardeners have found that by tilling deeply and enriching the soils heavily, more food can be

A *compost pile* makes valuable fertilizer and is a convenient way to dispose of garbage and garden wastes.

grown in less space with less work. In fact, as one who remembers the old-time garden, I am frequently amazed at how productive a small garden can be when it has been well planned, tended, and fertilized.

Manure is a time-tested soil enricher. Farm manures—cow, sheep, pig, horse, or poultry—are all good. Well-rotted manures are better than fresh ones for fertilization, provided they have been kept covered and haven't lost their fertility because they overheated or were leached out by rains. Old manures also give vegetables and berries a better flavor than fresh manure. Poultry manure has more nitrogen than others, so less is needed. In fact, it must be used sparingly, or it may burn young, tender seedlings or strawberry plants.

Both poultry and horse manure are considered "hot," and are valuable additions to a compost pile to help speed decomposition. Don't pile up big masses of either horse or poultry manures, however, without mixing in bedding or other green material, because much of their value can be lost by burning.

Many gardeners find it more convenient to use commercially dried manures. Although they are more expensive, they are easier to use, less smelly, and contain no weed seeds.

To get the speediest growth possible, a great amount of fertilizer is essential. It must be in a form that is readily available for plant growth, however. New organic gardeners are sometimes surprised if, after using hundreds of pounds of expensive bone meal, rock phosphate, kelp, green sand, and partly rotted compost, their gardens do not resemble those shown in the seed catalogs. All of the excellent materials they applied, unfortunately, were not able to help the plants because they take several months to decompose into a form that can be used. It is best to put them on in the fall and till them in so that they will be available to the plants a season later.

Although great amounts of fertilizer are good, too much can be applied, especially when it is chemical fertilizer. Gardeners have been known to reason that if a few pounds of 5-10-10 work well, twice as much of 15-15-15 would do an even better job. They are likely to be disappointed, because even a tiny bit too much will "burn" the plants, and may kill them.

We apply about 100 bushels of farm manure on our 50- by 60-foot garden each year, in addition to a large heap of compost. We also include occasional applications of wood ashes and rock phosphate.

There are several theories about trace elements in the soil. We haven't included the addition of trace elements in our own soil fertility program because we believe that the leaves we compost and apply to the soil are well supplied with all the essential minerals, since the roots of the maple trees go deep into the soil. We believe, also, that a soil full of organic humus is full of earthworms that bring trace elements up from the subsoil in adequate amounts.

Soil that is well supplied with manures and rich compost should be adequately fertile, but sometimes it doesn't supply quite enough push to give plants a quick start and the necessary speedy growth in early summer. Some gardeners use liquid chemical fertilizers for this purpose: Rapid-Gro, Peter's soluble fertilizer, Miracle-Gro, and others. Organic gardeners prefer liquid fish oil, liquid seaweed solution, or, my preference, a manure tea made of dried or farm manure mixed with water. Water the plant with any of these every week or two during the first four to six weeks of the growing season.

THE RIGHT pH

Although you may have added adequate fertilizer, if your soil is too acid or too alkaline, the plants will be unable to absorb the nutrients. Many northern soils are rather acid, but some unusual spots, including ours, have fairly alkaline soil. With frequent tilling, however, and acid rainfall, it, too, occasionally becomes somewhat acid. Organic gardeners who use lots of mulch, compost, wood ashes, and manure rarely have trouble with off-balanced pH.

The letters pH are commonly referred to as potential hydrogen. The pH or acid-alkalinity of soil is caused by the breakdown of some of the hydrogen atoms of the water in the soil, into positive and negative ions. The mineral and organic content of the soil affects this breakdown. Calcium limestone, for instance, causes alkaline or sweet soils; peat, sulfur, or aluminum cause sour or acid soils.

The chemical pH scale ranges from 1 to 14, with 1 being the most acid and 14 the most alkaline. Seven is neutral. Although

most soils are in the 4 to 8 range, good garden soils are usually
in the 5.5 to 7 group. When soil is too acid or too alkaline to suit
a particular plant, the plant is unable to use the fertilizer in the
soil, even though there may be an abundance of it. Some plants,
weeds, for instance, can grow on a wide range of soil types, but
others are more choosy.

Most vegetables grow best on soils with a pH of 6 to 7. Beans,
beets, parsnips, potatoes, pumpkins, squash, and turnips prefer a
slightly more acid soil (5 to 6 pH). Most fruits and berries also do
well on 6 to 7 pH soils. Blackberries, currants, gooseberries, grapes,
plums, and strawberries, however, prefer more acidity (5 to 6 pH).
Blueberries insist on an extremely acid soil (4 to 4.5 pH).

I believe that a small, low-priced soil test kit is a good investment
for any serious gardener. If your test shows that the soil is too acid,
by adding 10 pounds of lime per 100 square feet you will raise the
soil pH one point. Wood ashes also make a soil more alkaline. To
make the soil more acid, add peat moss, composted pine needles,
oak leaves, or cottonseed meal. Sulfur and aluminum sulfate also
lower the pH, and these are often used by blueberry growers. Four
pounds of sulfur per 100 square feet will lower the pH one point.

WATERING

Because the North has such a short summer season, it is important
that sufficient water be available to your plants during the critical
long growing days in June and early July. In years when rainfall is
scarce during this period, you may need to provide additional
moisture. Mulches on established fruit trees, berry plants, and
shrubs conserve spring moisture and make watering unnecessary.
Seeds or shallow-rooted seedlings lying in dry, bare soil, however,
become dehydrated rapidly, and watering may be necessary.

It should be done in early morning when there is less sun and
wind to evaporate the moisture before it gets to the roots. The earth
should be well soaked every time you water—the equivalent of
about an inch of rainfall. Light sprinklings only encourage shallow roots that dry out quickly. Two heavy waterings each week
are far better than a light sprinkling every day.

Trickle or soaker hoses are a good way to supply water along
rows or beds. Lawn sprinklers set on chunks of wood or stools to

SOIL REQUIREMENTS OF VARIOUS CROPS

Lime (over 7 pH)

Alfalfa	Cauliflower	Lilac
Arborvitae	Celery	Nasturtium
Asparagus	Clematis	Parsley
Barberry	Clover	Petunia
Cabbage	Geranium	Sweet Pea
Calendula	Hydrangea	Wheat
Carrot	Lettuce	

Neutral or near neutral (6½–7 pH)

Apple	Delphinium	Pea
Aster	Eggplant	Peony
Beet	Endive	Poinsettia
Broccoli	Fir	Poppy
Buckwheat	Fuchsia	Radish
Carnation	Gladiolus	Raspberry
Chives	Hollyhock	Rhubarb
Chrysanthemum	Iris	Rose
Corn	Marigold	Soybean
Cosmos	Melon	Spinach
Cucumber	Onion	Spruce (White)
Dahlia	Pansy	

Acid (5½–6 pH)

Bean	Oak	Rye
Begonia	Oats	Spruce (Red)
Blackberry	Parsnip	Squash
Bleeding Heart	Pepper	Strawberry
Currant	Phlox	Tomato
Ferns	Pine	Turnip
Gooseberry	Plum	Wildflowers (many
Grape	Potato	varieties)
Hemlock	Pumpkin	
Lily	Rutabaga	

Very Acid (below 5½ pH)

Azalea	Blueberry	Orchid

increase their height are also good if your water supply is adequate.

If peas, corn, potatoes, or other row crops are mulched with hay or a similar material, make sure the soil is well soaked before the mulch is applied, because light rains or even irrigation may not penetrate a heavy mulch. The crop will suffer, and you won't even be aware that it is drying out. The same thing can happen if a heavy mulch is applied to berry plants, fruit trees, or other perennial plants. To prevent drying out, either mulch them in the fall or when the ground is thoroughly wet in early spring, or after a long rain.

KEEPING AHEAD OF THE WEEDS

Since speedy growth is so essential, nothing should stand in its way, especially weeds and grass. All gardeners know that weeds are not desirable in the garden for appearance's sake, but few realize how greatly they retard the growth of the plants with which they coexist. Weeds not only "crowd" the good plants, but they also rob moisture, nutrients, and, in some gardens I've seen, even sunlight.

One of the best methods of controlling annual weeds is to spread a sheet of clear plastic over the bed for a few sunny days after it has been tilled, raked, and smoothed. The heat forces many weed seeds to sprout, then bakes them to a crisp so they will cause no trouble. When the plastic is removed, the bed is warm and ready for the planting of the seeds.

We know a few growers who like to cover the bed again, after the seeds are planted, making a greenhouse effect whereby the good seeds will sprout sooner amidst all the extra heat, and get a head start on the weed seeds further down in the soil. On a cloudy day this method is safe, but if you try it, be careful not to burn the new sprouting seeds. It might be beneficial to cover the bed each day in late afternoon and remove the cover in late morning for two or three days; but watch the seeds carefully. Replanting is not only costly in money, but in all the valuable growing time wasted.

Weed control must be continued all summer, especially if your garden is located where grass and weed seeds blow in from surrounding fields and pastures. If you garden in a village of well-mown lawns or on the edge of a forest, control may be easier.

Most commercial gardeners use herbicides such as Premerge and Dacthyl to prevent new weed seeds from sprouting. Home gardeners usually prefer not to use these powerful chemicals, and rely, instead, on cultivation, hoeing or mulching (in rows), or hand weeding (in beds).

Sometimes we forget that weeds are not the only competition in our plantings. Make sure your garden is located far enough from trees so that their roots will not steal nutrients from the rich garden soil, because in shallow soil roots of large trees may reach out 100 feet or more. Don't plant vigorous-growing raspberry, blackberry, elderberry, lilac, or similar shrubs with ambitious roots near your vegetable or flower garden.

RAISED BEDS

It is a common practice in cool climates to plant vegetables in beds that are raised a few inches above the surrounding area. The raised beds drain better, warm up faster, and accumulate heat that keeps the plants growing during cool nights and on cloudy days. Planting corn, cucumbers, melons, potatoes, squash, and pumpkins in this way has been common since the Indians found that by hilling up these plants they could get better yields. Tomatoes, peppers, eggplant, and similar warm weather plants also grow better in raised beds. Even the small-seeded plants like lettuce, spinach, radishes, chard, carrots, and beets can go in the ground earlier and will grow faster during the cool days of early spring when they are planted in raised beds. Because the soil in them freezes earlier and deeper than in level soil, however, they are not a good place to grow strawberries.

Sometimes the beds are simply made of soil piled into heaps about 6 inches high with sunken rows between piles. If they're not braced, however, rains gradually wash them down, so something should be used to hold them in place. Tires from cars, trucks, or tractors are sometimes used to make circular beds. Wide boards, planks, or cement blocks will retain long, narrow beds (see chapter 4).

Gardens on steep slopes can be made with permanent retaining walls holding the beds on the lower side. Sometimes these are made of stone, similar to the terraces on European hillside gardens. The soil in them thaws out quickly in the spring, and the beds provide good drainage and allow the plants' roots to soak up the heat of the summer sun.

SPRING FROST PROTECTION

It doesn't happen every year, but too often, after the garden is full of little green sprouting vegetables and the fruit trees are in blossom, the weatherman predicts, "Frost in exposed areas tonight, followed by possible snow in the mountains tomorrow."

Water is often used by commercial growers to protect their plantings, and it is a possibility for home gardeners as well. If you have a lawn sprinkler or two and plenty of water, you can often save tender seedlings by leaving the sprinklers running over them all night. Even if the seedlings are covered with ice by morning, they often survive if you keep the sprinklers going until the temperature warms above the freezing point.

"Covering up" is the standby protection against frosts, and in northern villages, on mornings after a cold night as you walk along the street you see every garden colorfully decked out in bedspreads, yard goods, and old sheets. Straw is used sometimes, but we don't have it readily available, so we use newspapers, old quilts, and anything else we can find. Corn that's grown an inch or so can be protected by hoeing the soil up over it, barely burying the plant. You can do the same to the potatoes. It's not necessary to rake away the soil the next day because the plants will soon push above it. We cover tomatoes, squash, and similar tender plants with cardboard cartons, which are good insulators. Plastic pots and pails aren't as good for frost protection, however, because the heat passes quickly through one thin layer of plastic.

More than once we've covered up the garden after dark with only the beam of a flashlight to show the way, but that is definitely not the best timing. If possible, cover your plants in late afternoon to seal in some of the day's heat before it has left the premises.

We've learned to remove the coverings in the morning after the temperature has warmed above freezing, even if there is a threat of another frost the following night. Plants can become overheated

WHAT IS FROST?

We sometimes think of cold as a wicked villain that can be thwarted by using the proper weapon. In fact, although heat is a real, measurable form of energy, cold does not actually exist. It is merely the absence of heat. Therefore, we never cover the garden plants to keep out the cold, but rather to keep in the heat.

Although we see white frost when dew freezes on the outside of plants, the injury takes place within the growing plants when cold freezes the sap or other moisture inside the leaves bark, flowers, buds, and roots. Since all plants contain more moisture when they are green and growing, that is when they are most susceptible to cold damage. During late fall, winter, and early spring, when plants and trees are dormant, they contain far less moisture and are less likely to be injured by cold.

and "bake" under certain kinds of covers, and if a heavy dew or rain weighs down the sheets or quilts, it may crush the tender seedlings.

Vegetables are not the only frost victims. When our fruit trees are in bloom we watch the thermometer very carefully. Usually the apple blossoms escape because they bloom later, but the plums, pears, and Juneberries bloom early and are very likely to be hit by frost. Strawberries seem to bloom habitually during the same June frost that kills our new tomato transplants if we're not careful.

It's easy to cover up tomatoes and a small strawberry bed, but how can you save a blooming fruit tree? We have wrapped a few limbs with sheets or burlap bags, but it was not too successful. I remember once saving part of our plum crop by running an irrigation sprinkler over the trees throughout the night. It took a lot of water, but the plums were worth it.

If a surprise frost catches you unawares, you can still save garden plants and fruit blossoms by washing off the frozen dew with a hose or sprinkler can of cool water—not ice water. This must be done before the sun hits the plants, or it will be too late. If you plan to use a hose for this purpose, store it inside, as we do now. Too many mornings we tried to water and found that the hose was frozen!

EXTENDING THE GROWING SEASON IN FALL

"If it doesn't get you at one end, it will the other," northern gardeners say about frosts. Fall frosts are especially frustrating because often the first one may come in late August or early September, and there may not be another for the next two or three weeks. Getting the plants through the early crisis often means a yield of extra bushels of tomatoes, cucumbers, beans, and corn during the remaining good weather.

When the weather report indicates clearly there is going to be a frost, and your experienced gardening friends agree—although

Covering up is a time-honored custom whenever a fall frost threatens.

sometimes they are all wrong—it is a good idea to devote some time to getting ready. Pick and store in the basement or garage everything that is already ripe, and prepare to cover those vegetables that are not quite ripe.

Just as in the spring, get out the large cartons, sheets, and blankets. In the fall the soil is usually much warmer than in the spring, so protect the plants in a way that takes advantage of ground heat by covering them in late afternoon before the earth chills, including plenty of soil surface under the insulation.

Corn and beans are difficult to cover, so turn the sprinklers on them if you can. Even if you save only part of the crop, it is usually worth the trouble. Some gardeners use kerosene heaters to ward off frost, but we've never had any success using them.

INSIDE RIPENING

Every year, in spite of choosing early varieties and covering them up faithfully, we have bushels of tomatoes that don't get ripe. Sometimes we pull out the whole vine and hang it in the greenhouse or warm shed, but this is messy. We prefer to pick off the larger fruits and spread them on a greenhouse bench or put them in a sunny window. Some people like to ripen them in a warm, dark place—a box in back of the kitchen wood stove, for example. They claim the flavor is better.

Apples, pears, plums, and elderberries continue to ripen after being picked, and green pumpkins, too, will often turn yellow and ripen in a greenhouse or on a sunny windowsill. None will increase in size, however, and only those fruits that are nearly mature are likely to ripen satisfactorily after they have been picked. Fruit that is too immature is more likely to rot than ripen.

CHAPTER THREE

HOW TO LENGTHEN THE
GROWING SEASON

Lengthening the growing season by providing an artificial climate for plants is nothing new. Europeans have done it for centuries, and settlers from England, France, Italy, and Spain simply continued the practice in North America. Not only did they start plants in hotbeds and cold frames for planting out later, but they also grew entire crops in elaborate rows of glass-covered frames. By the mid-1800's, hundreds of acres were being grown under glass in the Northeast. Only when the railroads began to transport cheaper produce from the South in the 1870's did they start to disappear.

Most of the gardeners I knew when I was a child were not interested in improving on Mother Nature, however. When the garden froze in the fall, that was the end of it, the way the Lord intended. My family usually started a few plants in the house, but most vegetable and flower seeds were planted in the ground on Memorial Day, or very close to it.

No cold frames were used, and although we gathered any ripe produce when frost threatened, we seldom covered plants and tried to save them. Because cows and chickens often broke loose and roamed around our farmhouse, the unfenced garden was planted a safe and considerable distance from the house and barn. This made it less accessible and much more difficult to tend and cover in case of frost.

Greenhouses were something for commercial growing or for the very rich, so there were none in our rural area. Although a few gardeners sent to Georgia for "started" tomato and cabbage plants, these were a rare extravagance.

With my limited gardening background I was quite surprised and not very young when I first met gardeners who used hotbeds, cold frames, hot caps, and greenhouses. They seemed like such a good idea for our cold climate, just as did having the garden close by the house.

STARTING SEEDS IN THE HOUSE

In northern Vermont the first Tuesday in March, New England's Town Meeting Day, is the traditional time to plant tomato seeds inside. When I was a child, sometime during the fall we dug up a pail of rich, black, loamy soil in the maple woods and put it in the cellar. In the spring the seeds were planted in old coffee cans or wooden boxes filled with that soil. The woods soil was not only rich, but it had less disease, fewer weeds and harmful insects than normal garden soil. We placed the containers near the big old wood stove until the seeds sprouted, then moved them to a sunny window. I can't remember when the plants didn't grow well.

Over the years, after electricity came to the back country, we tried many other methods of starting seedlings in the house, some much more successful than others. Often the success we had depended on the kinds of plants we grew. Some vegetables resemble weeds and need very little fussing over. Cabbage, cauliflower, broccoli, Brussels sprouts, and lettuce are all in this category and start easily, even in cool temperatures and poor light. Peppers, eggplants, tomatoes, celery, petunias, begonias, and many other plants need more care and attention, however. They like heat, lots of light, and exactly the right amount of moisture.

Sunny Windows

Adequate light is essential for starting most vegetable and annual flower seedlings. Many perennials, asparagus, and a few other plants sprout better with only a little light, but they, also, should be moved into the light as soon as they are well started.

Sunny windows are a good place to start most seeds if you have only a small garden. A good-sized bay window or picture window will provide a large enough area for starting lots of plants. A window facing east is best so that the plants can get the early morning sun; but if you don't have that exposure, any window facing southeast or south will do.

A lot of us keep our houses rather cool, and the low tempera-

Seedlings grow well in a *sunny* window.

ture may present difficulties, since most seedlings need warmth to thrive. At night it will probably be necessary to move flats away from the cold windows unless you hang heavy draperies or plastic window coverings. Even thermopane glass may not completely protect the seedlings from subzero temperatures. Place the flats near a register, radiator, wood stove, or fireplace at night and on cloudy days, especially during the first few weeks after planting when seedlings need the most heat.

Because the sun creates a great deal of heat as well as light, plants dry out easily. Heat from a wood stove or hot air furnace may also have a drying effect. Seedlings with shallow roots need more attention than ordinary houseplants, and we find it necessary to check the moisture in our flats several times on bright sunny days.

Many gardeners start too many plants and soon run out of sunny windows. I've seen plants growing in homes on tables, bureaus, and even on the floor in poorly lit areas. The seedlings tip toward the light and become tall, straggly, and pale. It's a difficult chore to transplant weak seedlings because they are so fragile, and they take a long time to recover after the transplanting.

If your light area is limited, limit the number of seedlings as well. Try not to plant too many, but if you can't resist, don't hesitate to throw out the weaker ones and save only those you can handle. Quality is more important than quantity, and you'll have better results with a few productive tomato plants than dozens of puny ones that begin to bloom just about the time the first frost hits.

Grow Lights

Since degrees of light and heat fluctuate so much in windows, we prefer to use grow lights for starting our plants. Their watering needs are easier to calculate, and additional light can be provided if it seems beneficial. The fluorescent bulbs give off heat enough to keep the soil warm, but not too warm. They can be placed close to the flats when the seeds are first planted, approximately 4 to 6 inches above them, then moved higher as the seedlings grow. This flexibility prevents the development of leggy seedlings that grow tall, weak, and crooked as they reach for light.

We start our seeds under 40-watt fluorescent lights in a cool room in our house in midwinter (January through March). Although the house temperature stays at 60° to 65° F, the temperature under the light stays at 75° to 80° F, partly because we use a clear plastic tent to hold the heat in.

Directly after planting the lights are left on for about twenty hours a day, and turned off only when the sun shines through the windows on the plants. Marigolds, cabbage, lettuce, and many other plants will germinate in less than two days; tomatoes and petunias in four or five days; and pansies in about a week.

A *grow light* is ideal for starting seedlings.

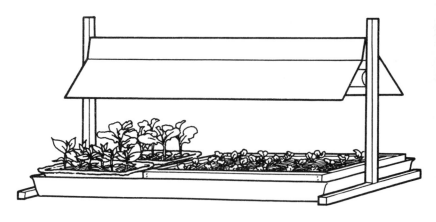

After the seedlings are up and growing well, we reduce the light to about ten hours, mostly at night, and move the light bulbs gradually higher, away from the plants.

It's convenient to have a timer for turning the lights on and off, to make sure they get the right amount of light. We prefer to set the timer to provide two or three shorter intervals of light during each twenty-four-hour period, rather than keep the lights shining continuously for the total time.

Grow lights fit in well with accelerated growth. Instead of starting our tomatoes on Town Meeting Day, we plant them any time from mid-March to early April, and they grow so rapidly that they do better than those we used to start in early March. The fast growth also seems to produce more healthy plants that better resist damping-off diseases.

Ordinary white fluorescent bulbs can be used as growing lights, but we have had better luck with both the pinkish-colored grow lights and the Agro-lights, both of which cost considerably more. These are available at hardware and garden supply stores.

Heat Pads

If you're not using grow lights and must rely on only a sunny window in a cool room or greenhouse, it makes sense to use bottom heat when starting your seeds, since seedlings warmed from below sprout many days earlier, have less disease, and produce better root systems. The heating-fermentation process of horse manure in hotbeds accomplishes this, as do electric soil cables when they are buried in the soil under a hotbed.

Neither horse manure nor soil cables are practical, however, for starting seeds in a cold room or cool greenhouse; but it works very well to use a heating pad with electric warming cables embedded in a tough asphaltlike mat. These mats, designed especially for gardening, are about 16 inches wide and 70 inches long, and are similar to those used in some industries to keep workers' feet warm while they stand or sit in cool places for long periods.

Place your seed flats on them and be sure to use a soil thermostat to prevent the temperature from rising too high. Fill a small flat or shallow pot with soil, and insert the tube of the thermostat in it. When the soil is warmed to the temperature you have preset, the mat shuts off automatically. Since it uses only 175 watts of electricity and is on only part time, power use is quite low.

Because seedlings grown on heat pads need light as well as heat and require air that is not too cool, this system is ideal to use in sunny windows, cool greenhouses, and basements under lights. We sometimes cover them with clear plastic when we use them in a cool place to create a greenhouse effect; the plastic sheet also cuts down the necessity of frequent watering.

Many garden supply houses sell both the pads and thermostats. Although they work satisfactorily, we have consistently had better results using grow lights under a plastic tent.

COLD FRAMES

Every gardener is familiar with the terms "hotbed" and "cold frame." Both are simple to build and operate, and can be valuable for home growers.

Cold frames are simply frames or shallow boxes with no top or bottom, often sunk partially into the earth. They are usually built of wood, but can be made of concrete, fiberglass, or other

Season-lengthening devices may be made out of almost anything, including windows and plastic gallon containers.

material. The top is covered with a glass window, a sheet of clear, flat fiberglass, plastic film, or a similar transparent material. Often an old storm window is used for the top and a layer of clear plastic is tacked to the underside of the window, leaving an air space between for better heat insulation. Usually the unit is constructed so the top slopes toward the east or southeast in order to collect the maximum amount of early spring sunlight.

With a cold frame you can start seedlings outside earlier than is possible without such protection. Since they provide no heat other than that of the sun, however, they can be used only in late spring and only for crops that don't object to cool temperatures, such as the cabbage family, lettuce, and many perennials.

Sometimes cold frames are used as "hardening off" beds for tomatoes, peppers, and other heat-loving plants that have been started indoors. Plants can be transplanted directly into the soil in the cold frames, or you can transplant them into flats or pots. The plants can then be gradually adjusted to the climate by opening the frame whenever the temperatures are warm enough.

A cold frame is a very useful season extender, especially if your home has no good place for starting seeds inside. There are drawbacks to it, however. It needs frequent attention, since the limited air space in it can warm up or cool off quickly. The cover must be opened slightly on warm days, more on warmer days, and taken off entirely on hot days. Since the weather may change frequently in the spring, you may have to adjust the frame several times each day. We have an acquaintance who lost hundreds of plants one recent spring day when she went to the store for an hour and a sudden hailstorm battered them.

Her experience was exceptional, of course. Although caring for a cold frame entails more work and attention than indoor growing, most gardeners agree that the exposure to the outside air produces plants that are more sturdy and healthy than those living a secure life in a warm window or greenhouse.

HOTBEDS

A hotbed is merely a cold frame with some type of bottom heat provided to warm up the soil, enabling growers to start plants a few weeks earlier than with a cold frame. Even when the snow

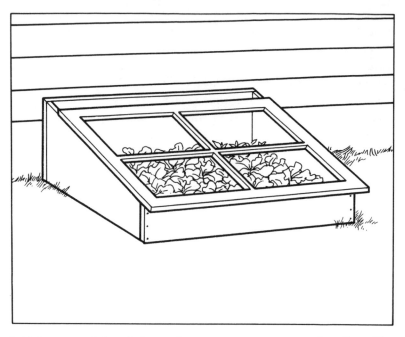

Cold frames and *hot beds* are low cost ways to start a lot of seedlings.

is deep, you can start plants that feel comfortable in warm sur-
roundings, such as tomatoes, peppers, eggplants, celery, and annual
flowers.

Soil cables are commonly used now for heating hotbeds, but
some gardeners, especially those without electricity, still use the
old-time method of fermenting manure to provide heat. Fresh horse
manure is the best choice, but fresh poultry manure can be used
too. Both heat up quickly when they're piled in a heap, dispensing
quantities of heat and strong fragrance. Cow, sheep, and pig manure
ferment much slower and with less heat, so they are usually not as
satisfactory to use.

To build our hotbed we first dug a hole about 2 feet deep in
a sunny spot sheltered from the wind. We dumped in about one-
and-one-half feet of manure, and covered that with about four
inches of good, sifted, sandy soil. Then we allowed the manure
to heat up for a few days before planting the seeds in late March.

We found that manure is tricky to use because it isn't easy to get the right amount. There must be enough to supply sufficient heat to keep the soil warm until the seedlings no longer need it, yet there should not be so much heat that they are baked to a crisp. Because of this problem we were glad when heating cables were introduced.

Soil cables provide an easy solution to the heat problem and eliminate the guesswork. We laid out ours in a series of loops on the bottom of the hotbed and covered it with a wire screen so that digging out the seedlings wouldn't disturb the cable. Then we covered the screen with 3 or 4 inches of sifted soil, though an artificial soil mix or other growing medium could also be used.

Soil cables need a thermostat, just as heating pads do, to prevent overheating. Sometimes the thermostat is built into the cable and preset at a temperature of about 75° F, which is about right for most plants. Others must be bought separately and can be adjusted to suit your requirements. If you must buy a thermostat, obtain one that works on soil temperature rather than air temperature.

Hotbeds with soil cables work very well. We have planted seeds in ours when the snow outside it was 2 feet deep. Many of the seeds came up in less than three days, and grew very well, even though sometimes the entire frame was buried by a fresh snowstorm for days.

The plants in hotbeds and cold frames must be as carefully watered as if they were grown indoors. Water them well in the morning and check the plants often throughout the day to see that they are not drying out. Always warm the water slightly. Use a bulb-type sprinkler or fine mist sprayer on the seeds so that you don't uncover them, and water the new seedlings gently to avoid breaking their fragile stems.

After the seedlings have developed their first set of true leaves, the heat can be shut off whenever the days are warm enough. Eventually it should be shut off entirely and the hotbed should be treated as a cold frame. Like a cold frame, on cool, sunny days the glass must be opened slightly for ventilation, and on warm days it can be removed entirely.

On cold nights and some early spring days the glass or whatever transparent material is used may not be protection enough.

It may be necessary to cover the whole bed with old rugs, insulation bats, blankets, or quilts. During prolonged cold spells you can save the plants by putting in a small light bulb and keeping it lit all night. One clever grower I know has a large bed with several storm windows covering it. During cold snaps he puts in a string of large Christmas tree lights to provide heat.

The hotbed and cold frame methods of starting plants have many advantages. With only a small investment you can start a lot of plants, since the initial cost of making and covering a frame is far less than building and equipping a greenhouse. Maintenance is much less expensive, heating costs are low, and property taxes are far more favorable.

The frames, however, need constant attention. Someone must be nearby every day to open them just the right amount to keep the plants from getting either baked or chilled. Large growers, in fact, sometimes install automatic electric openers that will adjust a series of frames, according to the weather conditions. In windy, rainy, or snowy weather we've found that caring for a frame can be difficult. The plants often need watering or transplanting at times when opening the windows would chill them.

For these reasons, many gardeners prefer to start their plants in a greenhouse, where it is possible to toil away on cold, stormy days and even at night. Greenhouses can be started earlier in the spring, or even operated all winter. By placing plants on different levels in a greenhouse, from the cool floor to the hot upper shelves, you are able to provide the right growing conditions for a variety of plants, such as spring bulbs that prefer cool soil, cabbage plants that like it warmer, and heat-loving pepper and tomato plants.

GREENHOUSES

Only a few years ago a greenhouse was like a swimming pool— something only a few could afford. With the development of plastic and fiberglass, however, the home greenhouse has become a useful part of many northern gardens.

Modern greenhouses differ tremendously from the early models. Although some still resemble their English prototypes and stand unattached, completely covered with transparent material, the new type is more efficient, cheaper to build and operate, and more of an energy producer. In fact, some actually produce more heat for much of the year than they consume. It's quite different from the days when greenhouses were such heavy energy consumers in the North that many large commercial houses were built near railroad sidings to facilitate delivering carloads of coal to them directly.

Builders carefully calculate how to make the most efficient use of sunlight, whatever the latitude, by properly positioning the house and the angle of the transparent panels to best catch the sun's rays.

Many greenhouses are attached to a home, and on sunny days blowers or fans are used to circulate the sun's heat throughout the house. Insulated panels or blankets are used to cover the glass at night to prevent heat from escaping. The trapped sunlight can

A *greenhouse* oriented north and south collects the greatest amount of morning *light* and *heat*.

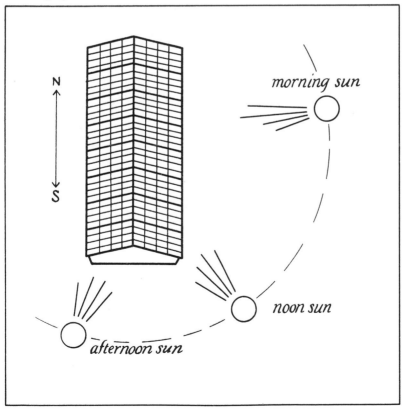

Scientifically designed *greenhouses* are designed to catch and retain the maximum amount of *heat* and *light* in spring, fall, and winter.

Homemade plastic or fiberglass *greenhouses* make it possible to grow *watermelons* and other difficult crops, even on *cold, windy hilltops*.

also be utilized to operate a water heater or to warm water before it enters the water heater in the house. At night and on cloudy days the heating system in the house can warm the greenhouse.

Even free-standing, large greenhouses can be efficient. They should be positioned to catch the morning heat, because in the cool of the morning it is important to get the early sun. At that time the extra heat is more beneficial than during the warmer afternoon. A greenhouse that runs from north to south, or northwest to southeast, collects more morning heat than one running east and west.

Since almost no solar heat is collected through the north and west greenhouse walls during the spring, fall, and winter months, it makes little sense to build these walls of expensive transparent material that will lose rather than gather heat. A solid wall, well-insulated and covered with black plastic or reflecting aluminum foil, should be used instead. Benches covered with black plastic and wood surfaces that are painted with a dark red or other dark stain also collect more heat from the sun than white or light-colored surfaces.

The ideal greenhouse in the North should be well protected from the north and west winds. Some eastern-facing, transparent vertical walls should be positioned to catch the low morning sun. Other angled transparent panels should be aimed to catch the higher midday sun from the south, and more vertical walls positioned to catch the last rays of the setting winter sun from the southwest. Arranging this odd shape is a tricky engineering problem, but such structures are being built and operated with success.

All sorts of clever ways have been invented to hold in the heat once you catch it. One of the best methods is to build a double wall of fiberglass, glass, or some other rigid transparent material on the outside and add a plastic film of vinyl or polyethylene on the inside, with about 4 inches of air space between them.

To prevent even further heat loss at night or on dark, cold days, blankets or insulating panels of styrofoam or other material may be used to cover the transparent walls and top. An especially neat way to assemble the light, large panels is to snap them into place quickly and easily with magnets that have been fastened to the glass and to the panels.

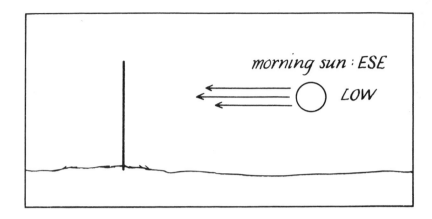

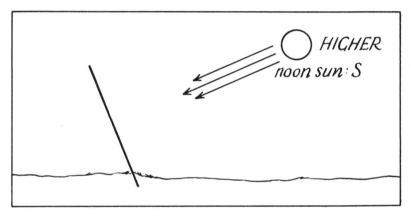

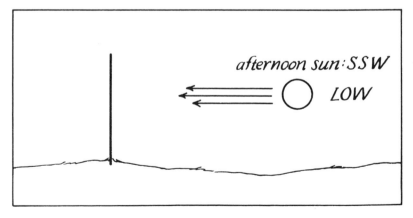

In the North the winter and early spring sun is very low. *Solar panels*
and *greenhouses* should be positioned to best collect the heat.

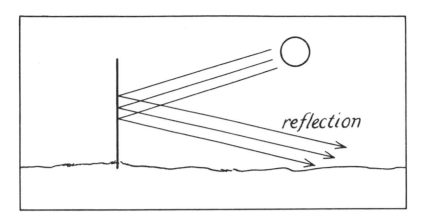

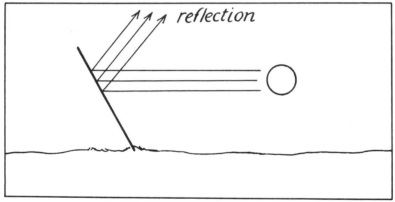

When sunlight hits glass at *oblique* angles, a great deal of heat and light are lost by reflection.

Rigid Greenhouse Covers

Glass is still one of the best coverings for a greenhouse because it lets in so much light. However, various less fragile rigid plastics developed in recent years are now being used—vinyls, fiberglass, acrylics, various polyvinylchlorides, and other materials formed in flat or corrugated sheets. Few of these materials are as clear as glass, even when they are new, and most seem to become yellow as time goes by. We once covered a greenhouse with fiberglass guaranteed for twenty years, but within eight years it had become badly discolored. The guarantee, naturally, was so carefully written it was worthless. Although some of the more recently developed plastics may be more durable, some are not made for subzero temperatures. We put a clear rigid plastic on a greenhouse door one fall, and when we shut it hard on a cold winter day, the material shattered as if it were ice.

Rigid plastics as greenhouse coverings have many advantages over glass. They are easier for the amateur builder to use, since many can be nailed or stapled directly to a wood frame. Most are shatterproof, but the more glasslike ones must be put on with strips of wood, as they must expand and contract with the weather, and in some cases driving a nail through them will break the material. Nearly all can be safely sawed with an ordinary power saw, and some can even be cut with heavy duty metal shears.

Plastic panels are better than glass to place on a greenhouse that lacks a permanent nonshifting foundation; changes in temperature or ground heaving from frost won't break them as easily as glass. They are also more resistant to hail, baseballs, rocks, and other flying objects, and, unlike glass, need no puttying—an annual chore on some glass houses.

There is a wide selection of materials from which to choose. Specialized books on the subject describe them in detail. Exolite, Lexon, Polygal, Filon, and many other trade names are on the market, and new ones are introduced and old ones discontinued so rapidly that any list is soon out of date.

If you plan to become a greenhouse gardener, contact manufacturers, study catalogs, examine recently built greenhouses, and visit flower shows and other trade exhibits where greenhouse materials are displayed. Talk to other growers, too.

Low-Cost Greenhouses

Many expensive glass greenhouses for hobby gardeners are on the market, but cheap, homemade ones can be just as useful for starting plants at low cost. My first one was made of cedar poles I'd cut myself. Each post was about 3 inches in diameter on the top end. I sprayed them with wood preservative and stretched polyethylene over the structure and nailed it on with thin, narrow wood strips. The only heat was a wood stove.

I started to use it only in mid-March after the coldest weather was over but still eight to ten weeks before most plants could be put outdoors safely. I'd already started some seeds in the house in February and early March and was therefore able to gain several months over outdoor seeding.

Since then polyethylene has increased in price a great deal, but it is still the cheapest greenhouse covering available. Unfortunately, the cheaper grades of plastic last only one season. They flutter in the wind, develop tears, rip easily wherever they are folded, and are a real pain to put on, especially on a breezy day.

New materials have been introduced that will last for several years, such as Monsanto 703 and Cloud Nine. Commercial poly-covered houses are often constructed with two layers of these coverings separated by air space. A small blower running constantly keeps the space between the two films inflated, which not only prevents it from fluttering in the wind, but also adds insulation to the house.

Underground Greenhouses

I have read a great deal recently about building greenhouses that, like hotbeds and cold frames, are partly underground. The method makes a great deal of sense because earth is such good insulation; and if the house can be built into a hill with its exposed area facing south, I believe this type might work very well. The one I

A *greenhouse* built partially *underground* can save building, heating, and maintenance costs.

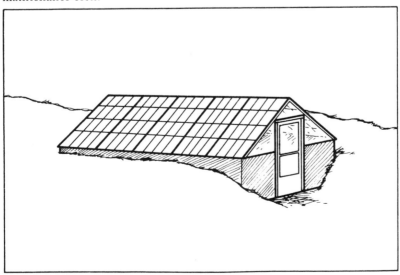

tried, however, was not successful, since it was built on level ground, and our heavy snows covered it for most of the winter and spring. Eventually it became very difficult to shovel off the snow to let in the sunlight—I ran out of a place to put it long before the end of the winter. If heavy snow loads are a possibility, an underground house should be especially well braced. It must also have a good drainage system to make sure that hard rains and melting snows won't flood the floor.

Greenhouses for Fun

In addition to the fact that greenhouses lengthen the gardening season, a fringe benefit of owning one is that it can be lots of fun. Working in a greenhouse on a cold, sunny spring day is a perfect cure for cabin fever, and cheaper by far than a trip to Jamaica. Green, growing seedlings are cheery, and if you feel extravagant, a few potted flowers or spring bulbs from a florist help to brighten up the house until your own plants begin to bloom. In a greenhouse you can shed your heavy jacket and boots and really "think" spring. One gardener I know has a couch in one corner for an afternoon sun-drenched nap. He claims it bakes away his arthritis!

Our greenhouse has a 200-foot coil of ½-inch black plastic pipe in the top to heat water for watering the plants. On sunny afternoons we have free, solar-heated hot water to use in the corner shower as well. The eighty-degree temperature inside is a perfect treatment for an early spring cold, too.

One of our homemade greenhouses has a small, above-the-ground swimming pool in it, and we enjoy swimming throughout a long season. The primary purpose of the pool, however, is for heating. It is amazing how the water holds the day's heat and keeps the greenhouse warm on cool nights. We have never used any auxiliary heat in that house, even when outside temperatures dropped below freezing; but we don't put our plants there until the coldest winter weather is over.

Heating

The high cost of heating a greenhouse can be a problem in the cold climate of zones 3 and 4. Each year we resolve to delay starting our greenhouse until the weather warms up; then the sunny midwinter days of late February and early March nearly always tempt us to get going. As we look over our living room full of seedlings and plants, we yield to temptation and start the greenhouse. Several weeks of winter follow, and, as our plants grow, so do our heating bills.

Gas, oil, wood, coal, and electricity are possible greenhouse fuels. Hot air, steam, and hot water systems are used, as are vented and unvented gas and kerosene heaters. Each system has its good and bad points. An oil or gas furnace with hot water pipes running under the benches is, most people agree, the ideal heating system. Unless you can attach it to your house furnace, however, such a system is impractical for the hobby gardener. A gas heater or an oil-burning pot burner with an outside vent is usually satisfactory, especially if it has thermostatic controls. An unvented space heater may produce too many fumes in a tight greenhouse to be satisfactory for the plants and for the gardener.

Whatever equipment you choose, if it depends on electricity it's a good idea to have available some form of emergency heat in case the power should fail. A battery-powered thermostat hooked to a house alarm can also save you lots of worry.

One year we decided to burn wood exclusively, but it was not satisfactory, probably because our smokestack wasn't high enough. The pipe or stack should be sufficiently high to create a strong draft, especially when a slow-burning wood heater is used, both for good heating and to prevent formation of creosote, which is bad for plants. The creosote piled up that spring, and we spent many anxious hours in the middle of the night wondering whether the fire had gone out entirely or if it was burning down the greenhouse. A few years ago we met one elderly hobby gardener who slept each night all spring in his greenhouse in order to tend the wood fire.

To save heating costs, keep the house as full of plants as possible, since plants store and release heat far better than air alone. If there are not yet enough plants, plain soil in pots or flats does just as well. Large garbage cans filled with water also retain heat.

Since warmth, whether supplied by the sun or by heaters, tends to gather at the top of a greenhouse, one or more small circulating fans or blowers insure an even temperature from top to bottom and will conserve heating costs. A large exhaust fan that will come on automatically and an intake ventilator are also essential for the days when the sun produces an abundance of heat.

Operating a Year-Round Greenhouse

Even before fuel costs rose, the maintenance of a conventional freestanding greenhouse throughout the winter in the North was too expensive for most home gardeners to consider. From late October to late February the temperatures are so low and the sunshine so scarce that it made little sense to attempt heating one unless you were a commercial gardener.

Today, surprisingly, operating a year-round greenhouse is more practical than it has ever been. As I mentioned, the house-attached solar unit can be an energy producer if its floor area is small, the sun-collecting area quite large, it is well insulated, and it is oriented carefully to gather the most sun possible.

When this type of structure is properly built, it will collect a lot of heat, even on cloudy days, which may be used to warm the dwelling and heat water as well as to grow plants. Unless it is filled with plants from floor to roof, piles of crushed rock, sand, or tall cylinders of water may be used to store the day's extra heat, keeping the room warm, or at least frost-free, during the night.

GROWING MEDIA

There is a good choice of materials for starting seeds, whether you operate a greenhouse or start seeds in your living room. Most growers prefer artificial soil mixtures like Pro-Mix or Gro-Mix, for they are less likely to contain disease organisms that kill young seedlings. They contain a combination of vermiculite and peat moss ground finely and thoroughly mixed with a small amount of plant nutrients.

Choose a medium that will hold moisture yet not become too soggy, and one that will allow plant roots to penetrate quickly. It should also be able to hold fertilizer that can be released slowly to the plants as they grow. The faster a seed can grow, the better its chances for survival.

The essential growing media includes:

SOIL—Be sure any soil you use is light, loose, and loamy for good root growth. Sterilize it with heat or a chemical such as Vapam, following all the directions carefully.

VERMICULITE—This exploded mica is often used in home insulation. It comes in different sizes, so choose a fine grade or grind it fine when you use it for horticultural purposes.

PERLITE—A very light, sterile material, perlite is good mixed with peat moss or can be used alone for covering seeds. Because it holds water and fertilizers less well than other media, it is not a good one to use alone. Choose a finely ground grade.

COMPOST—Thoroughly composted leaves or bark are excellent materials to mix with perlite or vermiculite, but too heavy and soggy to use alone. It, too, should be sterilized before use.

SPHAGNUM MOSS—Shredded sphagnum moss, either gathered from swamps or purchased, is a good, naturally sterile medium for starting seeds. It should be dried and finely shredded. Overwatering must be avoided, since its absorption ability is phenomenal.

PEAT MOSS—Excellent to mix with perlite or vermiculite, but a bit too heavy to use alone for growing most seeds.

ARTIFICIAL SOIL MIXES—Many professionally mixed products are for sale, including Jiffy-Mix, Jiffy-Mix Plus, Fafard Mix, Pro-Mix, and Metro-Mix. They are available at most farm supply stores and garden centers.

PLANTING

We use large, shallow plant trays (about 10- by 20-inch) to start our seeds; they are easy to handle and neatly fit the space available under our grow lights. It is always tempting to fill the trays too full of soil; however, we are careful to leave room for covering the seeds and still have space after that to water them.

SUGGESTED SEQUENCE OF STARTING SEEDLINGS

(For transplanting into the garden about June 1)

	Vegetables	*Flowers*
JANUARY		Begonias
		Double Petunias
FEBRUARY	Celery	Exhibition Dahlias
		Impatiens
		Pansies
		Seed Geraniums
		Single Petunias
		Tall Marigolds
MARCH	Eggplant	Asters
	Herbs	Bachelor Buttons
	Peppers	Coleus
	Tomatoes	Gloriosa Daisies
		Pinks
		Portulaca
		Snapdragons
		Zinnias
APRIL	Broccoli	Alyssum
	Brussels Sprouts	Dwarf Marigolds
	Cabbage	Other annuals
	Cauliflower	
	Lettuce	
	Melons	
	Pumpkins	
	Squash	

We use an artificial mixture, Pro-Mix, that has given us consistently good results for years. We break up the lumps, smooth the mixture level in the trays, and firm it down slightly.

Moisture is critical for sprouting seeds, and we must check to be absolutely sure the planting medium is well soaked with lukewarm water before we plant any seeds. Mixtures that contain sphagnum or peat moss sometimes resist getting wet, and it may require repeated sprinklings to get them thoroughly moist. Some growers soak each flat in a large shallow pan of water for an hour or so after it has been filled with artificial soil.

After the flats are thoroughly watered, they may be planted. I shake the seeds out of the envelopes, scattering them sparingly over the top. Some growers prefer to plant everything in rows, believing it easier to space the seeds more evenly and to transplant the seedlings.

Most of us have a tendency to plant seeds too thickly. Although we know we shouldn't, it is human nature to want to fit as many plants as possible into the small space available. Even if the packet contains too many seeds to fit in the flat, we may decide to plant them all, thinking they might lose their viability by the following year.

Seedlings that grow too close together, however, are spindly. They fail to develop either good tops or roots, and it is extremely difficult to separate them when transplanting without tearing apart their root systems. They also get disease more readily because air doesn't circulate around them well and the sun or grow lights never dry out the top of the medium. It is worthwhile, even if you must throw out seeds, to plant sparingly in order to get large, healthy plants. Those with strong root systems will hold a tiny ball of soil when you move them and be more certain to live. You might save the extra seeds to use in case the first planting fails.

Most of us must also guard against planting the seeds too deep. That tendency is often encouraged by outdoor planting of corn and potatoes, which should be planted deep so that they won't wash out in heavy rains. But fine seeds sown in indoor flats need be only lightly covered, and some growers never cover them at all. Instead, they sow the seeds on a slightly moist medium, cover the flat with a pane of glass or sheet of plastic a quarter inch or more above the soil, and let them sprout.

I like to cover all seeds with a fine grade of perlite, which dries out fast. Seedlings are less likely to become diseased if the top surface of the medium is rather dry most of the time. I barely cover the tiny seeds, like celery, petunias, begonias, and primrose; but the larger seeds must get a somewhat heavier layer. Up to one-fourth of an inch is necessary to support tall-growing asparagus plants, for instance.

WATERING AND TEMPERATURE

Although shallow-rooted new seedlings occasionally dry out and die from lack of water, too much moisture is a far more common cause of trouble. It is ideal to keep the medium at the bottom of the flat wet while seeing that the top remains as dry as possible. Although many gardeners water all their plants from the bottom to achieve this situation, this can be risky, for the top may then not get enough moisture. If you bottom water, check carefully to be sure the moisture reaches the top without making it too wet. After the seedlings are up and growing well, their roots will be able to reach further down for moisture, so keeping the top layer dry without depriving the seedlings of moisture will then be much easier.

If you water your flats from the top, gently sprinkle or mist them. We use a commercial rubber bulb-type sprinkler, but a plastic clothes sprinkler works fine too. Once the seedlings have begun to grow we continue to water them carefully. Heavy watering not only drowns the roots, but the force of water from a sprinkler can or hose may also wash tiny seeds out of the soil easily or break the stems of fragile seedlings.

Whenever it is possible, top watering should be done at a time when the flats will be exposed to sun or lights for a few hours afterward. Sprinkle the plants growing in a sunny window in the morning and those growing under lights just after the lights have been turned on. If you give plants moisture just before their growing area will be dark and cool, disease is almost certain to proliferate.

Although overwatering and low temperatures together present

perfect conditions for disease to start, either alone can induce trouble. Most seeds sprout best at a temperature of 75°–80° F, and they are much more likely to grow and resist disease if kept in that temperature range for much of the first two weeks after sprouting.

In our greenhouse the changeable weather in April almost always presents problems. On a sunny morning, when the temperature hits 80° F after a few minutes of sunshine, we may water the seedlings heavily. Then it suddenly begins to rain, not only throughout that day, but for several days. The greenhouse becomes chilly, and the wet plants don't dry out. We can turn on extra heat and put the most fragile seedlings under lights, but the plants have a rough time.

Seedlings that have just been transplanted also suffer if they receive too much water and low temperatures. Even the most rugged seedlings experience shock if they are transplanted into cold, wet soil; and delicate ones need special care.

Many troubles are caused by watering the seedlings with water that is too cold. Water that sits in the coils of black plastic pipe in the tops of greenhouses heats quickly, but we must remind ourselves to stop watering when the warm water is used up and wait for an hour or two until more gets heated. When we're watering seedlings in the house, we either let it warm to room temperature or we mix hot and cold water to make it mildly lukewarm. Be very careful not to use water that is too warm. We have killed little seedlings by "cooking" them without realizing it.

Our water supply comes from a spring. One April morning I put a thermometer in it as it poured from the faucet. It registered 34° F. To have poured that ice water on plants could have been fatal. Soils watered with cold water often take hours to warm up, and seeds will not sprout or seedlings grow unless they are warm enough. Damping-off diseases love the combination of low temperature and moisture.

Super-Water

Some gardeners are reporting a phenomenal speeding up of seedling growth by watering them with super-water, another name for ordinary water that has been boiled for a few minutes to force all the air out of it. It is then put carefully into a jar, pouring it down the side so that as little air as possible will become mixed with it. The jar is filled completely, sealed, and allowed to cool. The seedlings are watered with this each day.

The theory is that the plants can better utilize deaerated water, and therefore growth is speeded up considerably. Some people, however, feel that the improvement is psychic only and that plants will respond to any favorable extra attention, such as being talked to, prayed over, touched or turned each day, or having pleasant music played near them.

DISEASE CONTROL

Outdoor plants have many natural controls to help them battle against disease. Exposure to the wind and rain and climate in general makes plants more rugged, just as a maple is more sturdy than a greenhouse orchid. Also, the ultraviolet rays of the sun are present and kill off many disease organisms. Circulating breezes dry out plants and keep diseases from getting started in the moist conditions they like.

Plants grown in the unnatural conditions of a greenhouse, hotbed, or windowsill, however, are more vulnerable to troubles. Most diseases can be prevented by keeping everything very sanitary, by careful watering, temperature and light control, and by not planting the seeds too thick. Sometimes, however, in spite of our best efforts, disease does hit our seedlings, and some sort of remedy is necessary.

By far the most common disease is the one that strikes as the seedlings begin to look good. Just as we are congratulating ourselves on the superb job we've done, the plants suddenly fall over and die. It is called "damping off," a colloquialism for several diseases, including pythium, that attack not only newly sprouted seeds and larger seedlings, but sometimes even transplants.

These diseases are found in most garden and other cultivated soils, and commercial growers, whose profits depend on good crops, use every preventive measure possible to control it. Many use disease-free artificial soil mixtures or treat their soil mix with chemicals. Others sterilize the soil by steaming or baking. They sterilize the flats and all the tools they use, and carefully dust the seeds with fungicides and spray the seedlings every week or so.

After the seedlings are growing well, the growers are careful not to touch the plants or soil with tools, hands, clothing, or anything that hasn't been sterilized with a chlorine bleach solution. This kind of operating room cleanliness may seem like a lot of trouble for a home gardener, and may be necessary only if damping off becomes a serious problem.

Damping off is only one group of diseases that may bother seedlings. Another disease is tobacco mosaic, a virus that can be fatal to tomatoes, chrysanthemums, and others. Smokers of cigars, cigarettes, and pipes must be especially careful about handling plants, since it is easily contracted and difficult to control. It is best for smokers to wash hands thoroughly before dealing with any plants. We keep a sign in our greenhouse asking visitors please not to smoke.

FUNGICIDES THAT CONTROL SEEDLING DISEASE

CAPTAN—*One of the best fungicides for garden, orchard, and berry patch. It may damage sprouting seeds, however, so use it only after seedlings are all up and growing well.*

DEXON—*Dyes everything a bright yellow, long-lasting color that lets you see where you've put it—on plants, soil, hands, and clothes. Good for diseases on geraniums and other houseplants, as well as for damping off.*

BEN-LATE—*Very effective fungicide for seedling diseases. It is long lasting, but also expensive. Controls mildews on outdoor plants, too.*

Be sure to read and follow carefully all the directions on the package, and use fungicides only on the crops listed.

INSECTS

If a few tiny bugs appear in the seedlings in our house, as they sometimes do, we're always surprised, because we can't figure out where they've come from. Since the soil mix is sterile, we can only assume that they must have been hiding in the house plants.

Insects are not usually a major problem for indoor growers unless other nearby plants are already infected. Houseplants often have aphids, and the beautiful poinsettia you received for Christmas may have brought with it white flies, leafhoppers, or spider mites, all of which can spread rapidly and infect small seedlings.

Messy greenhouses can harbor insect eggs under benches, in piles of rubble, or in weeds growing in the aisles. Dirty flats or pots are another breeding ground. Open greenhouse doors or hotbeds let in flying outdoor insects on warm spring days, which can multiply rapidly in a warm, humid greenhouse atmosphere. It is possible to have a real invasion before you're aware anything is wrong.

Other insects can present problems too. One greenhouse grower had several failures with his lettuce crop before he realized that ants climbing up a post from the floor were stealing his seed as fast as he planted it!

The best way to control insects in a greenhouse is to disinfect it thoroughly with a strong insecticide and fungicide before plants or people will be spending any time in it. Ask your county extension service what is being recommended and what is legal and available.

Many insects that damage seedlings, either in the house or greenhouse, can be controlled with a regular spraying of Rotenone or by spot spraying with House and Garden Raid. Each time you water look over your plantings closely to see if any alien has staked a claim on them. Insect invasions can usually be checked quite easily if nipped in the bud, but a major epidemic is extremely difficult to eradicate.

The best defense is, of course, prevention. Use only clean flats and pots, and make sure any plants you bring in are *clean*. Be particularly careful about buying plants from garden centers, greenhouses, and from community plant sales, because the best of them are often infested with white flies and aphids. Look over any gift plants carefully, and perhaps quarantine them for a few days before putting them in the greenhouse or near your seedlings.

FERTILIZING SEEDLINGS

A new seed or seedling is delicate and, like a baby, is not ready for anything resembling a barbecued steer dinner. Gardeners, hoping to hustle the growth of their plants, frequently apply too much fertilizer and cause fertilizer "burn" that can weaken or even kill them.

A seed carries enough nutrients within it to sprout and maintain the seedling for a short time, but then it will need additional nourishment. Although nonorganic gardeners use liquid fertilizers such as Rapid-Gro or Miracle-Gro in weak solutions to feed new seedlings, I believe that organic fertilizers are a safer way to feed plants. When I plant I always mix with the medium a tiny amount of dried cow or chicken manure; it is then ready when the seeds need more food. Dried sheep manure may also be used.

After a few weeks, if growth seems to be slowing down, I mix manure with water, stir it well, and give the plants the brew in small doses. The greenhouse takes on an unusual fragrance, but it makes plants grow.

TRANSPLANTING

As soon as the plants get their first set of real leaves—the second pair that appears—it is time to transplant them from their seedbed. I place them 2 inches apart each way in flats or plant boxes, or put each in an individual pot if I have the room. I prefer to use pots whenever possible because single plants can be set into the garden with less damage to the roots than those grown in flats. Most herbs, vegetables, and annual flowers get off to a faster start in the garden if they are transplanted and grown for a few weeks in 3-inch pots, styrofoam cups, the bottom half of plastic-coated quart or half-gallon milk cartons, or frozen juice containers. Peppers, tomatoes, and eggplants should especially be as large and sturdy as possible to beat the short growing season. I like to pot them in the larger containers, those of 5 inches in diameter or more.

Sometimes we grow a few hybrid tomatoes in 8-inch pots. They

Early fruiting and large crops are the rewards for starting tomatoes inside *early*.

are usually in bloom and often have small fruits on them when we set them out in mid-June; and by July they begin to ripen, weeks ahead of the others.

Melons, squash, and other hard-to-transplant vegetables, as well as poppies, should be grown by planting the seed directly in a 3-inch peat pot filled with a rich soil mixture. We usually plant three or four seeds in each pot and remove the weaker ones if more than one grows. These can be set out easily when the weather becomes warm enough, with no shock or setback to the plants.

If you grow or buy plants in flats, you will probably have better transplanting results if you root-prune them a week or so in advance. With a sharp knife cut between each of the plants in the flat, dividing them into cubes. Cut to the bottom of the flat and water it thoroughly and immediately to help ease the shock of

Cut small plants apart in the flat a *week* before planting in the garden, to help prevent *transplant shock*.

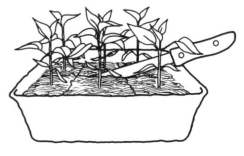

the damage you've done to the roots. By the time you set them out a week later new roots will have developed within each cube, and they will separate easily into neat, well-rooted plants.

Potting Soils

Ordinary garden soil is not the best medium for potting your transplants. In order to promote the fastest growth possible a potting soil should be loose, well supplied with nutrients, and sifted to free it from rocks, sticks, roots, and similar things. You can buy potting soil, although it may be expensive in large amounts, or you can mix your own.

We like to use a mixture of ⅓ rich loam from fields or woods, ⅓ sand, and ⅓ peat moss or compost, combining the materials when they are dry. To each 4 or 5 cubic feet (approximately one wheelbarrow load), we add a quart of dried manure, one cup of lime, and one cup of bone meal.

It's necessary to plan ahead in the North if you mix your own potting soil; if you don't, the materials may still be frozen when you want them in the spring. It seems to work best for us to mix ours in the fall and store it over the winter in garbage cans or plastic bags in the basement, garage, or greenhouse. The several months of storage time seem to "cure" the fertilizers and make a soil that encourages optimum growth, particularly if it is not constantly frozen. It is nice to have it ready to use in the spring instead of frozen in a pile outside.

Setting Out the Plants

Transplanting young seedlings is a critical process in the North. Those grown in a sheltered house or greenhouse environment instead of a cold frame should be "hardened off" by being put outside for several days before setting them out in the garden.

Put them out for the first time on a mild, cloudy day, or, if it is sunny, set them in a shady spot. At first they must be protected from wind and any cold, pelting rain, as well as from bright sunlight. Gradually, as they become acclimated, they can spend longer periods of being exposed to weather. Keep track of them, for they will dry out easily. Unlike soil in the garden, that in containers receives no moisture from the surrounding ground.

Set *peat pots* well below the surface of the soil to prevent drying out.

Plant the seedlings in the garden on a warm, rainy day, if possible, or if rain doesn't seem imminent, choose a cloudy day. If the weather is perfectly clear, with no clouds on the horizon, plant them in the early evening so that they won't be subjected to the hot sun before they get their roots well settled in the new soil.

Dig a small hole for each plant in the thoroughly prepared garden soil and fill the hole with water. Carefully remove the plant, also soaked with water, out of its pot and plant it in the muddy mixture, firming the soil carefully around it. Leave a slight depression around the plant, to catch future waterings. If the following day is hot and dry, cover up the new plants with boxes, pots, or paper bags to keep them shaded.

When you plant peat pots, soak them heavily first. Set them deep enough to bury the pots completely in the soil. Any part of a fibrous pot that sticks out of the soil will act like the wick of a lamp, bringing up moisture from the wet part of the pot below the soil surface, evaporating it into the air and drying out the plant.

If it doesn't rain, water your new transplants heavily every day in early morning for the next week. Those in peat pots will need even more water than the ordinary transplants, until the roots break through their pots and the plants become well established.

Hot Caps

Individual covers, usually called hot caps, make good miniature greenhouses for delicate transplants. You can buy the kind produced commercially, such as Hotkaps, which are made of trans-

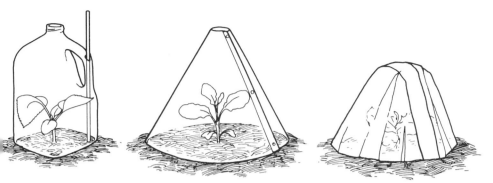

Plastic jugs, fiberglass cones, and *hot caps* protect tender plants; a stake pushed through a hole cut in the jug's handle keeps it from blowing away.

lucent waxpaper or plastic; or you can make your own by cutting the bottom out of a plastic gallon milk or cider jug. Anchor them solidly to the ground with a stake and leave the caps off. These make good heat collectors for warm-weather plants, yet they don't get too hot because they are not clear plastic and they have top ventilation.

Commercial fiberglass cones also serve as excellent heat gatherers and are useful in both spring and fall for frost protection. Their cost may limit their wide use, but if they are stored inside when not in use, they should last for years.

Fiberglass cones serve both as heat traps and frost protectors.

By putting out hot caps a few days before the plants are set out, the soil will be warmed beneath them and the plants will be happier when they are moved in. It is not necessary to "harden off" transplants if you are protecting them with hot caps, but you must water them.

Plastic Tents

You can build a plastic tent over a bed or row of tender seedlings or transplants to protect them on raw, windy days and collect heat from the sun, even if days are cloudy.

Some growers stretch clotheslines, ropes, or wires supported by poles over their plantings and throw plastic tents of polyethylene (usually of 4 mil thickness) over them, much as you would throw clothes over a clothesline. These may be used as heat collectors in the spring and for frost protection in the early fall. On windy days, however, the plastic must be carefully weighted or pegged down.

Since strings and ropes often stretch and sag, and occasionally break, some gardeners prefer to make shelters rather like greenhouses out of cheap lumber and posts or frames out of plastic or aluminum pipe. These are often constructed in the shape of a

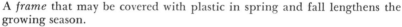

A *frame* that may be covered with plastic in spring and fall lengthens the growing season.

Bales of hay piled with an opening to the south make good heat traps to shelter tender plants.

Quonset hut or like a row of large croquet wickets. The plastic is stretched over them in such a way that it can be open at both ends for ventilation during the day and closed when necessary on cold nights. Only a few minutes of direct sunlight on a tight, clear plastic house will quickly bake the plants inside beyond recovery. If you tighten up this kind of structure for a cold night, be sure to rise early and open it the next morning.

In the heat of the summer the plastic is removed entirely. No matter how a tent is constructed, its purpose is the same—to collect additional heat in the soil around the plants so they will grow faster.

Sun Traps

If you live in a cold, windy area, you may be able to grow the warm weather crops successfully only by using a sun or heat trap.

You have no doubt noticed how snow melts much faster in a corner facing toward the south where two buildings meet. A heat trap in the garden does the same thing. In the prairie provinces of Canada, heat-loving plants are sometimes grown between two or three layers of hay bales piled up in a U-shape facing the sun. The structure is covered with plastic on cold days and nights in the spring and when frost threatens in late summer.

Buildings, hedges, and walls oriented toward the sun can all be used to collect heat for plants, or you can construct your own heat trap of boards or plastic fencing. Clear fiberglass fences, 2 to 3 feet tall, can be used to construct an open-top heat trap that will ripen tomatoes and peppers weeks earlier than those grown in wind-swept spots. We have planted our tomatoes in such an enclosure with great success.

You may want to use materials that are cheaper than fiberglass for the north and west sides of the fence. The structure can be made large enough for growing two or three plants, or as many as you want. With ingenuity, you'll be able to construct the ideal heat trap for your own needs and location.

PART TWO

Growing Food in the North

One of the more disturbing statements I have read in recent years was buried in a report published by the Department of Agriculture. It stated that the cost of energy now makes it more profitable for West Coast farmers to ship their produce to Japan than to the northeastern United States.

Whether or not this situation is likely to result in a food shortage, those of us in any area of the country that must import our supply can be assured of future enormous increases in the cost of store-bought food.

It presents an exciting opportunity, however, for northerners who have been accustomed to relying on southern California and Florida for winter eating. For nearly two centuries the North Country produced nearly all the food and energy it needed, and it can be done again. Since we must work within the limits of our climate, however, self-sufficiency will obviously require some changes in our diet—most of them good. Fresh, nutritious, flavorful fruits and vegetables untouched by additives and preservatives are not a bad exchange for hours spent in the garden.

CHAPTER FOUR

GROWING VEGETABLES

"Never plant a garden bigger than your wife can look after" is
the old Yankee admonition. One of our old herbals puts it differently: "Praise large gardens, plant small ones." Many people
become frustrated at keeping up with the demands of a large
garden. In the unhurried days of winter they order too many seeds
and put in more than they can either tend or eat.

I've known discouraged northerners who gave up vegetable
gardening for other reasons as well. Their tomatoes didn't ripen,
their newly sprouted beans froze, the woodchucks ate the peas,
or a blight struck the potatoes. They now eat vegetables that are
several days or weeks old and of doubtful vitamin content, just like
city folks.

It's a pity not to garden in the North because one of the big
advantages of living here is to taste the fresh vegetables, fruits, and
berries that grow so deliciously in the cool summer climate.

I won't promise that growing your own food supply in the
North is always easy. There are many problems when you try to
crowd six months of gardening into less than three, but I'll guarantee that it is worth the trouble.

LOCATION

A sunny, well-drained spot to plant your vegetables is essential. If
you have a place where the land slopes gently toward the south or
southeast, that is the best location for your garden, as described
in chapter 2. The early rays of the spring sun melt the snow and
warm the soil on this exposure far faster than on a northern or
western slope, especially if the area is protected from chilly
north and west winds.

If you can arrange, also, to place your garden where the soil
is already good, you'll save work and the expense of building it
up. Wet, heavy soils stay cold late in the spring, and gravelly ones

dry out too fast. Rich, light loam is best, and second best is a soil with good texture that you can improve.

Although a community garden is truly a blessing to anyone who has no other good spot available, it is a great convenience to have your garden close by your home. You can work in it at odd intervals whenever a few minutes of time are available, and if you check the plants at frequent intervals, it's easier to be aware when each vegetable is ready to harvest and to notice when bugs are attacking.

Locate your vegetables away from the fumes and dust of a highway, if possible, and a safe distance from any septic drainage field.

SOIL PREPARATION

The garden should, of course, be thoroughly rototilled, harrowed, or spaded deeply by hand before it is planted. Sometimes in the rush of spring I tend to cut soil preparation short, but experience has taught me that once or twice over the garden with the rototiller is not enough in our rather heavy soil. Well-tilled soil warms up much faster and has more air in it than poorly tilled soil. It encourages good growth, makes future cultivation and hoeing easier, and, last but not least, the weeds can be pulled out better.

The best time to till the soil is when it is fairly dry. After the garden has been cultivated, don't walk on it until you plant it, especially when it is wet, because your weight will compact the soil. Some gardeners put down boards if it is necessary to walk over a wet garden in the spring. Even after you've planted the seeds, try to avoid compacting the soil between the rows any more than necessary.

MELTING THE SNOW FASTER

Some years the snow depth on our garden may reach 5 or 6 feet on the level, and deeper where it drifts. Like most gardeners, we are impatient to get started in the spring, and it seems that the snow takes forever to melt. So, for years we have sprinkled wood ashes on the snow to make it melt faster. On sunny days the sprinkled area disappears much quicker, and it is often completely

Wood ashes or *powdered charcoal* may be used to melt snow quickly on sunny spring days.

gone a week or more earlier than the untreated snow. A further
bonus—it adds alkalinity to the soil. I have also used other dark-
colored materials, such as soil, sand, and powdered charcoal,
with good results. Although the material disappears into the soil
where you won't see it, nevertheless it remains there, so don't use
creosote, used motor oil, or other unsavory products.

FERTILIZER AND LIME

The wife of a well-known professor of our acquaintance received
from him, for her birthday gift, a load of manure for her garden.
Romantic it was not, but she couldn't have been happier. She was
a good gardener and realized the importance of fertilizer.

We are lucky to live near a farmer who is willing to part with
several loads of manure each year, which we put on our orchard,
berry plants, and vegetable garden. We prefer to get fresh farm
manure in the fall and put it on before the ground freezes so that
the urea that oozes out of it can soak into our soil instead of being
wasted. By spring the manure is aged and ready to feed the plants.

Whether you decide to use organic or chemical fertilizer, or a
combination of the two, is up to you; but don't fail to apply some
kind of fertilizer each year. If you can't get manure easily, you
may want to make your own humus by composting a variety of
organic wastes that are usually available, as described in chapter 2.

Over the years I have made many soil tests for gardeners, and,
with the exception of those plots that had been well fertilized recently, every test showed a need for nitrogen, phosphorus, potash,
and, quite often, lime. I seldom test for fertility any more, just
assuming that the soil needs manure or some other complete fertilizer every year. I do test for lime, because that may or may not
be needed.

In warm areas of the world it is possible to get along without
proper pH in the soil because the long growing season will compensate for the plants' slow growth. In the North, however, the
soil must have the proper degree of acidity-alkalinity if the plants
are to grow quickly. Northern soils usually range from a pH of 4.5
to 7.5. Since most vegetables grow best with a pH of 6 to 7, a soil
test is obviously essential. (See the list of different plants and their
lime preferences on page 32.)

Occasionally newcomers in our area attempt to garden without fertilizer, but the results are disappointing. A few trusting souls still feel, apparently, that all there is to farming is to put a seed in the soil and sit back and wait for the harvest.

To conserve fertility in the soil we run the rows across the slope of the garden instead of up and down. That way rain is less likely to wash it out. Many gardeners plant winter rye after harvesting the garden in the early fall to prevent the wind and rain from eroding the soil's fertility.

Some of the most successful gardeners I know have built up a fantastically rich garden soil by sheet-composting it. They have two plots of land of equal size for their garden and change from one to the other every three or four years. On the plot that is not being planted for a garden they spread layer after layer of manure, shredded bark, leaves, hay, rock phosphate, and all sorts of organic wastes for the first year or two. Then, after this is mostly decayed, they till it under and plant a cover crop such as oats, millet, or winter rye. When these are plowed under, they have a deep, lush soil, rich in everything a garden needs to thrive.

BUYING SEEDS

Most gardeners begin soon after the Christmas season to receive a variety of seed catalogs from all over the country. Most collections include the old-time, established places like Burpee and Harris, organic firms like Johnny's Selected Seeds, and, of course, Vesey's on Prince Edward Island, which is aimed at northern growers. Northerners may well wonder whether the location of the seed source makes a difference in how well it will grow in the North.

It definitely makes a difference, because seed from plants that are acclimated to the North grow far better here. However, usually we have no way of knowing where the seed actually was grown. Many northern gardeners bought seeds loyally from a Vermont firm for years, thinking they were grown in the Green Mountains. Most of us never realized that the company had only a large warehouse in Vermont and bought most of its seeds out of state, usually from the West Coast.

A few northern seed houses are growing part of their seed today, among them Johnny's Selected Seeds of Albion, Maine. Their catalog says: "A good portion of our seed is produced on our farm and by our organic growers in the U.S. and Canada." With many catalogs, however, all we can do is study the descriptions and the listed "growing days to maturity," make our decisions, and hope for the best.

If you select seeds in a retail store, look carefully at the description on the packet to check the length of time to maturity, and select only those varieties that will mature within your estimated length of growing season. Select varieties your family likes, and if you freeze vegetables or store them in a root cellar, choose kinds that are good for that purpose as well. You may want to choose one kind of beet that is ready early for tender beet greens, and another that matures later and is good for winter storage.

If you raise large amounts of certain crops, you may want to select more than one variety of each kind. Peas and corn are our main crops, since we like them so much and they freeze well for winter eating. We carefully choose kinds that ripen at different times so as not to have to stay up all night shelling and freezing.

Each year we experiment with a few of the new kinds, trying to find those that have the best flavor when they're fresh and those that taste best when they've been frozen. Sometimes catalogs tell you these things, but trial and error and observations of friends will tell you more accurately.

Some of us get overly excited with plant novelties and waste a lot of our gardening efforts on them. Many items in seed catalogs that catch our eye are of little practical value. A few gourds and similar plants are fun, yet so productive that a hill or two supplies your needs unless you plan to sell them. Yard-long beans, climbing tomatoes, and climbing strawberries, huckleberries, and similar plants are also interesting, but northern gardeners should not expect fantastic results from them.

Tobacco, peanuts, soybeans, lima beans, sweet potatoes, large watermelons, and similar things are all strictly warm-climate plants, although certain varieties may be worth a try in the North, especially if you use season-lengthening devices.

If your garden space is limited, you may want to grow only the crops that are difficult to purchase locally and buy the rest. For instance, you may want to skip growing potatoes and corn. They take a lot of room and work and deplete the garden soil greatly.

Often they can be bought easily from nearby market gardeners, as can tomatoes, pumpkins, squash, onions, and dried beans. You might like to plant a few of these popular crops for eating fresh and buy whatever you need for preserving.

Order your seeds as soon as you can after you receive the catalog if you send away for them, because some years seed crops are poor and supplies limited. Also, seed companies are likely to be more harried later in the spring and, we've found, more likely then to make mistakes in filling orders.

When the seeds arrive, or after you've chosen them from a store rack, wrap them in a plastic bag and store them in a cool closet until planting time. We like to separate ours into various lots as soon as they come, to save rummaging around for them later on. We group them according to the month they should be started.

SAVING YOUR OWN SEED

During the Depression our family and most of our neighbors raised a lot of our own seeds to save money, although at that time a package of seed cost only five or ten cents. Corn, beans, and peas were the most common ones, but we also saved lettuce, spinach, radish, tomato, pumpkin, squash, and cucumber seeds. A few beet, parsnip, turnip, onion, and carrot roots were often planted the second year also, to blossom and go to seed. It was difficult to get chard and members of the cabbage family to seed in our climate.

Anyone who likes a feeling of independence and wants to save money can grow seed. An added bonus for northern gardeners is the fact that when it is locally grown, it usually grows more vigorously and matures earlier.

If you intend to save and use homegrown seed, you must avoid mixing different varieties of the same vegetable. Only one kind of pea, one kind of corn, etc., should be planted in the same area. If you must grow additional kinds, space them several hundred feet apart so that they won't cross-pollinate. As corn is pollinated by the wind rather than by bees, the different strains need be only 100 feet apart.

Hybridizing seed is a science in itself. Home gardeners who save seed should not save any from hybrid corn, tomatoes, or similar vegetables. Although seed saved from these vegetables may grow and produce good results, it will not be as good as the original hybrid seed you bought.

Hybrid vegetables are grown from a controlled cross-pollination between two different varieties, and this cross-fertilization must be done each year if hybrid seed is desired. Unfortunately it is a rather difficult procedure for a home gardener to duplicate. Since many nonhybrid vegetables are of very high quality, plant these if you plan to save your own seed.

Members of the cucurbitaceae family often cross-pollinate each other resulting in a hybrid of the two. Don't plant pumpkins, squash, and gourds near each other if you plan to save the seed, or next year's vegetables may include a crop of squmpkins or puash!

Homegrown seed must be well-cleaned, carefully dried, and stored in glass jars or plastic bags in a cool place. Seed will keep a year or two under good conditions; after that it will begin to lose some of its vitality and sprout more slowly, or perhaps not at all.

How to Save Your Own Seeds

BEANS AND PEAS—Allow them to ripen completely and partially dry out while still in the ground. After they turn brown, pull the whole plant, dry them thoroughly, thresh and clean them.

BEETS, PARSNIPS, TURNIPS—Plant a few roots from your winter storage in the spring. These will bloom and produce seeds in mid- to late summer. Pick them after they are ripe. Shell and dry the seeds on sheets of paper or in flat pans.

CARROTS—Plant some roots in the spring. Gather the seed in late summer when it is ripe enough to fall off the stems easily. Dry on fine, meshed screens or papers. Make sure there are no plants of Queen Anne's lace or other wild carrots nearby, or they may cross with your carrots and make the seed worthless. To avoid mistakes some growers raise their carrot seed under screened boxes to keep out the bees, and pollinate the blooms by hand, transforming the pollen from blossom to blossom by hand with a soft brush.

CORN—Allow the ears to ripen thoroughly. Then pick them and pull back the husks, but leave them attached to the ear. Hang them in an airy, dry place, not touching each other, until thoroughly dry. Shell and dry additionally until they resemble seed corn you buy.

LETTUCE, RADISH—These usually go to seed by themselves in the garden. Pick them only after the seed is completely ripe. Gather lettuce seed when it starts to fall naturally. Shell radish pods when the seeds become dark-colored. Dry inside in an airy place.

CUCUMBERS, MELONS, PEPPERS, PUMPKINS, SQUASH, TOMATOES, WATERMELONS—Allow the fruits to ripen completely but not rot. Wash the pulp off the seeds and dry them on fine mesh screens or in pans.

WHETHER TO START YOUR OWN SEEDLINGS OR BUY THEM

If you have good plant sources nearby and like the varieties they supply, it saves a lot of trouble to buy your tomato, cabbage, lettuce, broccoli, cauliflower, pepper, celery, and similar seedlings all started and ready to plant. It makes it easier to get just the right number too.

Many people work away from home and cannot give seedlings all the care they need. If your home is kept cool, it may be difficult to start seeds without damping-off problems. With the high cost of seeds today, it may be cheaper and easier to travel even a long distance to get good started plants, rather than start your own.

There are, of course, many reasons for growing your own plants from seed. The plant supply in your area may be uncertain or the prices unusually high. You may want to grow an uncommon variety; you may use a large number of plants; or you may want some extra for friends or to sell. If you have a good place to start them and the time to care for them, it is satisfying and fun to grow your own from seed. We always enjoy watching the seeds progress from tiny sprouts to the transplant stage, especially in the late winter when we can almost see them grow.

If you decide to start your own, plan your seed-sowing schedule with the date of the last expected frost in mind. Our last frost of the spring is likely to come sometime between May 25 and June 15, so we count backward from those dates. See planting instructions in chapter 3.

PLANTING THE GARDEN

Each year we "plant" our garden on paper before we put the seeds and transplants in the soil; and we keep records so that the following years our crops can be rotated and any mistakes we've made can be corrected. Tall-growing corn or telephone peas should not be planted where they'll shade sun-loving tomatoes or peppers, for example, and zucchini vines should not crowd out delicate bean plants. Last year we planted dill for the first time, and found it grew so tall it shaded everything in the row behind it.

Spinach, lettuce, herbs, and other edible greens should always be planted a distance away from anything you might spray, such as potatoes, broccoli, cabbage, or others. If you plan to use herbicides, group together all plants that need the same treatment. You might like to place in the same corner those plants that must be covered for fall frosts.

If you follow your plan exactly, it isn't necessary to mark each row with the variety planted there. Our markers always seem to get lost before we start to harvest the vegetables, anyway. It is convenient to keep a record of the varieties you plant, as well as where you plant them, because if you have a memory like mine, you'll forget which kinds tasted the best and which didn't mature or were in some other way unsatisfactory and therefore should be omitted the following year.

Some gardeners hate to throw away any plants or seeds. If they start three dozen cherry tomato plants, they set them all out, even though three plants would supply all they want. Packets of cucumber, radish, zucchini, and others usually have more seeds than most people can use. It is a waste to plant them all.

Follow carefully the directions on each seed packet, and plant each kind of seed at the right depth. You don't want them to wash out in a rain, nor do you want them down so deep they'll take weeks to sprout.

The rows should be spaced for your convenience. I've seen some home gardens with rows spaced a foot apart and some that were 4 feet apart. If you hand-hoe or mulch, it's important to leave enough room between the rows so that you can walk comfortably after the plants are full-grown. Make them wide enough to admit the tiller if you cultivate with one, or a horse if you use that method to hoe and hill the plants. Above all, don't leave more room between the rows than you need. Not only do you waste rich soil and invite erosion, but widely spaced rows make a lot more work and look less attractive.

SUCCESSIVE PLANTING

Since the season is so short in the North, successive plantings of many crops are not practical. There are notable exceptions, however. Some vegetables, like radishes, mature and go by so rapidly that they must be planted repeatedly if you are to enjoy them for throughout the summer. Lettuce and spinach (which bolt and go to seed quickly in warm weather), peas, and early beets are likely candidates for successive crops. By planting short rows of these fast-maturing crops every week for three or four weeks or longer, depending on your estimated first frost, you'll have young and tender vegetables throughout the entire summer. It may be possible to put in two or three plantings of early corn in places where the growing season is somewhat longer than our usual seventy to ninety days.

In addition to those started plants of the cabbage family you set out, you may want to sow directly in the soil seeds of early cabbage, broccoli, and cauliflower, which will mature later, yet, being cold hardy, will still be ready before harvest time.

Growing another crop of vegetables in the fall is less common in the North than further south, although many people are doing it on a limited scale. Lettuce, spinach, radishes, chard, kale, and beets can be planted in mid-August and will provide a few weeks of good, tender eating before hard frosts. In some years edible pod peas will also mature.

FALL PLANTING

In an attempt to outwit the tricky spring weather some northern gardeners plant a few seeds of hardy plants in very late fall, just before winter. They reason that, since weed seeds lie dormant until spring, why shouldn't other seeds? Onion seeds can be successfully planted then, and some growers claim success with peas, radishes, and other crops, especially in years when snows come early and stay all winter.

My luck with this planting method has been limited; I've found that the weeds grow better than the seeds. It is also difficult to know exactly when to plant. If the seeds should start to grow during a warm, Indian summer week, they would be lost. If you attempt fall seeding, plant as late as possible before snowfall.

THINNING

I once visited a neighbor when he was weeding his garden. Instinctively I stooped to weed a row while we talked. Soon I forgot it wasn't my garden and was thinning out turnips at a great rate. Noticing his paled appearance, I sheepishly stopped.

"You know," he said, "I just can't ever bring myself to thin out anything. I realize that I should, but I can't. Maybe I should hire you to do it when I'm not watching. I just plant more of everything, hoping enough of them will turn out all right." He had an enormous garden, including three long rows of turnips, for his family of four. Since then I have seen many gardens only a quarter the size of his that were much more productive.

Even for those who love to garden it makes little sense to waste seed, fertilizer, land, and work growing hundreds of plants that will never be worth harvesting. Although it may require self-discipline, we should thin our plants so that each one will have room to mature without being crowded. Thinning is an important job wherever you garden, but it is especially practical in the North, where speedy growth is vital.

If you plant seeds sparingly, you'll save yourself much thinning out later on, especially with radishes, carrots, parsnips, beets, corn, turnips, and onions. Although peas and beans can be planted more thickly, there is no point in wasting seeds. Sometimes it helps to mix the smallest seeds with sand or dried coffee grounds before you plant in order to space them effectively. Follow the directions for spacing on your seed packages, both for thinning and for setting out transplants.

Usually it works best to thin root crops in stages, harvesting the

thinnings to eat whenever they are large enough. We look forward
to the first tiny, tender carrots of the season, the small beets, and
the fresh young greens. The taste of mature vegetables never quite
compares to the first of each in its season.

INTENSIVE GARDENING

Ruth and David Gaillard, who garden successfully near the top of
a windy Vermont mountain, practice all the methods northern
gardeners use to cope with their short season. They lengthen out
the growing time by using a greenhouse, protective covers, and
similar methods, and they are also masters in the art of speeding
up the growth of their plants and so harvest a large percentage of
their garden before the frosts begin.

The Gaillards, who are transplants from Washington, D.C., feel
that there are special advantages to encouraging fast plant growth.
It is less expensive than lengthening the growing season, requires
very little equipment, and takes less time and attention. Furthermore, in their case, it produces tremendous results in a small area.
They believe that they achieve the best results by intensive gardening.

Intensive gardening is a method of raising vegetables by growing
the plants in raised beds much closer together than is common. To
accomplish this a deep, well-tilled soil is necessary to make sure
the roots go downward rather than sideways.

To start a suitable bed, enrich the garden soil heavily with
manure or compost. Spade or till it deeply, at least a foot or more.
One good way to build up beds is to outline the area with 6- or
8-inch boards, stood on edge and held in place by posts to keep the
soil in place. The area should be an easy width to reach across, from
3 to 5 feet wide.

Loose soil is then shoveled into the beds to raise them 6 to 8
inches or more, making a total growing depth of at least 20 inches.
To warm the soil some growers lay a sheet of 4 mil plastic over
the bed for a few sunny days before planting.

In the North full sun is as necessary for intensive culture as it
is for any vegetable garden. For the plants to get an abundance of
sunlight and the soil to warm up rapidly, the beds should be on
land sloping gently to the south, be somewhat protected from north

and west winds, and be a rich, loamy-sandy mixture well supplied with manure and compost rich in fertility.

Besides nitrogen, phosphorus, and potash, the Gaillards add other elements, plus the proper amount of calcium, to their soil. They believe that some fruits and tomatoes, for example, ripen far faster in a soil with adequate magnesium, and that other plants need boron, zinc, manganese, molybdenum, cobalt, copper, and other elements in small amounts, but still more than most northern soils provide. Many garden supply houses now sell these trace element fertilizers, and a few extension services provide soil-testing services to determine if they are needed.

We have had excellent results from planting lettuce, spinach, and chard in raised beds. Carrots, beets, radishes, parsnips, onions, and similar plants also fit well into intensive farming. Even tomatoes, peppers, small-headed cabbage, broccoli, turnips, cauliflower, and Brussels sprouts can be grown in this manner, though most gardeners prefer to plant the larger-growing vegetables in rows, where it is easier to space them well.

Intensive gardening is especially beneficial for northern gardeners because the soil warms up faster in beds and the plants grow more quickly. As many plants can be grown in a small area, the method is made to order for anyone with limited gardening space. It also saves a great deal of hoeing and requires less fertilizer, since you are working with a relatively small total area.

Because the plants grow so close together, weeds present much less of a problem than when plants are grown in rows, and if the area is relatively free of weeds at planting time, almost no weeding

The *soil* in raised beds warms up faster. Seeds can be planted earlier and plants grow more quickly.

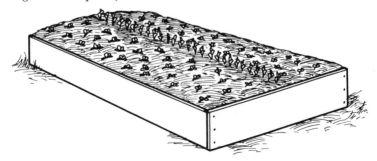

is necessary. If any do appear, they should be promptly removed. A weed-free bed is absolutely essential; delicate vegetable plants should not be required to share their plot with vigorous, pushy weeds.

By being crowded together, plants grow taller in an intensive bed. The earlier maturing vegetables should be harvested as soon as they are ready to make room for others to grow.

The method originated in Europe, where growing space is often limited, and it often goes by the name of "French Intensive Gardening." It is frequently used on terraced gardens at high elevations, where growing seasons are short and cool.

WEED CONTROL

I've always known that weeds are not desirable in a garden for appearance's sake, but I never realized how wretched they are until I first grew plants in large pots. Whenever I had two identical plants in the same kind of soil and in the same size container, and one had a husky dandelion in it, by the end of the summer that plant would reach only half the size of the one without the dandelion.

All weeds steal nutrients and moisture, and a few give off foul substances that are toxic to certain other plants. They are such rank growers that they slow down and sometimes stop entirely the growth of garden plants. A successful gardener must keep dandelions, kale, grass, and a hundred others under control from the beginning of the season rather than let them grow large and have to get rid of them later.

There are several ways to slow down weed proliferation. Careful soil preparation helps tremendously. By raking out as many grass and perennial weed roots as possible before you plant seeds, you can save lots of pulling and hoeing later. Keep the area around the garden mowed to prevent masses of weed seeds from blowing in. Use composted or dried manure rather than fresh manure, because the latter contains many more viable weed seeds; and if you mulch, use straw, leaves, spoiled ensilage, lawn clippings, or composted bark, all of which are more weed-free than ordinary, late-cut hay.

Another way to avoid the spread of weeds is to keep the ground covered by planting winter rye or millet as soon as the early peas, radishes, and spinach are harvested. It may be more practical, how-ever, if your season is long enough to replant the harvested area with more spinach, peas, lettuce, and other short-term crops.

Most organic gardeners hoe, cultivate, and hand-pull weeds throughout the growing season, although some people allow them to grow in late August, since the garden crop is usually mature by then. If you do allow weeds to grow in fall, pull them before they go to seed; once they've fallen into the earth they'll reappear as worse pests the next spring.

Rather than rely on cultivation and hand weeding, commercial gardeners often use various herbicides to eliminate weeds. Most are expensive, some are toxic, and I don't encourage their use by home gardeners. Nevertheless, some people feel that the risk is worth taking, considering the time and labor saved. The following herbicides are on the market and in common use.

Premerge is a yellow, evil-looking chemical that is sprayed on the ground just after planting corn, peas, beans, and potatoes to keep new weed seeds from sprouting for several weeks.

Dacthyl is used to control annual weeds in peas, beans, corn, and potatoes, and it is used on certain transplants, including tomatoes, cabbage, cauliflower, Brussels sprouts, cucumber, broccoli, peppers, pumpkins, squash, and melons. It should be used on transplants only, and not on spots where seeds of any of these plants will be placed directly in the ground.

Treflan, Vegetex, and others are also used for weed control on vegetable gardens, and *Aatrex (Atrazine)* is used on corn. All herbi-cides must be carefully applied at precisely the right time and in the proper amount for each specific crop, and some are suitable for certain soils only. Read the labels carefully before buying the products, store them in a safe place, use them only on the recom-mended crops and with the utmost care. Government regulations on chemicals change frequently, so check carefully to see if the chemical you intend to use is legal for the crops you have in mind.

MULCHES

One spring when I cleaned out our root cellar I dumped some old potatoes into the compost pile. They sprouted and grew through the partially rotted leaves and compost, and by midsummer had produced some of the most beautiful, solid potatoes I had ever seen.

The next year I decided to grow the potatoes under a thick mulch of leaves and hay, and the results were excellent. This method eliminated weeding and disease, and there were very few bugs. Harvesting was easy too. When we pulled aside the mulch, there were the potatoes. They tasted wonderful, and we continue to grow potatoes the same way whenever we can get the hay.

I've experimented a great deal with mulch. Sometimes, when I could get spoiled hay easily, I mulched the whole vegetable garden with it; other times, I spread it over only part. I discovered, as chapter 2 describes, that only cool-weather crops do well under a mulch that's spread early in the spring in the North. Peas, beets, carrots, potatoes, parsnips, turnips, cabbage, cauliflower, broccoli, Brussels sprouts, kohlrabi, spinach, chard, and lettuce all do well when mulched as soon as they are a few inches tall, but most mature a bit later than they do when unmulched. Corn thrives when it is mulched in midsummer, after it is well started, but other warm-weather crops grow better with no mulch or with a mulch of sand or plastic to attract the heat. An ordinary mulch is useful on

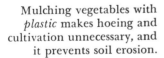
Mulching vegetables with *plastic* makes hoeing and cultivation unnecessary, and it prevents soil erosion.

these crops only during hot, dry summers, common in the Midwest but rare in the Northeast.

Mulch encourages frost damage by keeping the ground heat contained and away from the plants. Low-growing beans, potatoes, cucumbers, and melons especially need the ground heat on cool fall nights. On corn and other higher growing plant life, however, mulch does not seem to increase frost damage.

Unless mulch is removed at the end of the garden year, it becomes mixed with the soil, of course. It is therefore important to choose materials that won't hurt the soil in any way or create problems in planting the following spring. Or choose a material like plastic that can be picked up and reused. Be wary of covering a garden with uncomposted sawdust, partly rotted garbage, wood shavings, newspapers, magazines, asphalt roofing, or similar materials.

On the other hand, some materials that are excellent as mulch are dried or newly mown hay that's cut early, before its weed seeds ripen; partially rotted, shredded bark from a sawmill; spoiled ensilage from a farm; salt hay; or other weed-free materials that may be obtained economically.

Apply all mulch only when the soil is moist; light rains and irrigation will not penetrate it, and the soil could remain dry during part of the critical growing season, which would defeat the purpose of the mulch.

CONTROLLING PESTS

One of the worst pests in the North Woods attacks the gardener rather than the garden. Clouds of black flies in late spring and early summer can make planting and cultivating miserable for those of us who live near the fast-running streams where they breed. Only when there is a strong breeze is it bearable to be outside during the worst of the season, though we use bottles of various repellents, always hoping to find one that will work more than a few minutes.

The garden gets its share of insects too. Luckily, most of the worst bugs don't like our cold northern climate, and the worst epidemics usually take place during the rare warm, dry summers. We use as many natural controls as possible: hedgerows around the garden attract a variety of insect-eating birds; cutworm collars protect our transplants; marigolds, wormwood, and other insect-repelling herb plants scattered throughout the garden help too. Still, it often becomes necessary to spray the broccoli, cauliflower, cabbage, cucumber, eggplant, potatoes, tomatoes, and sometimes the pumpkins, squash, and turnips with Rotenone, Thuricide, or Sevin.

Diseases are often worse pests than bugs in the Northeast, because so many thrive in the mild, dewy evenings of midsummer. This is the time when the garden will likely play host to a variety of mildews, blights, rots, wilts, and other fungi. During a warm, moist summer it may be necessary to spray or dust Captan or some other fungicide on cucumbers, melons, peppers, potatoes, and tomatoes.

Although we get our share of insects and disease, wildlife is by far the worst garden pest in many rural northern areas. In spite of a high, tight fence, the deer, racoons, woodchucks, porcupines, rabbits, and even squirrels and mice seem to regard our garden as their restaurant. We've used hedges of wormwood, electric fences, various scents, lights, human hair in cloth bags, noisemakers, radios, traps, and guns—all without too much success.

Some growers even sleep in their gardens the weeks the corn is ripening, to fight off the racoons. Others employ a watchdog or enlist the help of hunting neighbors. Unfortunately, however, if you garden near a forest, you may never completely solve the "varmint" problem, and the best you can hope for is some degree of control.

Birds can be a dilemma too. Although they are beautiful to see and hear in the spring, and indispensable for insect control and eating weed seeds, they are less welcome when they are scratching out vegetable seeds or devouring corn on the cob. English sparrows, bluejays, starlings, and crows are the worst bird pests in our garden. After years of experience I know I can count on losing every kernel of corn as soon as it sprouts if I forget to put crow repellent on it. Last year a friend planted her carrot, parsnip, and beet seeds four times because the sparrows kept eating them.

Noisemakers and scarecrows help somewhat, as do fluttering strips of aluminum foil strung over the garden. All of these should be put out just before you need the control; otherwise the birds will become accustomed to them. If the birds are numerous and persistent, they will invade anyway, we've found. Some gardeners have discovered that plastic and rubber snakes frighten away some of the smaller birds, but not even these faze the big crows, who often pick them up and carry them off.

THE HARVEST

Last summer a young man who had been in my 4-H club a dozen years ago called to say that he and his family had worked until after midnight for several evenings picking, shelling, and freezing peas, and preserving spinach, beet greens, and beans. "When you showed us how to plant and take care of a garden," he said jokingly, "you never mentioned the long, hard work of harvesting."

Because of our late spring, in the North many kinds of vegetables and berries are ready to harvest at the same time. It may help to plant several varieties of corn and peas that will ripen at different times, to make successive plantings of beans and spinach at one-week intervals, and even to invite unsuspecting friends and relatives from the city to visit you at harvest time.

Although many foods taste better frozen, some of us worry that a power shortage might cost us our food supply if the freezer should fail. Canning and dehydrating, as well as root cellar storage, are

Drying fruits and vegetables is quick and efficient with a *solar drier.*

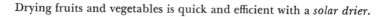

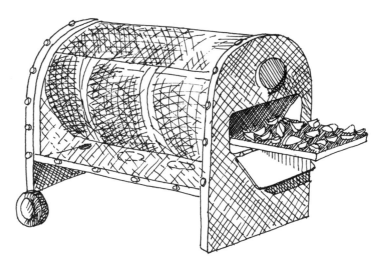

popular alternatives for gardeners who intend to be self-sufficient. One family we know dehydrated their entire vegetable and fruit supply last summer, and they report that the reconstituted food is delicious.

In earlier days drying racks in the oven or over a wood stove were used to dehydrate fruits, berries, and vegetables. Both solar and electrically-operated driers are available from Garden Way, Inc., in Troy, New York.

ROOT CELLARING

One advantage of a cold climate is that we can use it to help preserve our food. Long before anyone thought of a home freezer, our family kept chunks of homegrown pork and beef frozen in a cold back room for much of the winter. Like everyone else's, our stone-lined cellar with its dirt floor kept apples, potatoes, turnip, cabbage, beets, and carrots in fine condition. Unheated upstairs rooms and attics stored butternuts, pumpkins, squash, dried apples, corn, oats, and beans.

After we put a furnace in our cellar, we had to build a cool room in one corner for our storage space. The only temperature control is an outside window that can be closed on warm days and opened cool nights during warm spells in early fall and late spring. Many kinds of apples and vegetables keep in good condition there until April. Shelves at different levels provide a variety of temperatures. The bottom shelf holds the apples, which keep best at a temperature barely above freezing, and the potatoes, carrots, and beets, which prefer to be slightly less cold, are stored on higher shelves.

We store many things in our root cellar now. We've found it saves preserving time in the busy summer, and it's also nice to be able to eat "fresh" rather than frozen vegetables all winter. We dig potatoes before a hard frost in September, and gather the beets, carrots, and turnips in October before the ground starts to freeze. Although we used to pack them all in sand, we've found that layering them with dry maple leaves in plastic clothes baskets keeps them much fresher, and fewer of them rot.

It was years before I learned that not all crops should be gathered as soon as the first cold snap hits in September. Many root crops and some leafy vegetables continue to grow. The flavor of some, like Brussels sprouts, rutabagas, and winter cabbage, improves during the cool days in the fall.

Parsnips taste best if they're left in the ground over the winter and dug in the spring. Put in stakes in the fall, to mark their spot so that they can be dug through the snow if the ground hasn't been frozen. By spring the starches in them have been converted to sugar, and for a brief period they become our favorite vegetable.

WINTER GARDENING

As the winter prices of fresh greens grow higher, and iceberg lettuce shipped thousands of miles becomes less tasty, we're looking for new ways to grow our own. All over the North, herbs and green vegetables are being grown in pots in sunny windows, under lights, and in greenhouses, hotbeds, and grow frames. Although it seems like a good idea, many difficulties appear as gardeners try to grow greens for food in a completely artificial environment, especially when sunshine is scarce and temperatures are low. The results have often been discouraging.

But the outlook is improving. Innovative growing arrangements have been designed for winter use by the Rodale Experimental Farm in Emmaus, Pennsylvania. After a great deal of experimentation, several models of what Rodale calls "Grow Frames" have been developed.

The Grow Frame is similar to a cold frame, except that its transparent top is placed at an angle that will catch more of the low winter sun. The bed is also oriented toward the south rather than the southeast, as are spring-operated cold frames.

The only source of heat in the Rodale frame is sunlight transmitted through fiberglass and an insulating air space that's covered with a layer of polyethylene. The bed is heavily insulated below ground level with styrofoam to prevent frost from creeping in; and a styrofoam curtain is closed tightly over the top of the plants at night and on extremely cold days to hold the collected heat in a smaller area.

Well-screened, deep, rich soil is essential for good growth in a grow frame, just as it is in other intensive gardening beds. During the cooler months seeds should not be planted directly in the

Solar Grow Frame is
positioned to catch the
low winter sunlight.

frame. Plants are started, instead, in the house or greenhouse and moved to the frame after they are well established.

Occasionally gardeners find that growth is poor in a grow frame, even when they have provided good soil and the temperatures are right. They suspect that a lack of carbon dioxide may be responsible, since the frame is very tight, so they open the top whenever the outside air is above freezing. Some also burn a candle or a small amount of paper in a tin can inside the frame occasionally to add a bit of the gas to the air. Whether this is effective or not, I don't know, but it may be worth trying if the plants have not responded to other inveiglings.

Although these frames can be used for gardening all winter in many areas, winters where we live have proven too cold for January and February growing. We find our Rodale-developed frame ideal, however, for lengthening the fresh-greens season until December. After Christmas we start more seeds in our home, meaning the frame can be operational again in late February or early March. It gives us two or three extra months during the sunny springtime for eating fresh greens. Although it's necessary to shovel off the frame frequently so the sun can get through, the salads are well worth the effort.

In spring, when days are warm, the frame can be used as a conventional cold frame. For late fall and late winter use, however, the only vegetables worth planting are those that tolerate very cool temperatures. Many Oriental vegetables are especially suited for this type of culture.

The following are suitable for growing either in an outdoor grow frame, a cool greenhouse, or a basement cold frame.

CHICORY—Thrives when young, but may be prone to mildew as it gets older.

ENDIVE—Does rather well in grow frames, and is less bitter than plants grown outside.

GAI CHOY—Indian mustard with a distinct mustard flavor.

KALE—The dwarf, curled variety has an excellent flavor, better than when grown outside. It does well, especially in late winter.

KOMATSUNA—One of the most tender and mild-flavored of the Chinese Brassica. Grows slowly, but is very cold-tolerant.

KYO MIZUNA—Looks like endive and tastes very good in salads. A fast grower.

LETTUCE—Arctic King is one of the best, according to Mr. Wolf. Green Ice, Salad Bowl, Kagran, Buttercrunch, and Ostinata also do fairly well.

MICHIHILI—A Chinese cabbage available in many seed catalogs and featured in Oriental dishes.

PAK-CHOI—A Chinese white cabbage that can tolerate temperatures well below freezing.

PARSLEY—The curled kinds, such as Paramount, grow best.

SEPPAKU TAINA—Another loose-heading Chinese variety. Pick off the outer leaves and let the new inner ones grow. Stands temperature in the low 20's, but grows only when it is above freezing.

SHUNGIKU—The leaves resemble those of chrysanthemums. Use the young, tender shoots.

SIEW CHOY—Yellow bud radish. Mild mustard flavor, with light green hairless leaves.

SPINACH—It apparently needs more sun than it gets in midwinter, but thrives as spring approaches. Mr. Wolf has had good success with Monnopa.

TURNIPS—Tokyo Cross, Petite White, Express White grow even better than radishes. Harvest when two or three times the size of radishes, and eat raw or fried.

WINTER WINDOW GARDENING

If you don't have the right spot for a winter grow frame, you can still grow lots of greens all winter inside your home. Although, as I noted, most northern gardeners have had less than smashing success when they tried to grow greenery on a sunny windowsill, there are some kinds of vegetables that are excellent for this purpose. Ray Wolf and his friends at Rodale who developed the Grow Frame found that the greens that grow well in the frame are also ideal for cool weather window gardening, and can be grown even in unheated rooms if the temperature stays above freezing.

They discovered that, although Arctic King, Green Ice, and Buttercrunch do considerably better than most other lettuce varieties, the Chinese and other Oriental vegetables are even better for growing inside, since they were developed for sunpit gardening during China's cold winters. If left to grow to maturity, many of them develop a cabbagelike head; but when grown in a winter window garden, they can be picked like leaf lettuce. Since I have never been too fond of Chinese cabbage, I was delighted to discover that the leaves are more tender, less bitter, and have a pleasant, sweet, peppery taste when young and grown inside. Among our favorites are Komatsuna, Kyo Mizuna, Michihili, Pak-choi, and Seppaku Taina.

If you prefer a simpler type of indoor gardening, cut a few tops off beets and turnips and place them in shallow flats of earth or even soup dishes of water to provide winter dish gardens. Their greenery is attractive, and they are a tasty substitute for store-bought lettuce.

Besides growing the leafy vegetables, many indoor gardeners get part of their vitamins from sprouting beans and alfalfa seeds. We find them a tasty addition to the winter diet and a boon to the budget as well.

VEGETABLES FOR THE NORTH

Beans

There are many kinds of bush beans, and all are big improvements over the old stringy kinds that had foliage that rusted easily. Green beans, reddish purple beans, yellow wax beans, pole beans, and shell beans grow easily almost everywhere in the North. We can also grow certain varieties of shell and pole beans for drying and winter baking.

Some good green snap beans are: *Burpee Stringless, Contender, Harvester, Royalty Purple.*

Yellow varieties include: *Butterwax, Goldcrop, Pencil Pod Wax.*

Some good shell beans are: *Dwarf Horticultural, French Horticultural.*

Pole beans include: *Kentucky Wonder, Romano.*

Beans best for baking that will mature in the North are: *Cranberry, Jacob's Cattle, Red Kidney, Soldier, Yellow Eye.*

Although we usually buy the seeds from catalogs, our original dried bean seed came from a package of baking beans grown in Maine that we bought from the food counter at the local grocery store. We baked part of them and planted the rest. Now, when we thresh our Jacob's Cattle beans each fall, we save some of them to plant the following spring.

Baked beans are an old New England tradition that is rapidly regaining popularity. Not only are they rich in protein, but the dry beans can be stored for months or even years without spoiling. Make sure they are completely ripe before you pull them, vines and all, from the garden. Dry them thoroughly before threshing and storing.

All varieties of beans sprout and come up fast after they are

A convenient way to dry *baking-type beans* is to pull out the mature plants in late summer and stake them on a bean drying pole.

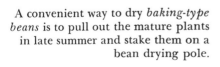

planted. Since they are very susceptible to frost damage and a row of beans is difficult to cover, don't plant them too early. It's better to hold off a bit, then soak the seeds overnight so that they'll sprout faster and make up for lost time.

Lima, mung, fava, and soybeans need a longer growing season than is usually available in the North, although there are some newly developed, early maturing varieties that make us hope that someday we, too, will be able to grow these protein-rich foods.

Corn

Corn not only takes a lot of room in the garden, it also robs a great deal of nourishment from the soil. The Iroquois changed the location of their cornfields often because the corn crop depleted their soil so rapidly. To grow it well you must provide generous amounts of manure or other fertilizer; and be prepared to fight with the coons, and possibly the bears and porcupines.

Although some gardeners have given up trying to raise it, and buy it, instead, from a market gardener, sweet corn, like peas and asparagus, tastes best when it is cooked and eaten only minutes after picking. This taste treat is impossible unless you grow it yourself. As I said before, some people compromise by buying a large amount to freeze, but still grow enough to be able to eat it daily in late summer.

We plant mostly hybrid corn, which is more vigorous and more frost-resistant than ordinary corn. There are now some high-quality, early ripening kinds available. We plant only the yellow or the yellow-white varieties, having found that most of the all-white kinds ripen too late for our short growing season. Any variety that requires more than seventy-five days to mature is too late for us, though your season may permit it. Our favorites are: *Butter and Sugar, Early Extra Sweet, Early Golden Bantam, Early Sunshine, Golden Jewel, Gold Mine,* and *Mevak.*

We grow several kinds all quite close to each other each year, which is good for a variety of flavor and a longer picking season. This is not possible, however, if you want to save your own corn seed. If so, you should grow only one kind, and it should be a non-hybrid.

Popcorn will grow in the North, but only the early kinds will mature, and it may be impossible to get any kind to ripen in the coldest areas. *Bearpaw* and *Japanese Hulless* are two of the earliest. Ornamental Indian corn needs a long growing season too, although certain varieties may mature in favored spots.

If you grow hard corn for drying and grinding, also choose only the earliest kinds. *Early Northern Flint* and *Mandan Bride* are both fairly early, and are good for cornmeal and animal feed. Your local farm store may be able to suggest others that are better for your area.

I've found that once I've picked an ear of corn, cutting off the stalk at ground level gives the remaining stalks more sunshine and room to grow—and corn definitely needs lots of room to grow. If you plant it too thick, thin out the weak plants so that the stalks are a foot apart. Hoe or hill up the soil around each stalk for better growth and to make it less likely to blow over in a strong wind or hailstorm.

Don't plant corn in one long, single row. Instead, plant several rows, even if they are short. Corn is pollinated by the wind; the crop will be small and the ears not full if the pollen from the male tassels on the top of the stalk doesn't blow on the silk (female) of an adjoining plant.

We've tried starting corn inside in peat pots in the hope of eating it sooner, but it matured only a few days earlier than that planted directly in the field, so it was hardly worth all the extra work. Instead, it is more practical to choose early-ripening varieties. Soak the seed for a day before planting, and plant it in a warm, sunny spot as early as is safe, that is, when you expect no more frosts.

If crows are a problem, remember to use a crow repellent on the seed. Hopefully your corn will be "knee-high by the Fourth of July," according to the old saying, and most of it will be mature before the first fall frost. Even a light frost changes the flavor of sweet corn considerably.

Peas

Peas are a cool weather crop and grow very well in the North. In fact, they grow best when the weather is cool. We usually divide the seeds and soak some in water overnight to make them sprout faster and ripen a bit earlier than the others, which we plant dry in the ground. The soaked seeds should be covered with soil as soon as they're dropped in the row, or they will dry out rapidly in the air and sun.

We like the tall-growing, telephone-type peas, such as *Aldermans,* because the peas are so big and easy to pick; but the extra work involved in putting up the fence during a busy spring sometimes makes us settle for a shorter-growing kind. *Alaska, Freezonian, Greater Progress, Laxton, Little Marvel,* and *World's Record* are all good. *Sugar Ann* is a new, delicious, high-quality pea that can be cooked and eaten pods and all, like snap beans.

Sometimes growers in the North have trouble with mildew on the peas. Just about the time the peas are getting ripe, the weather may be warm and the nights dewy, creating an environment that is just right for the fungus to grow. Because peas will grow well in cool weather, mildew can be prevented by simply planting them as early as the soil can be made ready in the spring. Then they will be harvested before the problems begin.

ROOT CROPS

Beets, carrots, parsnips, radishes, turnips, and onions all do well in the North. They need no special care, since all are cool weather crops, but it is important to prepare a deep, loose, rich soil for them, and to thin them sufficiently so that they will have room to grow to a good size.

Beets

Because they like a lightly acid soil, avoid heavy applications of lime or wood ashes where you plant them unless a soil test shows it's necessary. Scabby roots may result if the soil is too sweet. Quicker germination occurs if the seeds are soaked in water for a few hours before planting. Make sure that soil is hilled up around the plants slightly in late summer to prevent the roots from growing partially above the ground.

Our favorite beets are *Early Wonder, Detroit Dark Red,* and *Burpee's Golden* for early eating of both tops and roots; and *Winter Keeper* for root cellar storage.

Carrots

If your soil is heavy you may want to plant the short, stubby or globular varieties, such as *Golden Ball;* rather than the common, long-rooted kinds. We like *Chantenay, Danvers, Gold Coin,* and *Nantes Half Long.* But there are many other good kinds.

Onions, etc.

Like most northern gardeners, we grow ours from the onion sets available in most garden centers and hardware stores, but some people sow seed inside very early in order to grow the late-maturing, large Sweet Spanish and Bermuda types. Other onion-lovers order living plants already started from plant farms in the South.

Onions don't grow as well in heavy soil. Don't "hill" them up, but let them, instead, grow mostly above the ground. We pull them whenever they become large enough, and dry them on window screens laid flat and elevated so the air can move beneath them. When they are dry, we cut off the tops and store them in mesh bags in a cool room that stays dry and above freezing.

Shallots and leeks also thrive in the North. A good source for them is the mail-order herb specialty house, Le Jardin du Gourmet, P.O. Box 44, West Danville, Vermont 05873.

Garlic cloves can be separated and planted direct in the garden among other vegetables, for eating and as pest control.

Parsnips

Parsnips need a long growing season, but that is no problem because they keep growing even after frosts begin in the fall. They can be dug just before snow comes and stored in a root cellar or, even better, left in the ground to overwinter and become the first fresh-dug vegetables of spring—sweet and tasty. Don't leave them in the ground long after it begins to warm up or they will become "woody" and tasteless. Since parsnips have never been widely planted, a long list of varieties has not been introduced. *Hollow Crown* is the old standby, but *Model* is preferred by many gardeners.

Potatoes

Potatoes are a natural cool weather crop and no special care is needed to grow them well. As I mentioned earlier, there are many advantages to growing them under a thick mulch of leaves and hay, although most gardeners grow them successfully in soil.

Because potatoes are heavy feeders, like corn they need generous amounts of nitrogen, phosphorus, and potash in some form for good growth. Many gardeners believe that manure should not be used on potatoes, but we've found that composted or dried manure works fine. Unless the soil is extremely acid, lime or wood ashes should not be applied on land where potatoes will be planted or scabby spuds will result.

In late summer the potato tubers grow very fast, and they often grow right out of the ground. Fall rains may wash the soil off them too. To avoid this, unless you mulch them with hay, you must hill the soil around the plants to a height of 6 or more inches to keep them covered and out of the light. If not kept covered, the tubers will turn green quickly, develop a poisonous substance called solanine, and become inedible. Should you have some potatoes with green on them, don't throw them away; they may be saved for next year's seed.

We like to snitch some small early potatoes for cooking with our new peas in midsummer by burrowing into the hill, without pulling the vines. The results—new peas and potatoes in milk and butter are one of the taste treats of the summer. Potatoes can be dug and used whenever they are large enough, but we don't usually dig them for winter storage until after the first frost in September. We dry them slightly in a dark place so they won't turn green, and store them packed in leaves in the root cellar.

There are many varieties of potatoes. Unless you save your own or buy them from a neighbor, it is best to get certified, disease-free seed potatoes. Those specifically for eating, available in supermarkets, are usually treated with a chemical to keep them from sprouting and therefore are not good ones to plant.

Some popular kinds are: *Norland,* an early one, *Green Mountain, Kennebec, Red Pontiac,* and *Superior.* Others we have tried and like are *Irish Cobbler, Katahdin,* and *Lady Fingers.*

Most of the varieties of the so-called "Irish" potatoes do well in the North, but sweet potatoes are strictly a warm weather crop and should be grown only by gardeners who live close to Dixie.

Radishes

Radishes are a cool weather crop, and even in the North they may grow well only when planted in the spring or late summer. They bolt and go to seed quickly in the warmth of midsummer. There are many varieties. We find we like them all, although we usually choose the traditional red round kinds such as *Cherry Bell,* and *Scarlet Globe.*

Turnips and Rutabagas

Turnips and rutabagas like cool weather and are grown far north in Canada for animal and human food. Early turnips furnish good eating in midsummer, and the late rutabagas keep all winter.

Because these vegetables like cool weather, many garden books advise planting them only in late summer for fall growing. Naturally, this wouldn't work in the North's short season, so spring planting is recommended. We like *Purple Top, White Globe,* and the *American Purple Top* for early eating, and the *Red Chief Rutabaga* for winter storage. Rutabagas keep growing until late in the season, and are not dug until late September or early October when they have reached their optimum size and best texture.

GREENS

Celery, chard, chicory, endive, lettuce, spinach, and similar leafy plants grow to perfection in cool northern weather, and northern gardeners have an excellent choice of varieties. Because they feel at home in our climate, they produce for a much longer portion of the summer than when they are grown further south. All are quite cold-resistant and can be planted almost as soon as the soil is ready in the spring. The only greens we start inside are celery and a bit of lettuce to get an early crop.

Celery

Start the seeds by February if you want mature plants by mid-August. Celery seeds take a long time to come up, and they grow slowly. In midsummer, when the plants are about 6 inches high, if you want them blanched white, put a narrow board upright on each side of the row, or tie a magazine or piece of cardboard around each plant to keep the sun off the stalks. Celery can be stored in a refrigerator wrapped in plastic, or for a short time in a root cellar by burying the roots in moist soil.

Pascal is one of the most commonly grown varieties, but *Florida, Utah,* and *Fordhook Giant* all ripen earlier and may be better choices.

Chard

We like chard because it can be picked all summer long. If it gets tough, it can be cut down to about 2 inches from the ground and will grow a new batch of fresh greens, even in hot weather. Although I don't like the flavor of chard quite as much as that of spinach or young beet greens, it is more productive than most spinach crops, and we wouldn't be without it. Our choice of varieties include: *Rhubarb* (red stemmed), *Lucullus,* and *Fordhook Giant.*

Chicory (French Endive)

For a winter gourmet treat grow blanched chicory, a somewhat involved and lengthy process made easier by checking the price of it in the store, if you can find any!

Plant the seeds early in the spring, thin the plants to 4 inches apart, and let them grow. In the fall, dig the whole plant, cutting off all but an inch of the top and shortening the ends of the roots to 6 inches. Plant them upright in a dry, sand-soil mix in the bottom of a deep box, and store in a cool root cellar.

In midwinter, bring the box into a cool room and water the soil thoroughly. Fill the box with 8 additional inches of sand or sawdust. In three or four weeks they will push through the sawdust. Cut them off at the base for your winter salads.

If the price of coffee is making you somewhat heady, dry a few mature chicory roots, roast and grind them, then perk or boil them for an ersatz coffee brew.

Lettuce

In the cool North you can enjoy lettuce all summer by planting a new batch of seeds every week or two until the weather gets hot. Head lettuce may have difficulty making a solid ball if it's growing in direct sun, so you may want to plant it on the north side of your corn patch, where it can enjoy the shade from the corn on midsummer afternoons. Leaf lettuce, also, benefits from being shaded for part of the day in July.

Some of the best hard head varieties are *Grand Rapids, Great Lakes, New York No. 12, Tom Thumb,* and *White Boston.* Good loose head and leaf lettuce kinds include: *Buttercrunch, Black Seeded Simpson, Lobjoits Green Cos, Oakleaf, Paris White Cos,* and *Salad Bowl.*

Spinach

As spinach has the reputation of going to seed quickly in hot weather, plant it early and eat or freeze it as soon as it is ready. Several varieties produce over a longer season than the old common *Bloomsdale.* Among them are *Northland,* and *Long Standing Bloomsdale.*

New Zealand spinach is not a cold weather plant, nor is it a true spinach, though it resembles it somewhat. The plants, since they are better adjusted to warm climates, will produce all summer, however, if you keep them cut. To get a very early crop of New Zealand spinach, soak the seeds for twenty-four hours, fill up several 3-inch peat pots with good soil, and plant two or three seeds in each pot, about mid-April. Set the started plants outside after all danger of frost is over.

THE CABBAGE FAMILY

Seeds or started plants of the cabbage family can be planted out in the garden quite early, since even a moderate frost doesn't hurt them. Be sure the plants are spaced 15 to 24 inches apart to allow them room to grow. Sometimes, when we set out transplants, we tuck a few seeds in the soil between each plant, which gives us another later crop to replace those we cut early.

Most of the cabbage family is susceptible to the common cabbage worms, and dusting or spraying with Rotenone, Thuricide, or Sevin is usually necessary. Keep out the cutworms that often attack newly set out transplants by putting little paper collars around them. Styrofoam cups with the bottoms cut out and set into the soil work well.

Broccoli

Broccoli plants thrive with fertilizer. To give them a lift in mid-season if they are growing slowly an additional dose may be necessary. Liquid manure or a tiny bit of dry plant food can be used. Pick the heads when they are full of rich green buds, before the yellow bloom appears. Another batch of smaller heads will then grow, which can be used until late in the fall. Late-growing broccoli seldom needs spraying because the worms almost never bother it.

Calabrese, Green Duke, and *Premium Crop Hybrid* are all good kinds for the North, but there are many others, as well.

Brussels Sprouts

These are best as a fall vegetable, so there is no reason to start inside plants too early. We are always surprised at their productivity. Each year we think nothing is going to happen to them, and suddenly, about September, their stalks are covered with tiny little cabbages. Their flavor improves after a light frost. Because of their cold resistance, you can pick them almost until snow falls; then pull up the stalks that are left, and store the whole plants by burying their roots in soil in the root cellar for winter eating. *Jade Cross Hybrid* and *Long Island Improved* are good kinds. *Catskill* doesn't grow quite as tall as the others.

Cabbage

There are many kinds of cabbage, so it may be difficult to make a decision about what to grow. There are early, mid-season, late, Savoy, Chinese, and red-leafed kinds. We have not had good luck in having the latest varieties mature, even when we start the seed inside. Luckily, this is no problem, because there are so many early kinds that are excellent. For our small family we have decided that the small and medium-sized heads are more practical to grow and use than the giant ones, although sauerkraut lovers might disagree. We like to raise some early ones for summer eating and some later ones that we can leave in the garden for fall use; then we wrap any extras in plastic bags and store them in the root cellar.

Varieties include:

EARLY—*All Head Early* (large), *Earliana* (small), and *Golden Acre* (medium)

MID-SEASON—*All Seasons, Flat Dutch, Wisconsin*

LATE—*Penn State Ballhead, Surehead*

SAVOY—*Ace, Early Perfection, Late Drumhead*

CHINESE—*Michihili, Wong Bok*

RED—*Red Acre, Red Rock, Ruby Red*

Cauliflower

Like broccoli, these are heavy feeders, and small heads result if they are undernourished. If you supply both the fertilizer and room to grow, however, the heads will be large. Some gardeners tie the upper leaves over the heads to keep the flowers snowy white, but in our cool climate we rarely bother. However, we are careful to pick the heads before they start to yellow and get "ricey."

Setting out some started plants and growing a few others from seed provides both early and late cauliflower. Since the plants like sweet soil, make sure their spot in the garden is well supplied with lime.

We put a great deal of cauliflower in our freezer for winter eating, and eat lots of fresh heads during the late summer, both raw and cooked. *Monarch, Snowball, Super Snowball,* and *Snowking* are early kinds that do well. *Purple Head* is a later ripening variety that adds color to your cuisine.

Kohlrabi

When I saw my first kohlrabi, I had no intention of eating such a sinister-looking object. It resembles a cabbage, but is much more solid. It tastes a lot like a turnip, though its flavor is even better. Because it is so dependable and ripens early, it is a good vegetable for the North, and a lot of good eating can be raised in a short row.

Like all vegetables, they should be picked at their prime. Don't pick them too early, but use them before they lose their firmness and grow to their full size.

Kohlrabi hasn't been widely grown in North America, so few varieties are available. You'll be content with any of the two or three kinds your seed company offers.

HOT WEATHER CROPS

Many vegetables we plant in our northern gardens were first cultivated in much warmer climates. Melons, peppers, and tomatoes came from South and Central America, for instance. Naturally a great deal of care is necessary to get them to flourish in a region where we often wear our parkas for a large part of the summer. To grow them successfully, we must keep in mind that all of them are fond of heat and extremely sensitive to frost.

All the hot-weather crops ripen faster if you pick off part of the forming fruits when they are small. The strength of the plant will then go into the growth and ripening of the rest. Pick off any small fruits that form late in the season and can't possibly ripen to help "energize" the larger fruits and hasten their maturity. Hot weather crops include both vine fruits and bush fruits.

Heat-loving vine crops such as melons, cucumbers, squash, and pumpkins grow best when planted in hills.

VINE FRUITS

These usually grow on fleshy vines and produce flowers that may be either male or female. All of them are heavy feeders. Plant them in full sun, protected from chilling winds, and provide an abundance of fertilizer so that they will ripen before frost.

The vine crops are usually planted on raised beds of soil covering a pile of manure. We dig a hole about 2 feet across, and 4 inches deep, put in a couple of buckets of farm manure or rich compost, and layer soil on top of the pile of manure, making a circular bed about 3 feet across and 8 inches high. Six or 8 seeds are planted in each bed and later thinned out as they grow, so only two or three of the huskiest plants remain.

Although all the vines are easily killed by even a light frost, if they are left uncovered, the fruits of pumpkin and squash will not be hurt unless the temperature gets very low. Green pumpkins can be ripened by leaving them in a sunny warm room or greenhouse for several days.

Cucumbers

These are the earliest ripening of all the vine crops except possibly summer squash, and little problem is encountered in getting a crop; but they, too, like to grow in a warm place out of the cool wind. Started potted plants will help assure you an early crop, although you may plant the seeds directly in the hill. Cucumbers produce heavier and for a longer period if they are picked as soon as they are ready to eat or pickle.

Burpless Hybrid, Early Fortune, Long Green, and *Straight Eight* are some common kinds.

Melons

Muskmelon and early watermelon will mature in much of the North, even when the seed is planted directly in the garden. Where we live, however, it is more reliable to start the seeds inside in late April, and to plant them out in June under hot caps or a plastic tent. Large watermelons are impossible to mature in most of the North unless they are grown almost entirely in a greenhouse, but the smaller, early-ripening kinds do well.

The *muskmelon bed.*

Muskmelons that are grown under a plastic tent will ripen rapidly and be protected from killing frosts.

Minnesota, Midget, Sweet Granite, and *Sweet n' Early* are all early-ripening muskmelons. *Golden Midget* and *New Hampshire Midget* are round, early-ripening home garden-type watermelons.

Pumpkins and Squash

Although pumpkins and winter squash both like warm weather, the Indians grew them successfully in the Northeast for centuries. To get a crop it is important that they grow rapidly after planting.

Acorn, Butterboy, Butternut, and *Hercules* are early-maturing, small-sized winter squash. *Golden Hubbard, Blue Hubbard,* and *Green Hubbard* are larger-growing, later-maturing winter varieties.

Spookie and *Sugar Pie* are good, early-ripening eating pumpkins. *Connecticut Field* and *Jack o'Lantern* are good Halloween pumpkins and may be used for feeding animals.

Summer squash needs only two months to ripen, and can be grown even where frosts come early. *Crookneck, Casserta, Green Cocozella,* and *Zucchini* are all prolific bearers and easily grown.

BUSH GARDEN FRUITS

The solanums, including eggplant, pepper, and tomato, have all received a black eye recently because of the fear that they may be a prime cause of some forms of arthritis. Probably this won't discourage their consumption very much; for they have long been favorite foods in our diet.

All are tropical or semitropical plants, and thrive only when the temperature is high. In order to grow them we must select only the kinds that ripen early, start them inside in late winter, and set them out whenever we think all frost danger is past. Even then, they must be kept warm and sheltered if they are to continue to grow rapidly. Plastic jugs, polyethylene tents, and other heat collectors help keep them warm on cool days. We sometimes encircle each plant with two or three black, heat-absorbing automobile tires piled on top of each other. Other gardeners surround them with a mulch of clear or black plastic. Some even grow them in large pots on a terrace or porch.

Like most gardeners, we keep them off the ground by staking or growing them on racks. In late summer we give them a shot of

To grow *eggplant, pepper,* and *tomato plants,* one method is to encircle them with two or three black, heat-absorbing automobile tires piled on top of each other to provide the warmth they require.

Epsom Salts dissolved at the rate of two tablespoons in a gallon of water, pouring a pint around each plant. The extra magnesium helps ripen the fruit faster. All solanums prefer a slightly acid soil, so we don't put lime or wood ashes where we plant them.

The bush garden fruits must be picked before a frost unless the plants are well protected. Green tomatoes will ripen in a warm kitchen, sunny window, greenhouse, or warm, dark closet, but peppers and eggplants will not.

Ropes are used to support *polyethylene sheets* for covering a field of tomatoes when fall frosts threaten.

I have always been puzzled by the fact that many of my gardening friends don't like to eat any of the bush vegetable fruits, yet they would never dream of planting a garden without them. They no doubt feel their reputation as gardeners is established by whether or not they can successfully grow these challenging fruits. A vegetable garden doesn't seem quite complete without them.

Eggplant

We have just about given up trying to grow these. It requires so much extra care to keep them warm on our windy hill that we feel they're not quite worth the trouble. If you live in a more favorable spot, or have time to coddle them, you will probably have good results. They are very vulnerable to insects, so be ready to control the bugs right after you set out the plants; a few potato bugs or aphids can wreck a good-sized plant in a few days. Keep them watered and don't hoe around them too deeply or you may damage their shallow roots.

Dusky, Hybrid, Early Beauty, and *Slice-rite* are early-ripening kinds.

Pepper

Although red and green sweet bell peppers are easier to grow than eggplant, most gardeners find them more difficult than tomatoes. They do well in a hot season, and growers use the same heat-gathering tactics as with tomatoes. Sweet peppers usually mature earlier than hot peppers, which may not be worth the trouble if your season is short.

A Canadian acquaintance of ours, Bart Hall-Beyer, who has gardened in the Yukon, Quebec, and northern Alberta for many years, has developed some interesting methods of coping with short seasons. One of them is digging his pepper plants in the fall before frost and keeping them inside as potted plants for the winter. He sets them outside again in late spring the following year when frost danger is over. Because they are well established, the plants bear earlier and for a longer time. He has been able to keep the same plants thriving for several years using this method.

Early Calwonder, Early Pimento, King of the North, New Ace, and *Sweet Banana* are all early-ripening sweet peppers.

Hungarian Wax, Large Cherry, and *Long Red Cayenne* are some of the earliest-ripening hot peppers.

Tomato

The perfect tomato is to vegetable gardeners what the tea rose is to flower gardeners and the ripe peach to fruit growers—the badge of success. It is a real test of gardening skill for a northern gardener; and it seems to be the goal of every gardener in zones 3 and 4 to mature a large crop of giant-size tomatoes.

Since many of the largest-fruiting tomatoes ripen late, some northern growers put a lot of work into accomplishing this. *Beefsteak, Beefmaster, Big Boy, Marglobe, Oxheart, Ponderosa,* and *Rutgers* need to be started in midwinter, and the plants grown to nearly full size before setting out in order that they ripen their large fruits before frost.

Less competitive gardeners like ourselves settle for the smaller-fruiting but earlier-ripening kinds: *Earlicrop, Earliana, Early Girl, Fantastic, Fireball, Firesteel, Pixie, Rocket, Big Set, Sun Up, Swift, Valiant,* and other more reliable sorts.

You may allow more sunlight to get to the fruits by pruning off a large part of the dense limb growth that forms on some varieties and by tying the plants to a sturdy stake with strips of cloth. Take off the surplus small fruits, also, as described at the beginning of this section.

CHAPTER FIVE

TREE FRUITS

In the 1950's, when I first became determined to replace the aging farm orchard my ancestors had planted more than a century earlier, I discovered that information about establishing an orchard where growing seasons are short and winters are long was nearly non-existent. Like other aspiring fruit gardeners, I wasted hundreds of dollars trying different varieties and cultural methods. I sent to the Midwest for trees that were grown in zones 6 and 7 and grafted on dwarf rootstocks imported from England. When they encountered their first northern winter, most of them just curled up their roots and died. The two or three that survived grew slowly and became diseased. Almost none lived to bear fruit.

It frustrated me that I was failing to grow fruit trees when my ancestors had obviously had such success. It was some time before I discovered that the early settlers succeeded because they bought their trees locally or grafted their own, choosing varieties that their neighbors were growing. By planting locally grown trees they had not only hardy varieties but also ones with hardy roots.

Once I chose varieties that were suited to our climate, I began to get good results. Then, after learning how to graft as the old-timers did, I rescued some of the superior but nearly forgotten old varieties from the few surviving ancient orchards and propagated them on hardy, small trees grown from locally produced seed. At last my orchard got under way.

The situation has changed somewhat in a few decades, and it is easier today to find suitable trees for the North. The increased interest in fruit growing has inspired the development of many hardy varieties. Hardy rootstocks, some of them semidwarf, have been introduced as well. Cultural and pruning methods that help prevent winter injury have been discovered or rediscovered.

Although growing any crop in the North is a challenge, the

northern gardener's chances for growing beautiful and tasty apples, plums, and pears are now better than ever before.

CHOOSING VARIETIES

Because our northern zones have a wide variety of soils, different extremes of temperature, and varied lengths of growing seasons, it is difficult to say for sure what will and what will not grow. Certainly in the "doubtful" list I would place peaches, most apricots, nectarines, figs, quince, persimmons, sweet cherries, and most varieties of plums, although there are people in favored areas of zones 3 and 4 who may experience some success in growing these fruits. Many kinds of apples, sour cherries, and pears will not grow, either because they are not hardy or the growing season is so short.

Nearly all fruit trees that are sold have been grafted. If you buy a small McIntosh apple tree, the part that was below the ground was grown by planting a seed or by dividing an existing apple tree root. The part above the ground grew from a tiny branch removed from a large tree that was already producing McIntosh apples. The two parts were joined together in a surgical process called grafting.

Since the fruit tree you buy is really two trees in one, it is important that both the good top and the "wild" roots are hardy enough to plant in your northern location. Few fruit trees are hardier than the old-fashioned Yellow Transparent apple, for example, yet if you bought one from a Tennessee nursery it might have been grafted on a Ben Davis apple seedling grown in zone 7, and you would never know it. Such a tree would probably have trouble adjusting to a zone 3 climate.

The popularity of the dwarf apple tree has discouraged a lot of northern growers. They buy trees that look nice and may thrive for a summer or two, then be winter-killed. Usually there is no inkling in planting leaflets or in nursery catalogs that Malling, the most common rootstock for dwarf apples, is of English origin. Although some varieties of Malling are more hardy than others, all may have trouble growing in the coldest part of the United States and Canada.

APPLE VARIETIES FOR ZONES 3 AND 4

Extra-early

YELLOW TRANSPARENT—First apple of the season. Soft, juicy, great flavor. Bears large crops, even when young.

Early

ASTRACHAN, RED—Old-time apple with wonderful flavor. Ripens over a long season and bears young.

BEACON—One of the best cooking apples ever, and good eating for those who like tart apples. Tree grows fast and is a heavy producer. Fruit is large, red, and makes good sauce, pickles, and pies.

DOLGO CRAB—Colorful small apple for pickles, juice, and jelly. Unpicked fruits hang on the tree for winter birds. Good pollinator for other apples.

DUCHESS—Old-time apple with superb cooking qualities. Excellent for cider too.

LODI—Huge yellow apple, of the Transparent type, but firmer.

PEACH APPLE—Wonderful old-time eating apple with lots of juice, good for cider too, and fine for sauce. Yellow with red blush.

QUINTE—Brilliant all-red apple with excellent flavor for eating fresh. Doesn't keep well, but you won't have trouble getting rid of them. Bears heavily.

RED DUCHESS—Like the old-time Duchess, but with a redder skin, and more attractive.

VIKING—A new apple from the Midwest. Of the Beacon type, this is also good eating right off the tree.

Fall-Ripening

MELBA—Early ripening McIntosh-type apple of excellent flavor.

RED SUPREME—A novelty apple that is all red, including the blossoms, skin, and flesh. Small to medium-sized fruits. Makes colorful applesauce, jelly, and juice.

WEALTHY—Old-time eating and cooking apple that keeps until December. Bears heavily, even when the tree is young. Red fruits of medium to large size.

WOLF RIVER—Old-time variety, producing giant-sized, red apples. Quality not so good, but once prized for baking.

Late Fall Ripening—for Winter Storage

BETHEL—Large, red-striped hard apple of good quality. Stores well for midwinter eating. Old-timer.

BLUE PEARMAIN—Dark-red apple of fine quality. One of the many fine old apples becoming popular again.

CONNELL—A Delicious-type apple that tastes very good, yet overwinters and ripens in a short season.

CORTLAND—Excellent flavor. Keeps in an ordinary root cellar until April, and is good eating and cooking. Apple is a big, beautiful, reddish-blue. Tree is healthy and vigorous.

FAMEUSE—Ancient apple of Canadian, possibly French, origin. Small to medium size. Very tasty and crisp. Red with white flesh.

FIRESIDE—Good quality apple from the Midwest. Excellent flavor and good keeper.

HONEYGOLD—This new apple resembles the Golden Delicious in both appearance and flavor, but it is more hardy. Needs careful pruning, and the fruit should be thinned heavily to get large-sized fruits. Don't pick it too early; a few frosts will improve the flavor.

LOBO—This McIntosh-type apple is from Canada, where it is often preferred over the Mac. Looks and tastes much the same except that it is more red. Ripens a few days earlier too.

McINTOSH—This old-time favorite northern apple needs no description. Keeps well into January in a cool root cellar.

MINJON—Small to medium-sized. Red fruit of the Jonathan type. Produces heavy loads of fruit each fall. Fruit hangs on the tree so well that if it's not picked, it will stay on for most of the winter.

POUND SWEET—Another golden oldie. Yellow-green apples of large size and sweet flavor.

PRAIRIE SPY—Large, red, late-ripening apple similar to the Northern Spy, but more hardy. Keeps well until spring.

ST. LAWRENCE—Bright red apple with excellent flavor. Old-time favorite.

SPARTAN—Another of the improved varieties of the McIntosh. Sprightly flavor, usually regarded as better than the regular Mac. Keeps better too.

TOLMAN SWEET—Greenish yellow, medium to large-sized fruit. Sweet flesh. Highly regarded as a fine baking apple in the nineteenth century. Good for sauce and requires less sweetening than most apples.

HARDY PLUM VARIETIES

ABUNDANCE—Large, red purple. Needs sheltered place to grow.

LACRESCENT—Small, golden-yellow, sugar-sweet plum with a small stone. Ripens early.

PIPESTONE—Giant, red, juicy plum of outstanding quality. Ripens in August and bears heavily.

REDCOAT—Large, sweet, red, late-ripening plum.

SUPERIOR—Large red plum of high quality, and a heavy producer. Ripens early September.

WANETA—Medium-sized red plum. Comes in great numbers in early September. Excellent quality.

HARDY PEAR VARIETIES

LUSCIOUS—New pear of real excellence. A fine addition to any fruit orchard. Moderately hardy.

PARKER—Large yellow pears of high quality. Hardy and reliable. Ripen in early September.

PATTEN—Good-sized yellow pear. Sweet, juicy, and with fine-grained flesh. Hardy.

CHERRIES

Although we have not had success with cherry trees, even hardy, sour, pie cherries, the hardiness of the trees doesn't seem to be the reason. In our climate an inherent virus apparently becomes active, and the trees succumb when they are five or six years old and just beginning to bear well. In zone 5 and in favored parts of zone 4 this is not a problem, and all of the following are worth a try. All have red fruit.

EARLY RICHMOND—One of the earliest and hardiest of the older kinds.

METEOR—Newer hardy kind. Good fruit, on a semidwarf tree.

MONTMORENCY—The most popular of the pie cherries.

NORTH STAR—Another new kind, one of the hardiest, and a dwarf-sized tree.

APRICOTS AND PEACHES

Neither apricots nor peaches have survived our winters and our short growing season, but they are being grown in zone 5 and sheltered parts of zone 4 quite successfully. Most growers describe the quality of the fruit as somewhat lower than that of the varieties grown in more charitable climates, but still good. All have yellow fruit.

Apricots

MANCHU—A South Dakota introduction.

MOONGOLD and SUNGOLD—These two are often planted in pairs for pollination. Both are University of Minnesota introductions.

SCOUT—This variety from Canada bears while quite young.

Peaches

RELIANCE—Probably the hardiest peach. From New Hampshire.

SUNAPEE—Also from New Hampshire. Not quite as hardy as the Reliance.

HARDINESS OF APPLE ROOTSTOCKS

ALNAP—This hardy apple from Sweden is now being used as a rootstock for semidwarf trees, but it has not yet proven entirely satisfactory in the North.

ANTANOVKA—A Russian apple variety grown in northern Europe. Numerous seedlings have been named and propagated. It is hardy, but northern growers report irregular growth habits.

DOLGO—Seeds of the Dolgo crab are planted and used for rootstocks for many of the apple trees grown in the Upper Midwest. They are hardy and produce a large tree. One of the best rootstocks for the North, even though it suckers badly.

HOPA—Hardy, similar to the Dolgo. It is less used because the smaller seeds are harder to gather, clean, and plant.

MALLING—Twenty-seven different East Malling rootstocks have been introduced (Nos. EM 1 to EM 27), and 15 Merton Malling stocks (Nos. MM 101 to MM 115). These originated in England, and most have not proven hardy in northern orchards. EM 9 and EM 26 are the most dwarfing, and EM 27 is one of the hardiest of the group.

OTTAWA—The Canadian Government has originated several rootstocks that show promise. Twenty-two Ottawa varieties have been tested and numbered. Ottawa No. 3 currently appears to be the one best suited for producing a vigorous dwarf tree. Sometimes it is used as an interstock. An apple seedling is grafted to Ottawa No. 3; a year later it is grafted to the variety wanted, producing a semidwarf, medium-sized tree that is hardy and vigorous.

ROBUSTA No. 5—Many of the orchard trees in Eastern Canada and Northern New England are grafted on Robusta No. 5, a vigorous-growing, hardy crabapple. It does better in the Northeast than elsewhere because it tends to start growing too early where winters are not long and cold. Like the Dolgo, it suckers badly, and it may be necessary to prune it frequently throughout the summer to keep the suckers controlled.

Canadian nurseries like to bud-graft this understock high, about 2 feet above the ground instead of at ground level, believing it results in a hardier tree.

STANDARD OR SEEDLING—Apples grown on seedling stock are usually sold as standard, or full-sized trees. Seedlings may be McIntosh, Delicious, Rome, Winesap, or whatever variety is common where the seedling is grown. Native crabapple seeds, such as Columbia, Siberian, or Sylvestris, are sometimes used as rootstocks.

Home orchardists who wish to grow a few trees for grafting are likely to get the best results from planting the seeds of a good-quality, vigorous-growing tree, such as Duchess, Dolgo, Yellow Transparent, or a similar variety. Good apples grafted on seedlings from sour, wild trees found in hedgerows may pick up some of the characteristics of the wild trees, and the fruit may be late in ripening, harder, and more sour. Therefore, wild apple seedlings are usually not the best choices for understocks.

PLUM ROOTSTOCKS

Usually plums do well in the North only if they are bud-grafted on native, wild plum seedlings. Although plums can also be easily grafted on wild black cherry and even chokecherry trees, these sucker so badly that they are impractical.

Unlike most fruit trees, good plums can be grown from seed. Stones planted from quality plums have a better chance of producing worthwhile fruit than when either apple or pear seeds are planted. It takes many years for the seedlings to bear, however.

PEAR ROOTSTOCKS

Seeds from Bartlett, Patten, Parker, or similar pears produce hardier rootstocks for the North than the more commonly used Callery pear seeds, although the latter are more disease-resistant. Dwarf pear trees are not good choices for northern growers, since they are grafted on quince seedlings, which are not hardy in cold sections. Pears can also be grafted on apple trees, though these grafts usually live for only a short time, and are not worth the bother.

GRAFTING

Many of us prefer to graft our own fruit trees and find it exciting to create our own orchards. Grafts of good trees may be either purchased (see appendix) or collected from old, abandoned orchards, or solicited from neighboring fruit growers.

Several varieties can be grafted on one tree for an unusual specimen, although these trees are difficult to prune and can be recommended only as a novelty.

LOCATION

It is nearly as important for northern growers to choose the right spot for their fruit trees as to choose hardy varieties. If you have only a small lot, your choice of planting areas will, of course, be limited. But if you have plenty of room, give your trees the spot most to their liking.

In the North a southern or southeastern exposure is ideal. Northern-facing slopes are usually much too cool. To thrive, fruit trees must be placed where the sun shines nearly all day. Don't plant them where buildings or trees will shade them now or in the future. They also need plenty of room to grow, and they won't be happy if their roots are restricted by pavements, nearby trees, pools, ledges, or other confinements. Since the tops must have room to spread as well, find out the height and width the trees will attain when mature, and give them proper space when planting. Be sure there are no low, overhead wires they may touch in future years. From experience I know it's no fun to prune around wires.

If you have room to shop around for a planting site, choose a spot where cold air doesn't settle on frosty nights. Valleys at the bottom of long slopes or steep hills are poor places for orchards; late spring frosts are likely to hit when the trees are in full bloom. Early fall frosts can also be hazardous, killing tender new growth or ruining the fruit before it is ripe.

Fruit trees don't grow well in wet soil, so avoid planting them where the ground is moist all year round. We once tried to extend our orchard to a spot on our property where the ground was damp much of the year, with disastrous results. We lost every tree.

Espaliers make it possible to grow heat-loving fruit trees and grape vines in sheltered, sunny locations on fences and buildings.

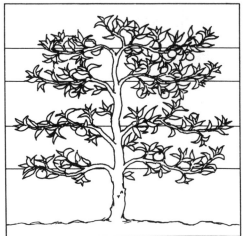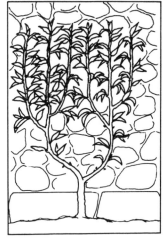

When the ground is uneven, plant on the high spots so that hard rains and melting snows won't cause puddles of water to cover the roots for several hours and drown them. A gentle southern or eastern slope, or well-drained flat land, such as would be suitable for a vegetable garden, is the best location for fruit trees.

Even if your property is so wet that there is no suitable place on it for fruit trees, there are still ways to grow them. If you don't mind the work and expense, you can usually drain part of the area, or you can build a raised mound of soil 10 feet or so square contained by railroad ties, stone walls, cement blocks, or logs for each tree that is 18 inches or more high. Choose good, light soil, well-supplied with manure and compost, and add lime if necessary.

PLANTING

Since the growing season for fruit trees in the North lasts only about six to eight weeks, a new tree must be planted carefully in the spring if it is to begin to grow immediately instead of taking all summer to get adjusted. Do everything to make the new tree feel right at home from the outset. Then the first, and possibly the second, season's growth won't be lost.

Most fruit trees are bought bare-rooted, with their roots wrapped in packing material to keep them from drying out, or they are wrapped in a ball of peat. Trees bought this way should have their roots soaked in a tub of water for twenty-four hours before planting. If the top has not yet been cut back, take off approximately one-third from the top of the tree to compensate for the loss of all the fibrous hair roots that were lost when the tree was dug.

Although many people find it difficult to cut off part of a tree they have paid for, the initial pruning is one of the nicest things anyone can do for a new tree. If it is not done, the top will begin to grow before the small root system is ready to support it. The growth of the roots should keep a bit ahead of the top growth, not only to ensure that your tree has a better chance of surviving, but so that it will be healthy and vigorous.

Supply your new tree with nutrients, and water it two or three times a week if it doesn't rain heavily. Manure tea is excellent food for young trees, and useful also as a pick-me-up for older trees that are making poor growth. Liquid fertilizers like Rapid-Gro and

Miracle-Gro will also give trees a boost, but the directions on the label must be followed carefully, since feeding the trees too often or too heavily will "burn" them. It may also stimulate a fast, weak growth that causes limbs to break easily in a strong wind, or winter-kill in an early frost. After the first of July don't give the trees any kind of fertilizer, or you may get a great deal of fragile, late-summer growth.

Don't let grass and weeds crowd your new tree. If you don't mow around it every week, mulch it heavily to a distance of 3 or 4 feet from the trunk to suppress all weeds. Keep renewing the mulch each spring or fall for at least several years. Weed and grass competition is one of the leading causes of poor tree growth.

The best kind of tree to plant, if it is available, is one already growing in a large pot of soil or a ball of soil. The fine feeder hair roots are intact and can start growing at once. No pruning is necessary when you plant the tree; but, after planting, it should be fed and mulched as carefully as a bare-rooted one. Unfortunately, potted or balled trees are not always available in hardy varieties.

TRAINING THE TREE

When you cut the top off your new fruit tree, you stop the tree's natural urge to send its main thrust of growth upward. Some training will probably be necessary to get the tree to resume its upward growth, or it may, instead, grow into a large, weak bush with many upturned limbs. By pinching and snipping during the first two summers, try to get the tree to develop a "Christmas-tree" look, with one central stem that has side branches coming out at slightly upturned angles. They should reach out at the bottom and taper to shorter branches toward the top. This shaping makes a strongly branched unit and one that lets in the most sun for ripening the fruit.

Plum and cherry trees are more difficult to prune in this manner than apple and pear trees. Eventually they will grow into rather weird shapes, whatever you do. Nevertheless, it is better to train them to grow in this shape for the first years and not let them form heavy side limbs that will eventually split apart.

Keep an eye on young trees to make sure they are not leaning in the wind. On the top of our hill, although we have a windbreak

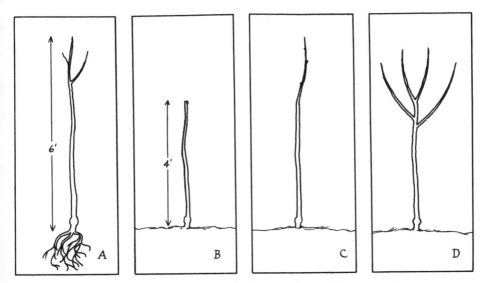

PRUNING YOUR NEW APPLE OR PEAR TREE

Bare-rooted apple or pear trees (*A*) should have their tops cut back about one-third at planting time (*B*). Pinch off new side buds to allow only top growth the first year (*C*) instead of as in *D*. (Potted trees do not need to be cut back at planting time.) The next year, train the tree to grow to look similar to *E* and not *F* or *G*. Make sure the lowest branch is at least 4 feet above the ground. Throughout its early life, try to shape the tree like a Christmas tree, with one central stem, branches coming out at slightly upward angles (*H*).

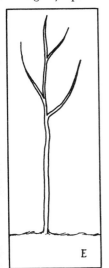

growing, most of our trees start to tip over, eventually, if they are not staked.

MULCH

I use lots of mulch around our fruit trees. A thick layer of paper, hay, shredded bark, leaves, shavings, or other organic material not only suppresses weeds and grass, holds moisture in the soil, and protects the roots from low temperatures, but also encourages earthworm activity that loosens the soil and consequently promotes better root growth.

If these benefits were the only ones that mulch provides, I would certainly go to the trouble of spreading it around the trees. But it has other attributes as well. Because of its insulation properties, a thick mulch prevents sudden temperature changes in the soil and tends to keep the roots cool during the first warm days of spring. Often a mulch insulation delays the blooming of a tree by several days. You'd think this might not be desirable, but in the North it is very beneficial, since the first warm days of spring are often followed by a cool spell and a frost or two. By blooming late the blossoms often escape this frosty weather. Pear and plum trees bloom very early and are especially vulnerable to being caught in a late spring frost. Our mulch has saved them, I'm sure, many times.

A delayed blossoming period also allows several additional days for bee populations to build up their numbers and thus better pollinate the trees. Winters in the North are hard on bees, and many of them die; but a few warm days in spring help the hives to recoup their losses.

My favorite mulch, especially for young trees, consists of several layers. First I spread about 2 inches of farm manure or compost. I prefer a compost made of shredded hardwood bark that we get from a sawmill, some composted leaves, and a few quarts of dried chicken or cow manure. This layer fertilizes the tree and stimulates as much growth as possible during our short growing season. Then, on a rainy day, I put down a second layer of several thicknesses of newspapers and magazines to conserve the moisture in the soil and to prevent grass and weeds from growing and stealing all the nutrients. Finally I add a 6-inch layer of hay or a thin covering of shavings to hide the ugly paper and keep it from blowing away. I've found that this mulch promotes fast, steady growth, even during dry summers. As it rots during the summer, it adds fertilizer and humus for the tree. I renew it each spring while the soil is still wet.

I have never had much success in using a mulch of crushed rock on fruit trees. It doesn't suppress the weeds adequately, add fertility, or insulate. Nor have I had success with sawdust. I find it packs too hard and robs nitrogen from the soil; and rains don't penetrate it easily. Some gardeners, however, swear by each method and apparently get excellent results.

FIRST FRUITS

When a tiny, healthy young tree produces its first fruits, the urge is almost irresistible to let the fruit mature so you can taste it. Resist the temptation! It is a mistake to let a new tree bear while it is still small. Not only does premature fruiting weaken the tree greatly, at the expense of future crops, but bearing too early in life may even kill it if the first crop is too heavy. Seed production demands a great amount of energy from the tree.

If your tree is still young when it begins to bear, pick off any forming fruits when they are small—about the size of marbles. Once the tree is as high as your head and well branched, it should be allowed to form only one or two fruits the first time it bears.

Not only is it hard on the tree when it bears at too young an age, but the first fruits may be small, misshapen, and not flavorful. If you give the tree a chance to grow a few years before letting it produce fruit, it will, hopefully, reward you with an annual crop of good fruit thereafter.

FRUIT PESTS

As with growing vegetables, the wildlife are one of our bigger problems. Rabbits and mice like nothing better than to chew up a young apple tree that is unprotected by hardware cloth or a plastic tree guard. When I went into the orchard one morning and found that half a dozen hungry deer had broken a hole through the fence and devastated a large planting of tiny fruit trees, I yearned for a location where the deer and antelope don't play. I suppose I should rejoice in the fact that while we live near a wilderness where deer abound, bears hoot in the backyard, and wolf-coyotes howl in the nearby woods, at least air pollution is not a big problem.

Northern growers face a different list of pests than their neighbors farther south, but ours are probably no worse than theirs. Our cold winters and isolation certainly account for fewer insect troubles, and some of the more serious diseases, such as fireblight, don't usually become epidemics as they do in warmer climates.

Nevertheless, disease and insects abound wherever there are fruit trees, and some kind of spray program is necessary if you want to grow perfect fruit. Your local extension service can best supply you with information on how to spray your orchard, including when to spray and what to use.

Apple scab is one disease that may be worse in the Northeast than elsewhere, thriving as it does in the cool, moist climate. During dry, warm summers it is often not a problem, but during rainy seasons orchardists sometimes must spray at weekly intervals for much of the summer to control it. Organic gardeners often use a dormant spray—a mixture of one pint of No. 30 motor oil, ¼ cup of liquid detergent, plus three gallons of water. They spray their trees in early spring before any growth starts. This not only kills a lot of hatching insect eggs, but it also deactivates a great many apple scab spores that have overwintered on the trees and in the soil. Growers who do not garden organically rely on Captan or a similar fungicide, plus a good insecticide, for their spraying.

Fortunately for gardeners who don't like to spray anything at all, some trees are quite resistant to apple scab. Unfortunately, many northern favorites are not on the list. The entire McIntosh family, including Barry, Cortland, Lobo, Macoun, Melba, McIntosh, Milton, Quinte, Spartan, and many others, are all very susceptible to scab and need lots of spraying, as do Astrachan, Fameuse, Honeygold, Prairie Spy, and some of the ornamental crab apples.

Hardy apples that are most resistant to apple scab and therefore need less spraying are: Beacon, Bethel, Connell, Dolgo Crab, Duchess, Lodi, Minjon, Peach, Wealthy, Wolf River, and Yellow Transparent. Several new varieties, whose hardiness is uncertain, are also scab-resistant: MacFree, Nova Easygro, Prima, Priscilla, and Sir Prize.

Northern orchardists have one problem southern growers need

never worry about. If your planting is in snowmobile territory, mark your young trees well. Many riders go out at night and are not likely to see a small, unmarked tree.

PRUNING IN THE NORTH

We once had a lone apple tree that must have been at least a century old. It grew in a pasture some distance from the orchard, and cattle and horses grazing beneath it for years had forced it to grow very tall, above their reach. Although I never found out what variety it was, everyone said that when the tree was younger, it had produced bushels of excellent fruit. I remember climbing to what I thought was a terrifying height for a small child, some 25 feet through the dark interior, past hundreds of little, sour, green apples, to get the few large red gems that ripened at the top of the tree.

I felt then that the tree was playing hard to get with its choice apples, and was saving them only for someone willing to pay the price. Later I began to understand how important sunlight is to ripening fruit, especially here in the North, where the days begin to get quite short just as the fruit starts to get its color.

Orchardists everywhere prune fruit trees for the same reasons: to let sunlight into the tree, to thin out the number of limbs bearing so that the tree will bear fewer and larger fruits, and to get rid of

Thin out branches of older trees to cut down on bearing surface so fruits will be fewer but larger, and to let in valuable sunshine to ripen the fruit.

deadwood and broken branches. They also prune to remove limbs growing in the wrong direction and to eliminate older wood that is no longer producing well.

Although pruning in the North is not unlike pruning elsewhere, there are some differences. Home orchardists in other regions can get by if they do a heavy pruning only once every two or three years. In the North we have found that it is very important to prune our trees annually if we are to get the best results. By taking off a moderate amount of wood each year, there is less heavy regrowth and, therefore, less winter injury. Also, if an older tree has not been pruned for several years, or perhaps has never been pruned at all, it is not a good idea to try to get it in shape all at once. Instead, spread the pruning over several years. Some northern orchardists like to do any necessary heavy pruning in late fall directly after fruit-picking is over; they believe there is less regrowth if it is done at that time.

Occasionally I meet fruit growers who feel that pruning can be done at any time the orchardist has the urge to do it. Most professionals, however, agree that the best time is when the leaves are off the tree and the wood is not frozen. I like to do ours on a sunny, mild day in late March before the sap begins to flow in the fruit trees, so that they won't bleed as much. Since we live in a spot where snow gets deep, I try to do it when there is a hard crust and I can walk around easily without snowshoes.

For many years it has been the custom to paint the wound after a limb has been sawed off. The paint is supposed to help seal out the weather and heal the wound faster. Recently, however, much evidence has been collected that seems to prove that painting is of little value, and we might as well save the expense. Smaller limbs can be clipped off and left untreated, and larger ones, an inch or more in diameter, can be covered with a patch of plastic held in place with electrical or duct tape. This keeps out the weather and apparently promotes better healing.

THINNING THE FRUIT

Overbearing weakens a fruit tree. Both pruning and thinning help to prevent large crops that come only occasionally, and to encourage a tree to bear a crop of good fruit every year. When fruit trees are

A. *Unthinned fruit*

Left untouched, older trees produce an abundance of small fruits (*A*). Thinning the fruit enables those remaining to develop to their optimum size and quality (*B*).

B. *Thinned fruit*

young, they bear large, beautiful specimens as a rule, but as they grow older, the fruits get smaller, mostly because the tree produces far too many of them. Although by pruning off some of the branches, you help to curb part of its overbearing, the tree will still be likely to produce too many fruits on the limbs that are left. Even limited overproduction results in smaller fruits and a tendency of the tree to bear only every other year.

In an attempt to correct the biennial-bearing habit of the tree and to increase the size of the fruit, we spend several beautiful June days thinning fruit—when we'd rather go fishing. We have found that the procedure must be done with self-discipline, since throwing away potential fruits is contrary to the frugality that struggling Northerners are reputedly either born with or quickly acquire. Picking off 80 percent of the crop and dropping it on the ground is a traumatic experience, even if you know it is done for a good reason.

We begin to thin out the fruits when they are about marble size, directly after the natural drop has thinned them somewhat. We make sure that the apples, pears, and large plums we leave on the tree are no closer than 6 inches apart. (We don't thin crab apples, small plums, or pickling pears.)

The difference is astonishing. The fruit ripens earlier, is much larger, and each one is usable, with almost no culls. The trees bear fewer fruits but more bushels, because each fruit is large. Far fewer seeds are produced, and because it takes more energy to produce seeds than flesh, the tree remains more healthy than if it had exhausted itself in bearing a large crop one year, then taking the next year off to recover.

PREVENTING WINTER INJURY

Fruit tree hardiness is determined nearly as much by the length of the growing season as by low winter temperatures. Although Reliance peaches may be hardy to $-25°$ F, as the advertisements claim, they are not hardy in a ten-week growing season. Instead, they continue to grow throughout the month of September, and get winter-killed when our early fall frosts damage their unhardened wood.

Most fruit trees originated in the warm climates of southern Europe and Asia, and many have not adjusted to a growing season that lasts only seventy to one hundred days. European and Japanese plums, peaches, apricots, grapes, nectarines, figs, and even some varieties of apples and pears have the habit of growing late in the summer and often continue growing in the fall, which makes them poor choices for northern climates.

In the areas that border Lake Champlain many varieties of apples, plums, cherries, pears, grapes, and even some of the hardier peaches can be grown. The water keeps the air warm until late in the fall, and the first hard frost may not hit until mid-November. A few miles away from the lake, however, the first frost usually arrives in early September, and quickly curtails the growing season.

After the lake becomes frozen in midwinter, both areas experience the same low temperatures. Furthermore, high winds from the lake may make the chill factor even lower in the lake-bordering areas than in the more outlying, sheltered spots.

Although February temperatures may reach $-25°$ F in both places, the long growing season near the lake makes it possible to grow a wide variety of fruits there, whereas twenty miles away most of these fruit trees would be winter-killed.

Since many of us live in an area that is not as favorable, we have found that we must choose only hardy varieties that can adapt to a short growing season. However, if you want to try your luck at growing a few "exotics" or borderline plants that haven't quite adapted to your spot, by using these methods you may help to control their growth in late summer:

1. Avoid using any fast-acting chemical fertilizers, or, if you feel you must use them, apply sparingly and only in early spring.

2. Mulch the trees heavily to conserve moisture so that they will have good growth during the early summer. Water during early summer dry spells also; you don't want late summer rains following a dry June and July to stimulate lush growth in August and September.

3. If late growth persists, cut it off or pinch it back as soon as it begins to grow. This process is easy on dwarf trees, young trees, and espaliers, but more difficult on mature, standard-sized trees.

4. Prune your trees in the fall, directly after you harvest. Trees pruned at that time make less heavy regrowth, and are therefore less likely to be damaged by early frosts.

5. Avoid planting in areas where late spring and early fall frosts are common. The wood of many fruit trees hardens quickly once the growth stops. Even a few days added to the growing season can make the difference between success and failure.

6. In a period of lush, late-summer tree growth, let grass or weeds grow under the trees in order to deplete the supply of soil nu-

trients. By removing the mulch, or ceasing to mow, you can often accomplish this. Some orchardists, instead of letting the weeds grow, plant winter rye or another crop to discourage late summer tree growth.

Experimenters are trying chemicals to slow down late growth. They are using the growth regulators used by florists and greenhouse bedding plant growers to keep petunias, poinsettias, chrysanthemums, geraniums, and other plants short and bushy. Although the use of growth regulators on fruit trees, broadleaf evergreens, and small fruits has been mostly experimental, in recent years some orchardists have been using them to keep their fruit trees small. Northern growers have been particularly fascinated by the idea that preventing any late summer growth might also prevent winter injury and **make it possible to grow some of the less hardy trees. The spraying is usually done directly after the first flush of growth in early summer, with repeat sprays made later if necessary.**

Planting deep makes it possible to grow hardy roots on tender dwarf appletrees. Leave a depression so roots can breathe (*May*). Fill in partially in mid-summer and mulch the roots heavily before winter. The following spring, fill in to ground level, and the new hardy roots will grow above the graft. This method is useful when a tree variety is only available on dwarf roots.

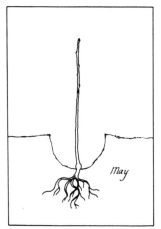

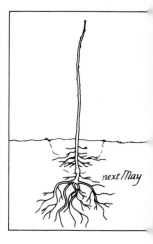

Many times I have wanted to try out a new variety of apple, only to find it was available exclusively on tender dwarf roots. It took some extra fussing, but often I have been able to get my "experiments" to survive. I plant the tree a little deeper than I would an ordinary one, leaving a depression about 5 inches deep around each tree. Gradually through the summer I fill this depression with soil, thereby finally getting the graft union buried about 6 inches below ground level without smothering the tree roots by burying them too deep at first.

In a short time some new roots develop above the graft, and they gradually replace the tender ones. It is these new roots that cause a full-sized tree to grow.

While the tree is growing its new roots I mulch it heavily before winter, to protect it whenever the snow cover is inadequate. I also choose a sheltered location for the tender trees, one that is protected from extreme winds. Many that would winter-kill in our more exposed spots do fairly well when they're hidden behind a tall windbreak.

SUNSCALD

The bright spring sun is a welcome sight; however, when it shines on the dark bark of a young tree, it is the prime cause of a great deal of "winter" injury. The most hardy trees may be affected, as well as the tender ones. The sun's warming of the bark and the cambium cells underneath on a cold day causes a considerable change in the temperature of the tree. The trouble comes when a cloud covers the sun, or a sudden cold north wind comes up. Either condition causes the tree's temperature to drop suddenly. The cells freeze, and the bark splits open.

If you notice that this has happened to your young trees, tack the loose bark back to the trunk of the tree with thumbtacks as soon as possible, and seal the crack with a tree dressing available in most hardware and garden stores. If you discover old sunscald wounds, scrape away all the loose bark and cover the bare wood with tree dressing or tree paint. Recover the opening every year or two until new bark covers it completely.

Sunscald usually takes place on the southern or southeastern side of the trees. As the name indicates, it looks as if the bark has been scalded or blistered, causing a large crack to appear. It particularly affects young trees that have spent their early life protected from the sun by being crowded in nursery rows. They are especially vulnerable to sun and chill when planted in an exposed field.

Sunscald is most common in March and early April. It can strike medium-sized as well as small trees, and some seem to be more vulnerable than others. Surprisingly, we've found our superhardy Yellow Transparents to be especially susceptible.

Preventing sunscald is, of course, better than trying to cure it; and many of us paint the bark on the sunny side of our trees with sun-reflecting white paint. We've found that an easy way to treat a small orchard is to thin the outdoor-type latex house paint with water and spray it on with a small tank or trombone-type sprayer; or, if you have only a few trees, they can be easily painted with a spray can or brush. The painting should cover the tree trunk from the ground to just above the point where the branches start. Re-paint the trees every two years until the bark begins to get tough and rough.

Sometimes home gardeners with only a few trees wrap them with spiral strips like a bandage, using a material called "tree wrap" to prevent sunscald. Others use aluminum foil, crimping it tightly to the stem of the tree to keep it from blowing away. Wraps and foils must be removed after sunscald danger is over in the spring to let the bark "breathe" in the summer sun, and to allow the new bark to harden before winter.

ICE, SNOW, AND ROAD SALT DAMAGE

Ice storms can strike nearly anywhere, and late winter storms of heavy, wet snow can be especially harmful by breaking the branches off even young, strong trees. Although these hazards cannot be prevented, measures may be taken to protect them.

To help prevent breakage, prune the fruit trees so that they have a strong branch structure. Be sure to cut off weak and rotting limbs from large, older trees to help prevent eventual ugly wounds.

Icy crusts settling down as the snow melts from below are a prime cause of limb breakage in snow country, so don't allow fruit trees to

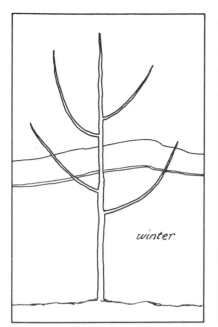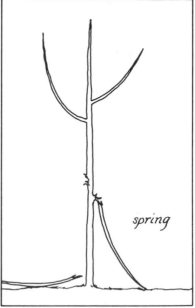

Heavy snow drifts with a layer of icy crust often break lower limbs from trees as the bottom snow melts and the crust settles, taking branches with it.

branch too close to the ground where snows are likely to get deep. Plant your trees where large deep drifts of snow don't accumulate, and a safe distance away from roadsides where snowplows pile up large amounts.

If you live near a highway that is paved or likely to be paved in the future, avoid planting trees where melting snow and salt will run onto their roots.

HARVESTING

How much frost can ripening fruit tolerate at harvest time? Some gardeners think that tree fruits are like tomatoes, and they rush to pick them all before the first frost. By picking them too early, their flavor doesn't have time to develop fully. Actually, apples, pears, and plums can stand a light frost with no trouble; and winter apples can even tolerate a moderate frost. Don't pick Cortland, Prairie Spy, Greening, Connell, Honeygold, Spartan, or McIntosh before they are ripe unless a really hard frost is coming. We consider it's a hard frost when the ground freezes slightly and water in a bucket ices up.

Making *cider* is a fall ritual on many northern farms and homesteads.

Moderate frosts will damage plums and pears, and some early apples. If you have misjudged the weather and these fruits become frosted, it is not necessary to throw them away. If they are used immediately, they may be cooked, canned, or frozen—or the fruit may be made into juice.

It isn't easy to guess when a damaging frost will strike, and all of us sometimes pick our fruit too early or too late, just as we do our corn and tomatoes. Apples are ripe when their seeds turn a dark brown, and plums when they are covered with a powdery bloom. Pears should be picked when they are well developed, have reached their proper color, separate from the tree easily, yet before they are ready to eat. They are one of the fruits that must be picked before they are completely ripe. If they're allowed to ripen on the tree, they rot quickly.

All fruit bruises easily, but some is much more vulnerable to rough handling than others. Hand-pick all the fruit you don't plan to use immediately; fruit shaken from the tree bruises and spoils rapidly.

STORING FRUITS

The North's cool fall weather makes it an ideal place to store fruit. Apples, plums, and pears can be kept a few weeks in sheds and barns after picking, until hard frosts begin. Even early-ripening fruit keeps rather well if it is stored out of the sun in a cool place. The hardiest varieties of plums and pears last only a limited time, but some hardy apples are excellent keepers. Before hard frosts we put these winter-storage apples into a frost-free root cellar, where they are kept just above freezing in a rather moist atmosphere. Some varieties, such as Bethel, Connell, Cortland, Prairie Spy, and Spartan, keep well most of the winter.

FRUITS SUITABLE FOR THE NORTH

Hardiest of all—suitable for zone 2:

Apples	Pears	Plums
Adanac	David	Bounty
Heyer	John	Dandy
McLean	Tait-Dropmore	Norther
Moris	Tioma	Pembina
Patterson		
Rosthern No. 15		

Next hardy group—suitable for zone 3:

Apples	Pears	Plums	Cherry Plums
Astrachan, Red	Golden Sweet	LaCrescent	Compass
Beacon	Luscious	Pipestone	Red Diamond
Bethel	Maxine	Toka	
Blue Pearmain	Mendel	Underwood	
Chestnut Crab	Parker	Waneta	
Connell	Patten		
Dolgo Crab			
Duchess			
Fameuse			

Apples
Fireside
Haralson
Lodi
Peach Apple
Pound Sweet
Red Baron
Red Duchess
St. Lawrence
State Fair
Sweet Sixteen
Tetosky
Tolman Sweet
Viking
Wealthy
Wolf River
Yellow Transparent

Suitable for favored spots in zone 3 and all of zone 4:

Apples	*Pears*	*Plums*
Honeygold	Duchess	Ember
MCINTOSH FAMILY:	Kieffer	Redglow
Barry	Seckel	Redcoat
Cortland	Lincoln	Superior
Early McIntosh		
Jerseymac		
Lobo		
Macoun		
Macspur		
McIntosh		
Melba		
Milton		
Quinte		
Spartan		
Minjon		
Northeast Greening		
Prairie Spy		
Regent		

Worth trying in favored parts of zone 4 and warmer:

Apples	*Apricots*	*Cherries*
Baldwin	Manchu	Early Richmond
Cox Orange Pippin	Moongold	Meteor
DELICIOUS FAMILY:	Scout	Montmorency
Red Delicious	Sungold	North Star
Double Red Delicious		
Starking	*Peach*	*Pears*
and others	Reliance	Bartlett
Empire	Sunapee	Clapps Favorite
Gravenstein		
Jonathan	*Plums*	
Northern Spy	Dietz	
Prima	Mt. Royal	
Priscilla	Stanley Prune	
Yellow Delicious		

CHAPTER SIX

THE BERRY PATCH

When I first started growing small fruits on our farm in the northern mountains, I tried everything in the catalogs I could afford. Red raspberries were my first crop, soon followed by strawberries, currants, and gooseberries. Then I ventured into blackberries, black and yellow raspberries, boysenberries, loganberries, grapes, and blueberries. Unfortunately, most of the latter group either died over the first winter or limped along for a brief time, never producing more than a berry or two.

Now, years later, I'm successfully growing many of those same kinds of berries that had failed when I first planted them. I've found varieties developed especially for the North, and have picked up a few growing tricks on how to handle those kinds that are not especially suited for our climate.

Since my first ventures, several new berries have been domesticated and marketed. Elderberries, juneberries, and Saskatoons are three of my favorites that have expanded the choice for northern gardeners.

Many small fruits grow best in areas where the summers are cool. Mountain-grown strawberries develop a sweet, rich flavor matched only by wild strawberries. Elderberries, currants, gooseberries, and most red and yellow raspberries thrive in cool climates and organic soils. In my opinion, any northern gardener who doesn't grow these fruits is missing a good bet.

In addition to the fact that most small fruits are hardy and taste good, they are rich in vitamins, grow well in a wide variety of soils, need little room and little care, are inexpensive to buy, and plantings last for years. Unlike the tree fruits, they begin to bear within a year or two after they've been planted, and most reach full production quickly.

If you plan to add small fruits to your garden lot, choose those that will grow best for you within the limits of your area and in your type of soil. Many may be used as ornamentals, and they are excellent bird attractors. In fact, many times we wish the birds were not quite as fond of the berries.

Red and yellow raspberries will thrive in the widest range of growing conditions, and need the least coddling. Currants and gooseberries are even more rugged; but the fact that they must not be planted within 900 feet of any white pine trees severely curtails their use in many areas. Both bush fruits often carry a disease called blister rust that can be fatal to white pine.

Although other small fruits are more fussy, they can, nevertheless, be grown in the North. Most black raspberries are not hardy enough to grow in zone 3, but several varieties do grow here. Strawberries are the least hardy of any of the small fruits, and must be covered for the winter unless snows come early and lie deep over them. Highbush blueberries require a very acid soil, and grow well in zones 3 and 4 only in a sheltered location. Wild elderberries are as hardy as raspberries, but the named varieties suffer minor winter injury in exposed locations.

The garden huckleberries listed in many seed catalogs are really not berries at all, but bush garden fruits closely related to the tomato. They may be grown in the North if they are started early inside. Although they are not good for eating directly off the bush, many people like them cooked in pies or as a sauce.

Although our family likes to eat the small fruits fresh and in all the traditional ways, including sauce, pies, jams, jelly, and ice cream, we have recently begun to appreciate them in fruit juices as well. Our gooseberries, currants, elderberries, raspberries, grapes, and strawberries all go into tasty, healthful juices that make tropical drinks pale by comparison.

There are many ways to extract juice from small fruits, but juice making got a big boost at our home with the addition of a steam process juice extractor. The fruit is steamed and its colorful liquid comes out boiling hot for easy preserving in rubber-stoppered bottles, or it may be frozen, or made into jelly, fruit leathers, or wine.

Not only do we use small fruits, but also crab apples, apples, plums, wild cherries, grapes, rhubarb, and vegetables. All make delicious drinks by themselves or in mixtures with each other, or with cider, orange juice, and other liquids. The juices, alone, make our fruit cultivation worthwhile.

A steam process *juice extractor* makes it easy to preserve juices of fruits and berries.

SOILS AND FERTILIZERS

Most small fruits will grow under difficult conditions and in poor soil. All of them do much better, however, with care, good soil, and annual doses of fertilizer. To get healthy, fruitful plants you should also protect them from weed and grass competition, prune out old deadwood regularly, control their diseases, and protect them from harmful insects and animals.

I've met people who believe that bush and bramble fruits are so hardy they can live anywhere, although they would never dream of planting tomato plants in an untilled hayfield. On the contrary, newly planted small fruits should have a rich, well-tilled soil in which to get started. If possible, till a generous amount of farm manure (100 bushels per 2,000 square feet) thoroughly into the soil where row or bed crops such as blackberries, strawberries, and raspberries are to be planted.

The bush fruits should be treated as small trees, and the area around each one fertilized before the new plant is set out. Add additional fertilizer over an increasing area each year as the bush grows and its roots spread out.

Manure applied very late in the fall or early in the spring is an excellent fertilizer for established bush fruits (blueberry, currant, gooseberry, elderberry) or bramble fruits (raspberries and black-berries). We use commercial dried manure or farm manure, either fresh or from an aged pile. It should be spread around the base of the bush fruits or between the rows of the bramble plants, and the rains will wash it in. Farm manures may be used at the rate of a quarter bushel or more per bush, or per 3 feet of bramble row; dried cow or sheep manure should be applied at the rate of one pint per bush fruit, or about 50 pounds per 50 feet of bramble row. If poultry manure is used, however, cut the amount used to half, because it is very potent.

By applying the fertilizer in the early spring or late fall, it is readily available to the plant when it makes its fastest growth in early summer. This is especially important in the North. If plants are fertilized in midsummer, they will start to grow, and late sum-mer growth must be discouraged, because if the plants do not harden their wood by the time of the first frosts, winter injury will result. Many of the highbush blueberries, blackberries, some varie-ties of black raspberries, and even some hybrid elderberries tend to grow late in the summer and are prone to early frost injury.

If manure is not easily available, composted leaves and garden wastes combined with other fertilizers may be substituted. If you use chemical fertilizers such as 5-10-10, or liquid plant foods such as Rapid-Gro, be extremely careful not to overstimulate plant growth in late summer, especially when there is a lot of rain in August and September. Follow carefully the instructions on the bag or those recommended by the extension service for your area.

LIME

The same glacier that pushed so many rocks into our soils also left behind a variety of soil types. For instance, in our area pockets of acid and sweet soil sometimes lie side by side.

Most northern soils, however, present no major problems for growing most small fruits unless the soil is extremely acid. For the fastest early summer growth soil pH should be between 5.5 and 7 for raspberries, elderberries, currants, and gooseberries. Blackberries prefer between 5.5 and 6.5; strawberries between 5.0 and 6.0; and blueberries grow well only if the pH is extremely low, from 4.0 to 4.5.

Lime or hardwood ashes may be added to the soil if it is necessary to raise the pH for raspberries, elderberries, currants, and gooseberries. On the other hand, if you want to raise blueberries, look for a spot that has naturally acid soil, and one that has not had wood ashes or lime added to it recently. If you don't have a naturally acid soil, you can lower the pH yourself (see chapter 2).

As I explained earlier, organic gardeners usually have fewer acid-alkalinity problems than chemical gardeners. When sufficient natural fertilizers are available in the soil, they seem to be more readily available and feed the plant more evenly than chemical fertilizers, even if the pH isn't exactly right.

MULCHES

Like fruit trees, small fruit plants thrive under thick organic mulches. I feel they're indispensable for many reasons. They help keep plants in their natural state, just as if they were growing in the wild. They prevent the soil from washing or drying out, and they add fertility to it. They encourage earthworms and keep the soil cool. They also help protect the roots of the more tender plants, such as highbush blueberries, which can be damaged by cultivation and by cold. A heavy mulch also eliminates the weed and grass growth that creeps in to steal moisture and nutrients from the berry plants and diminishes plant growth and fruit production. The weed seeds are prevented from reaching the soil where they can sprout; or, if they do get to the soil, mulch keeps the young seedlings so heavily shaded that they usually don't grow.

Mulch should be put on or renewed in early spring, after the plants are fed. We find, just as with fruit trees, that one of the best ways to eliminate weed and grass competition on the bush fruits is to place a layer of paper plus a layer of hay to hold the paper in place, over the manure or compost.

We mulch the brambles with heavy layers, 2 to 4 inches thick, of shavings, shredded bark, leaves, hay, spoiled farm ensilage, or a similar material, spreading it over the fertilizer.

Some growers feel that mulch makes strawberry plants more vulnerable to bloom injury by keeping the earth's protective heat away from the plants during early summer frosts. Although unmulched plants are less likely to be damaged during a very light frost, not much protection would be noticeable during a heavier one, 26° F or lower, so most gardeners, including myself, feel that the many advantages of mulches on strawberries far outweigh this possible disadvantage.

PEST AND WEED CONTROL

If you don't use heavy mulches around your small fruit plants, some alternate form of weed control will be necessary if the plants are to make a fast growth and produce well. Sometimes currants, gooseberries, and blueberries are planted as ornamentals in the landscape where a heavy mulch might be too obvious and unattractive. Mowing and clipping around them will keep them weed-free.

Row crops—the strawberries, blackberries, and raspberries—are often cultivated or rototilled instead of mulched to eliminate weeds and grass between the rows. Some commercial growers allow geese to feed in their berry plantings before the fruit forms, to check weed growth. Others use chemical herbicides such as Dacthyl to keep unwanted vegetation under control.

Insects are seldom a major problem for small, backyard berry growers. Disease should not be, either, if we use only certified plants and resist the temptation to set out uncertified or gift plants dug from a friend's patch. Don't even plant any from your own patch unless you are sure they are free of disease.

If possible, keep your strawberry bed 100 feet or more from the potato patch, from tomato plants, and from delphiniums, since potatoes and tomatoes harbor wilts, and delphinium plants often contain cyclamen mites that often bother strawberries.

TRANSPLANTING WILD BERRIES

Sometimes I'm asked if it is practical to move wild raspberries, blackberries, blueberries, elderberries, and other small fruits into the garden; and if their size and productivity will be increased by fertilization and other care.

In my opinion, usually it is not sensible to bypass a century or more of progress by not planting the improved kinds of berries—especially blueberries, raspberries, and strawberries.

Some wild blackberries, on the other hand, are of rather good quality, and some that have "gone wild" may quite likely be seedlings of earlier cultivated varieties. Since most garden varieties sold in catalogs are not hardy in zones 3 and 4, if you find some wild blackberries that seem of excellent quality, they are definitely worth rescuing.

The same may also be said of blueberries if your growing area is so exposed that growing the highbush varieties would be impossible. The small wild bushes can be easily protected by snow and low windbreaks, and even if the berries are small and the yields low, they are better than none at all. Furthermore, the plants are attractive and the berry flavor superb.

The best time to move any plants from the wild in the North is in the early spring. Choose medium-sized plants. Cut back all the top branches to about 4 inches from the ground and take a large clump of soil with each plant, disturbing the root clump as little as possible. Water them heavily, and pack the soil tightly around them when you set them into their new locations.

THE BRAMBLES

The brambles grow native throughout the North. Raspberries and blackberries grow wild even in Alaska. Although some of the cultivated varieties that have been developed in warmer climates are more limited in their growing area, many of the high quality introductions are extremely hardy.

Red raspberries are one of the most dependable, especially the summer-fruiting kinds; and the yellow are nearly as reliable. Many of the purple and black raspberries and most of the cultivated blackberries have trouble growing well in the coldest sections, although there are some of each kind that do well on our windy hilltop. Most of the fall-bearing raspberries (everbearers) are hardy and ripen their summer crop successfully. Unfortunately, however, only a few varieties ripen their fall crop early enough in the season to escape the first frost where short growing seasons are the rule.

Cut back *raspberry* and *blackberry bushes* before winter, so heavy snows won't break them over. Stake or support them with a low fence if necessary.

Brambles need little special care in the North. As elsewhere, the old canes must be cut back to the ground after bearing, and suckers either cultivated or mowed off when necessary to keep the plants in rows narrow enough to manage efficiently.

We always cut a foot off the top of each cane just before winter. Cutting them back makes the canes stiff and sturdy, and eliminates a lot of winter breakage. Even with cutting back, most kinds of raspberries and blackberries need a fence or other support to hold them up off the ground when they are loaded with heavy fruit.

Spur blight, a disease that causes the canes to die in early summer, may be a problem in the more humid areas of the North, especially in wet summers; but this can be easily controlled by using Captan or Ferbam.

Raspberries

Wild raspberries are abundant in the North. They can be found wherever there has been a recent tree-cutting operation, since Nature uses them as a cover crop to fill in for a few years while new trees get established. In fact, some people feel that there is no need to plant culivated ones, since the wild ones are so plentiful.

Perhaps. But the cultivated varieties taste nearly as good as the wild ones. The berries are larger; and the bushes are more productive, last four years, and, best of all, they are available. Every day during the raspberry season we pick several pails full in our backyard without stumbling around in the underbrush, or encountering bears.

Most people agree that raspberries are one of the best northern fruits. They are fast-growing and, as they bloom late, their blossoms are never bothered by frosts; and both roots and tops are hardy.

There are hundreds of American and Canadian red raspberry varieties, but some of the tried and proven good ones that are readily available are *Boyne, Camby, Chief, Newburg, Madawaska,* and *Taylor.* All are considered hardy and worth planting in zones 3 and 4. *Latham,* the old standby, and *Viking,* another favorite, have been nearly abandoned because the former got disease easily, and the latter grew so tall it was hard to stake. Our favorite is

Newburg, because it is disease-resistant, low-growing, and very productive, with high quality fruit.

Amber is considered one of the best yellow-pink varieties. It has a superior, very sweet flavor, and bears over a longer season than the reds.

The fall-bearing varieties of red raspberries that we've found most reliable are *August Red* and *Fall Red.* Fall bearers produce a summer crop on the canes that grew the previous year, and another crop in September on canes grown the same year. Most gardeners, because they grow regular raspberries as well, are interested only in a good-sized fall crop. To get the most berries then, you must cut the canes to the ground each fall right after the berries are harvested, so there are never any year-old canes to bear fruit during the summer.

Many fall-bearing raspberries do not produce well in places where the first frost comes before late September. *Indian Summer, September,* and *Heritage* all ripen too late for areas like ours with short growing seasons.

Black and purple raspberries grow differently than the red and yellow kinds. They form new plants, not from suckers growing from the roots, but by "tipping." The top of the cane bends over and forms a new plant by rooting where it touches the soil. Growers often extend their plantings by bending over additional canes and covering their tips with soil until new plants have rooted. After they are well rooted, these can be dug up and replanted.

Don't plant the red and yellow raspberries within 100 feet of the black and purple varieties, since the latter often have a disease. It doesn't noticeably affect them, but can cause trouble by infecting the reds and yellows.

We've had good luck with *John Robertson,* a hardy black raspberry that tastes, not too surprisingly, just like black raspberry ice cream. *Lowden* is another variety that may possibly grow well in zones 3 and 4, but we haven't had as good luck with it.

Purple raspberries worth a try in sheltered spots are *Sodus* and *Brandywine.* Both suffer winter injury, however, if the canes are not buried in the snow when temperatures drop below −20° F. *Brandywine* produces a huge berry of unusual flavor, as the name suggests, and the bush is vigorous and quite hardy.

Blackberries

Blackberries grow wild, as a cover crop, just as raspberries do. They ripen two to three weeks later than raspberries, and I remember picking them beside the road as I walked to school in September.

There are two distinctly different types of blackberries, and most of the named varieties of both that are commonly offered for sale are not hardy in zone 3 and most of zone 4. The upright kinds grow much like the red raspberries. The trailing ones, called dewberries, produce long canes that are usually tied to a fence or posts somewhat like grapevines.

Usually the roots of both the upright and trailing varieties are hardy even in the Far North; however, the canes often are not. Since fruit is borne only on the canes that grew the previous year, if they are winter-killed there are no live year-old canes, and no fruit is produced. Each year where they are not hardy, the blackberry patch is a jungle of dead canes from previous years, plus the new sprouting ones.

None of the trailing blackberries (dewberries) are regarded as hardy in zones 3 and 4; and few of the upright-growing blackberries can be grown in northern areas. *Snyder,* an oldtimer, is one of the hardiest, but is seldom propagated any more because it is very little larger than many of the good wild varieties.

Darrow is considered one of the hardiest currently available in the catalogs, but other more suitable kinds for the North will likely appear as soon as they have been thoroughly tested and stocks can be built up.

If you decide to try some of those hardy kinds now available, or transplant some from a friend's patch or a wild area, plant them in a place sheltered from the north and west winds, and where snow will come early, drift deeply, and stay late. Keep them separated from your garden and all other plantings, because if they get established and grow, you'll be amazed at the hundreds of new little plants that will come up everywhere, often as far as 20 feet away from the row.

STRAWBERRIES

At first glance there is probably no good reason why any northern gardener should even attempt to grow cultivated strawberries. The

plant is less hardy than a peach tree and begins to suffer damage
if the temperatures fall to 20° F. At ten degrees the injury can be
serious, and at temperatures below zero, the plant is likely to die.
The large-fruiting garden strawberries are improved varieties of a
West Coast native, so they are obviously more at home where winters are mild. They can survive in the North only if they get the
protection needed from the surrounding earth and are insulated
from the cold temperatures by a mulch or heavy layer of snow.

Six to 8 inches of snow is considered adequate protection when
temperatures fall to zero, but more snow is needed if the temperature goes much lower. In winters past, when it occasionally got even
colder than that in January with no snow, strawberry plantings in
the Northeast suffered badly.

Although snow is good insulation for plants, ice is not. Your
strawberry beds should be graded in such a way that no pockets
form that will catch pools of autumn rain, or water from midwinter
thaws. Even when the plants survive a rough winter, fruit yield
can be greatly reduced because cold temperatures injure the fruit
buds of unmulched plants.

Varieties

Unfortunately for northern gardeners, not much of the work that
has been done to develop new strawberry varieties has been with
hardiness in mind. Most of the older kinds are still the most
hardy and best for us to grow. Before you make a large planting,
check with growers in your area and with your state extension
service to see what grows best under conditions similar to yours.

Premier (the old *Howard 17*), *Catskill, Sparkle,* and *Dunlap* are
old standbys and considered the most reliable for the North. *Fair-
fax, Midway, MicMac, Raritan,* and *Redcoat* are new varieties that
are nearly as hardy, and do well even in zone 3.

Since frosts at blossoming time effectively destroy your crop, late-
blooming varieties can be an advantage. Commercial growers want
to get their berries on the market as early as possible, but home
growers don't need to hurry, and may want to consider some of the
later-blooming and ripening kinds. *Albritton, Jerseybelle, Marlate,
Redstar,* and *Sparkle,* when mulched for the winter, have done well
in northern home gardens.

Everbearing varieties are usually not too successful in the North.
Although they bear a few berries every day, there are seldom enough
for freezing or for use in large amounts unless you plant a great
many. *Fort Laramie* shows promise as being a hardy everbearer.

Bare-rooted and potted strawberry plants are available for spring
planting in most areas. Bare-rooted plants are far cheaper, usually
from one-fifth to one-half the price of the potted ones. With potted
plants, however, you can establish a bed quickly, and they can be
safely set out in summer or fall if you miss the spring season.

Of course, after your bed has become established, you may take
new plants from it for future plantings, as long as disease doesn't
invade your patch.

Garden books and magazines frequently suggest planting strawberries in barrels or large crocks full of holes, or in pyramids. While
this is novel and can be quite successful where winters are kinder,
covering up such a structure for winter can be a chore and is not
usually very practical in the North.

Planting

Grass and weeds give strawberry growers a lot of grief. Because
strawberries are so low-growing and noncompetitive, keeping the
weeds under control is difficult; but it is necessary, or you may lose
the plants before they even begin to bear.

The best way to control weeds is to get the soil in excellent shape
before setting out the plants. One way to kill off all the vegetation
is to grow a cultivated crop such as corn or potatoes the year before
planting. Some growers clear their prospective planting sites by
spraying a herbicide such as Round-up several times in the spring
before planting, or during late summer or early fall previous to the
spring planting. Other gardeners cover the area for a year before
planting with plastic or old metal roofing, to kill off the grass and
weeds.

Just before you plant, till thoroughly and enrich the soil with
lots of manure, compost, or a complete fertilizer. A loose, moist,
rich soil will encourage the rapid root and top growth necessary
to produce husky, potentially productive plants before the short
northern growing season is over. Strawberries are heavy feeders, but
they are so shallow-rooted that adequate fertilizer and moisture

This newly planted *strawberry bed* is arranged in a compact size for easy care and covering in case of frost.

must be near the top of the soil. For this reason, watering may be absolutely necessary in dry years.

Because each breeze that blows past the bed all summer probably contains weed seeds, it's important continually to get rid of new weed and grass seedlings all season. Herbicides such as Dacthyl and Dymid prevent new seeds from sprouting and are widely used. Organic gardeners, however, prefer to hoe, cultivate, or to use mulches that prevent the weed seeds and the soil from getting together.

Two methods of growing strawberries are used by home gardeners in the North. The matted, or runner-row, method is most common and is nearly always used by commercial growers. The hill method is often used by home gardeners if growing space is limited. The name "hill" may be misleading, because it refers only to spacing. Never plant strawberries in raised beds in the North, because they winter-kill much more easily.

The matted row: Set the plants 18 to 24 inches apart in rows that are at least 3 feet apart. If the soil is at all dry, water them thoroughly at planting time and every day or two thereafter for the next two weeks, unless it rains. Watering is particularly important in the North, because it is necessary to get the new plants established and growing as quickly as possible so that a good number of runner plants will form before the short growing season is over. For the same reason, plant the bed as early in the spring as the soil can be worked. Unlike vegetable seeds, strawberry plants don't need warmth and will become established faster in a cool, moist soil.

Toward the middle of the summer, if all goes well, the runners that form new plants will have begun to grow. Direct these along the row in both directions from the parent plant to make sure the row will be well filled with plants by the end of the summer. In windy locations it may be necessary to pin down the runners with small twigs or stones to keep them neat in their rows instead of growing all over the bed.

The hill method: Set the plants 15 to 18 inches apart in each direction to form a bed. If you plant more than three rows, a 3- to 4-foot row for walking should be made between each bed. Unlike the matted row method, all runners should be cut off the plants as soon as they start to grow. Each plant will grow very large and produce enormous berries. The advantage of the hill method is that if grass and weeds are effectively kept out, the planting can last five to ten years. The matted row system, on the other hand, will probably need to be replaced after the first crop is harvested.

We like to spread a sheet of 6 mil black plastic over the area we're going to plant. Then we cut slits every 15 to 18 inches into

Planting potted strawberries in a bed mulched with black plastic makes it possible to grow these delicious fruits with little work, even in the weed-prone North.

which we insert the plants. Packing a concave depression around each plant on top of the plastic creates a saucer that will catch rainwater to irrigate them. To hold the plastic in place on windy days, we weigh it down at various places with rocks, old tires, boards, or bricks. Black plastic cut in long, narrow strips can also be used to control weeds between rows in the matted row system.

Sheets of old metal roofing or yellowed fiberglass removed from buildings or greenhouses instead of plastic may be used as weed suppressants in the matted row system, and in the hill system, as well. The long strips of roofing serve as weed barriers between the rows and shorter pieces of aluminum, fiberglass, or similar durable material can be cut to fill the spaces between the plants in the hill system. Be sure rainwater can run from the roofing into the rows, however, and is not merely carried off to the ends of the bed. It may be necessary to punch holes in the material here and there to accomplish this. Asphalt roofing, which is definitely not good for the soil, should never be used as mulch. We like to cover the plastic or metal mulch with shavings, shredded bark, or a similar material to lessen the summer heat and to improve the appearance.

Spring Frost Protection

Each day in spring brings forth new blooms and each new one is a delight. But with our fruit blossoms always comes a bit of anxiety. Will the plums, pears, and apples get caught in a spring frost this year? Or will it arrive a bit later and hit the strawberry blooms that are close to the ground where the air is coldest?

It is the nature of strawberries to bloom early. Because they are shallow-rooted, they react quickly to a few warm spring days. A mulch may help delay their blooming by keeping the soil cool, but there is no guarantee that even a heavy mulch could hold them back until after the last spring frost. Spring frosts are sneaky, as I've mentioned before. The days preceding them may be warm and sunny, and often there is little warning that a temperature drop is about to happen.

Commercial growers use frost alarms to alert them when danger threatens, so they can turn on their sprinkler systems. Small home gardens can be protected by using a lawn sprinkler, or by covering the plants, as you do the vegetable garden, with sheets, bags, blankets, newspapers, or anything that offers protection. Since the ground usually has not collected very much heat early in the spring, plastic sheeting, we've discovered, is usually not an adequate covering, because heat is lost rapidly through a single layer of plastic.

Strawberry blossoms are injured by the frost in the same way fruit tree blooms are, by the damaging of the tender tube that carries the pollen from the pistil to the base of the blossom. If the flower has already been pollinated, a light frost won't hurt it, so a good supply of honey bees in the neighborhood is good insurance against spring frost damage.

Winter Protection

Covering the beds with straw mulches (hence the name of the berry) has long been a common practice, since the strawberry buds that form in the crown of the plant the season before they bloom are sensitive to temperatures much below 20° F.

Straw is still one of the best covering materials. It insulates well, does not pack tightly until late in the winter, contains few weed seeds, and, when the plants are uncovered in the spring, it makes a good mulch between the rows to keep the berries clean at picking time.

Unfortunately, straw is no longer easy to get in most places. Instead, we use spruce, fir, or pine boughs, which work very well. They are clean, don't pack tightly, and are easy to get in large

Cover strawberry beds with straw, shredded bark, or evergreen boughs in late fall just before the ground starts to freeze.

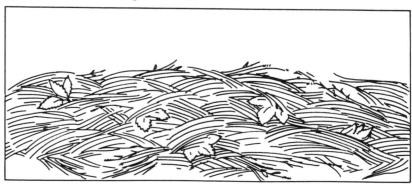

Next year's strawberry shortcake sleeps, snugly protected, under this bed covered with spruce boughs and snow.

amounts. Shredded bark from sawmills is often used as a cover by commercial growers in our area. Microfoam, a material used by nurserymen to cover up small plants, may also be used, but it is fairly expensive. Hay, leaves, sawdust, and shavings all cause problems, as do fiberglass, rock wool, and other home insulation that mats down when it gets wet. Use enough covering, whatever material you choose, to insulate the plants effectively against extreme cold and sudden temperature changes.

Where we live the snow nearly always comes early, lies deep, and stays until late spring, so little, and occasionally no cover is necessary, but we believe in spreading some kind of protection as a precaution. Where the ground stays bare, freezes deeply, or thaws and freezes intermittently for much of the winter, a thick mulch is absolutely essential if the berries are to be successfully overwintered.

Wait to cover your berries until about the time the ground begins to freeze nights in the fall. There may be danger that the plant will keep growing if you cover it when the ground is still warm.

The time you uncover the plants is as important as the timing of covering them. Wait until the last hard frost is over, and uncover them on a cloudy, rainy day, if possible. If that kind of day doesn't appear, uncover them in the late afternoon so the sun's bright rays won't hit the new, pale green growth before it has a chance to get hardened up a bit by being exposed to the weather.

THE BUSH FRUITS

The bush fruits are like miniature fruit trees, and quite unlike strawberry, blackberry, or raspberry plants. American cranberry, currants, gooseberries, blueberries, and elderberries are very long-lived.

I once found a very thorny gooseberry bush growing by a house foundation far out in the wooded back country. It must have been well over a hundred years old, but it was loaded with several quarts of large, sweet, greenish-yellow fruits. I had a good time eating my fill and wondering about the people who had cleared that hillside, built the house, and left one living gooseberry bush as a reminder that they had been there. I dug up a little sprout, brought it home, and planted it in mid-July. Happily, it lived and produced!

All the highbush American cranberry, currant, and gooseberry varieties I have tried seem to be hardy in the North, as are the wild elderberries. The canes of cultivated elderberries sometimes suffer some winter damage in the coldest weather, and a few kinds ripen so late some years that the frost damages the berries before they are ready. Blueberry varieties vary greatly in hardiness. Only those suitable for cold climates should be planted in the North, and they should be placed in a sheltered location.

The bush fruits do well on most good garden soil as long as it is not too heavy, gravelly, or wet. Elderberries will grow where it is somewhat more damp, and are often planted where the soil is too moist for gardens and fruit trees.

Currants and Gooseberries

Currants and gooseberries are two of the best small fruits for the North. Frost never bothers the blossoms, and winter cold doesn't hurt the plants. Both produce big crops of colorful and delicious fruit each year with little attention. Because grapes are not easy to grow in our region, the currants and gooseberries make nice substitutes. We enjoy them in all the ways we use any fruits, and use them even more because they ripen early in the season, before most other fruits are ready.

A few states prohibit the planting of currants and gooseberries altogether, or within certain areas, because they are likely carriers of blister rust, a disease that is fatal to white pine. In most states, however, the law states that they may be planted as long as they are not within 900 feet of white pine. Blister rust doesn't hurt the berries in any way, but they are the Typhoid Marys of the plant world, so investigate the laws in your state before you plant them.

Currants come in red, white, and black varieties, although the reds are by far the most popular. Red currant pies, jellies, and juices are beautiful as well as tasty. Many connoisseurs feel that white currants are somewhat sweeter than the reds, which are slightly tart, even when ripe; but few nursery catalogs list them.

Black currants are most likely to be carriers of blister rust and, by law, the plants cannot be sold in most states. Although some fruit lovers cherish black currants, I am not one of them, because I find the flavor and odor of most kinds rather strong and somewhat musky; but some of the newer kinds are rather good. Both white and black varieties are more popular in Canada than in the United States, and disease-free black currants are now being developed in that country.

Red Lake is still one of the best red currants. Other good varieties are *Minnesota 71, Cherry, Wilder,* and *Perfection.*

White Grape and *Imperial* are among the best white currants, and *Imperial* is probably the better of the two. *Manus, Consort,* and *Boskoop* are black currant varieties that are raised and sold in Canada. *Consort* is blister-rust resistant.

If you've ever tried to dry the fruit of the red or white currants, you may feel that the northern climate makes the results different from the dried currants available in stores. Actually, the commercial dried "currants" are not currants at all, but a variety of small grape.

Our visitors of European origin usually become excited when they see our gooseberry bushes. They miss the huge gooseberries of Europe, which are almost impossible to grow in North America because our climate encourages disease problems fatal to the plants, and very few nurseries sell them. There are, however, some large-fruiting North American kinds that produce grape-size berries. *Welcome* and *Red Jacket,* both reds, are delicious eaten out of hand when ripe. *Green Mountain* is a large, green-yellow variety. Other common kinds are *Pixwell, Champion,* and *Houghton.*

Gooseberries are among the hardiest of fruit plants, and are very productive.

Currants and gooseberries have very few pests that trouble them. A light dusting of Rotenone or other garden dust may be necessary when the leaves first appear to control the worms that may rapidly strip the foliage off the plants. Currants sometimes get mildew on their leaves and fruit during warm, moist weather if the air circulation about them is limited by buildings or other plantings. Giving them lots of room is the best prevention, and gardeners who don't object to chemicals may spray with Ben-Late as soon as the symptoms appear, to help control the disease.

Birds love currants, so we grow a few extra plants for them, or we wouldn't have any fruit for ourselves. Luckily, they seem to tire of the berries early in the season, or go on to something else, kindly leaving some of the crop for us.

Heavy winter snows sometimes break off some of the older branches of both currants and gooseberries, so we prune the bushes every three or four years to get rid of the brittle wood that is vulnerable to breakage and no longer produces well.

Elderberries

In Europe during the Middle Ages the elderberry enjoyed a place of honor few fruits have ever attained. It was credited with amazing health-giving powers and said to cure everything from arthritis to gout. Even the flowers reputedly contained healing powers for many ailments.

We have a friend who reports that her arthritic lameness has been definitely improved after a few weeks of drinking elderberry juice on a regular basis. The sipping of a bit of elderberry wine each day for medicinal purposes may not have been a joke after all, and the prim and proper little old ladies who imbibe may actually have their health in mind.

Whether or not elderberries can cure the aches and pains that are aggravated by cold, damp climates, they are excellent for northern gardeners, especially for *busy* northern gardeners. They require little care, and are nearly as hardy as the currant and gooseberry.

Elderberry plants grow so readily and the fruit is so tasty and useful, it is sometimes tempting to plant too many of them and to plant them in the wrong places. Because they usually grow eight or more feet tall, they will shade other plants growing nearby, if you're not careful. They grow prolifically and may spread rapidly, so don't plant them in your vegetable or flower garden or in the midst of your other berries. Put a row of them, instead, in a back corner where you can mow around them with your lawn mower. Be careful not to overfertilize them. If you give them little or no extra feeding, they will probably grow better, and fewer of their branches will be winter-killed.

Birds love elderberries. We've planted a few early-ripening wild plants to enable the birds to get their fill of those so they will leave the hybrid varieties alone. The wild ones are also useful as cross-pollinators for the larger-fruiting hybrids.

Although they take time to pick and process because they are so tiny, we make gallons of rich-flavored elderberry juice for good winter drinking, and freeze the berries, uncooked, to go into muffins and pies. They may also be made into wines, toppings, or jelly.

Several new, large-fruiting hybrids are available in many nursery catalogs. Plant two or more kinds for good pollination. *Adams, Johns, Nova, New York 21,* and *York* all grow well and survive northern winters. They ripen a bit later than the wild elderberries, so only those that mature before frost are worth considering. *Johns* and *New York 21* seldom ripen all of their fruit in our area, so those kinds should be avoided where fall frosts come early. If a frost threatens, we sometimes bring nearly ripe berries indoors, and they continue to ripen.

As I mentioned earlier, many new hybrid elderberries suffer winter injury. Usually this is no big problem, however. Unlike blackberries and blueberries, elderberries bear on new wood, so new sprouts from the ground and from uninjured wood produce a huge crop of fruit, even in those years when they've suffered severe winterkill.

Blueberries

The delicious highbush blueberries are the most difficult to grow of the bush fruits. I'd estimate that fewer than 50 percent of the attempts to establish a good blueberry planting in zones 3 and 4 are really successful. They are fussy about soil, cannot tolerate wind, need careful pruning, and are sensitive to overfertilization. Since the plants are expensive and it takes at least ten years for one to reach peak production even under the best conditions, northern gardeners should experiment with a few plants before starting a large plantation.

In spite of growing difficulties, home gardeners are raising blueberries successfully all over the North, often on soils and in locations quite unsuitable for commercial production of the fruit. It not only requires more work in the North than it would to establish a patch further south, but it also takes more patience because the plants grow very slowly. An apple tree planted the same day may reach prime bearing size before a blueberry bush.

Blueberry lovers feel they're worth waiting for, however. The fruit is large and tasty; the bushes live for decades, are productive and disease-resistant, and few animal pests bother them. Only the birds seem to be a nuisance; they will quickly grab most of the crop if they're not thwarted in some way.

A pH of about 4.5 is a basic soil requirement. Aluminum sulfate is the chemical most often used to make soils acid, although many gardeners feel the berry flavor is better if sulfur is used, instead. Four pounds of sulfur will lower the pH of 100 square feet (10 feet by 10 feet) of garden soil about one point. One pound of sulfur scattered around five medium-sized blueberry plants should lower the pH of the soil from 6.5 to 4.5. Organic gardeners prefer to use only natural materials to make the soil acid: cottonseed meal, peat moss, thoroughly rotten sawdust, pine needles, or oak leaves.

If your soil is of the limestone type with a pH of 6.5 to 7; if the water in your spring or well is quite "hard" ; and if American arborvitae (white cedar) grows well naturally in your area, it is probably just as well to buy your blueberries rather than try to grow them. You can make the soil acid, of course, but since every rain will percolate more lime up from the limestone subsoil, it will be a constant battle.

Care for blueberry plants as you do other semihardy plants, fertilizing them at the proper time to help harden their new growth before fall frosts begin. Put on a generous layer of farm manure just before winter or first thing after the ground thaws in the spring, and cover it with a heavy mulch of pine needles. Rich compost can be substituted for the farm manure, or you can use cottonseed meal or dried manure.

We've found that blueberries in the North must be pruned much differently than in the South. I've seen bushes fifteen years old that had never been pruned, yet they were producing far better than those of the same age that had been pruned. Every few years,

On a *mature blueberry bush* (A), the only pruning necessary in the North may be to clip back the twiggy ends every few years (B) to let in light and to increase berry size.

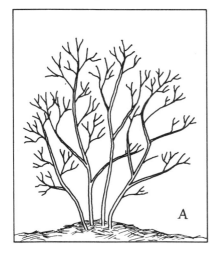
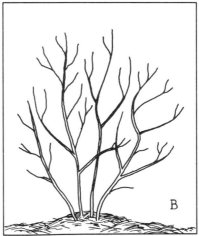

however, we prune lightly to get rid of the little twiggy growths at the ends of the branches, doing the clipping in late winter or early spring before growth starts so that the plants will continue to produce large berries. Although growers in New Jersey may renew their whole plant every four or five years by severe pruning of part of the aging wood each year, northern gardeners should never consider such drastic action.

We have had very good luck growing *Northland,* a somewhat dwarf plant, which is hardy and productive. Although its fruit is somewhat smaller than that of other highbush varieties, it is of very good quality. Other plants recommended for northern growers are *Blue Ray, Blue Crop, Earliblue, Jersey,* and *Meador,* a new one developed especially for cold climates.

Juneberries (Amelanchier)

The native *Amelanchier,* or Juneberry, is getting a lot of attention these days. Selections of outstanding wild plants have been made for many years, and experimenters are crossing these, hoping to produce even better fruit. Thus far, no sensational improvements have taken place as they have in the past with strawberries and blueberries, but the new fruits are definite improvements over the small, seedy, native ones, and show great promise for northern gardens.

Amelanchier canadensis, commonly called Juneberry, serviceberry, or shadbush, depending upon where you live, and the *Amelanchier alnifolia,* commonly called the Saskatoon berry, are sometimes found in nursery catalogs, though neither is yet commonly grown in the Northeast. The Juneberry is a native of the eastern United States and Canada, and, in our area, is the first white flowering tree in the spring. The Saskatoon is more commonly found in the prairie provinces of western Canada.

I was quite surprised to learn that people in western Canada often drive seventy miles or more to pick this delicious fruit, and plantations of fifty acres are now being established as "pick your own" ventures and to sell the fruit to nearby canneries and freezing plants.

Although both the Juneberry and the Saskatoon closely resemble the blueberry in fruit size, the bush is much hardier and does not require an acid soil. The bushes are actually small trees, 6 to 18 feet tall, and are planted 6 to 8 feet apart.

One of the reasons the *Amelanchier* family has not been more widely planted in the eastern United States is because the tree is very susceptible to cedar apple rust, or juniper rust. The juniper is not commonly grown in many cold regions, however, so this should not be a serious problem. *Juniperus scopulorum, Juniperus horizontalis,* and *Juniperus virginiana* are the most serious hosts of the rust disease, which also affects apple, pear, flowering crabapple, hawthorn, and quince trees. The native juniper of the Northeast, *Juniperus communis,* or pasture juniper, that often covers worn-out, pastured hillsides, is not one of the culprits that causes the rust.

One of the improved varieties of *Amelanchier canadensis* is the *Regent Juneberry*. Named varieties of *Amelanchier alnifolia* listed in catalogs or currently being tested include *Altaglow, Erskine, Forestburg, Improved Smoky, Northwine, Pembina, Porter, Smoky,* and *Wright*.

News of these exciting fruits is well worth awaiting, and they look very promising for the colder regions.

OTHER SMALL FRUITS

Bush Cherries

Midwestern nurseries often list *Nanking* and *Hansen's* bush cherries, and recommend them for northern climates. Although they haven't winter-killed, we have not had good luck with any of the different ones we have tried. None seemed to fruit well, and all eventually got a disease and died. Some of our gardening friends in North Dakota and Minnesota, however, raise them very successfully, and are enthusiastic over their compact size and the huge crops they produce.

Highbush Cranberries

Some catalogs get carried away describing the good points of this native shrub. It is a beautiful ornamental, with attractive foliage, white flowers in early summer, and red berries that hang on all winter. If you wait until after a frost hits the berries, it is possible to make a good-tasting jelly from them, but they are not a substitute for the bog cranberry, which is a member of the blueberry family. Some nurseries list several improved varieties, including *Andrews* and *Wentworth,* but most plant experts can see little difference between these and a good native Viburnum.

If you decide to buy some cranberry plants, get the American *Viburnum trilobum* rather than the European *Viburnum opulus* if you want them for eating. Although the latter are much more showy, and we use many of them for Christmas decorations, the fruit is so bitter it is inedible—even the birds don't touch it!

Experimentation is going on with many other native fruits—chokecherry, beach plums, buffaloberry, and many others—and researchers hope to develop fruits that are as hardy as their wild ancestors, but larger and better flavored. We certainly wish them every success.

CHAPTER SEVEN

GRAPES FOR THE NORTH

A few years ago a visitor at our nursery told me of his plan to establish an acre of grapes on a nearby hillside for the purpose of starting a northern wine industry. I tried my best to discourage him, and finally convinced him to try a dozen grapes first, to see how they grew, before he undertook such an ambitious venture.

Reluctantly he agreed, and three years of good weather followed. There was very little winterkill, so the vines flourished and began to bear quite a bit of fruit. As he harvested his first crop, he became somewhat resentful, naturally, that he hadn't planted an entire acre and perhaps more. I was beginning to dread his visits.

Then we had a real "old-fashioned" winter, the kind that hits the North Country at least once every seven or eight years. Nearly all his beautiful vines were killed outright, and the rest died back to the ground. When I last heard from him, he was considering a planting of rhubarb and elderberries for his vintage. They will probably be a big success.

I was also disappointed at his loss, for I was beginning to think that perhaps he had come upon the secret of northern grape growing. Every gardener dreams of having a few grape vines. They seem, as in Biblical and Roman times, to signify abundance, luxury, and fertility.

Unfortunately, most nursery catalogs do little to point out to gardeners in cold climates that our chances of creating a vineyard are slim. The art of grape growing was developed around the warm Mediterranean even before most of the ancient civilizations began. As people moved across northern Europe and finally to America, they brought the grape with them.

The foreign grapes were not happy in New England's cool, damp climate, and very few were successfully cultivated here until Ephraim Bull of Concord, Massachusetts, began crossing the European grapes with the wild American fox grape. Finally, after thou-

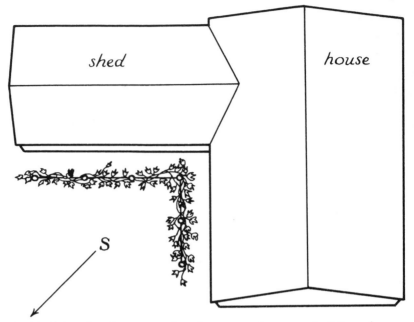

An ideal location for grape vines is a spot where two buildings form a sunny, south-facing corner. An equally desirable spot may be created by hedges, hills, solid fences, or walls.

sands of attempts, he developed the Concord, and the grape industry of the New World began.

Most hardy grapes that we grow in the North are descendants of the *Concord;* and fruit experimenters at the University of Minnesota and other places continue to develop hardy grapes of outstanding quality. What's more, the new ones will ripen even in a short season, which the famous *Concord* will not.

Although I tried repeatedly to grow grapes in the same open field where I was growing apples and berries quite successfully, planting after planting died over the winter. Since my experiences were similar to those of many other northern gardeners, I almost concluded that grape growing could take place only in areas south of the Green Mountains. Before giving up, however, I investigated some rumors I had heard about some farmers who had a few old vines that had borne for years around their farms. At first, it looked as if they had exceptionally hardy strains of *Brighton, Fredonia,* or *Worden* grapes; but the cuttings they gave me, although they rooted and grew, overwintered no better than the ones I had been buying.

Only when one elderly horticulturist mentioned that grapes don't like cold winds did I have an inkling about why I'd been losing all my vines. All the successful plantings I had seen were in warm pockets created by woods, hills, buildings, or stands of evergreens, where the vines were bathed in the warm morning and afternoon sun, yet sheltered from the cold north and west winds. Grapes were heat lovers, like watermelons, tomatoes, and eggplants!

I planted my first successful grapes in the backyard, where a greenhouse wall on the north and a tall arborvitae hedge on the west make a warm corner. If you supply the heat, you can grow grapes. Chances are you can create a heat trap if you don't have a spot on your property that is naturally warm and protected. I have seen grapes growing happily snuggled close to old barn foundations, fiberglass fences, and stone walls.

SOILS AND FERTILIZERS

A sandy soil is best for grapes, just as it is for most other warm weather crops. In fact, the colder the climate, the lighter the soil should be. Grapes start to grow later in the spring than most plants, which is fortunate because grape leaves, buds, and blooms are all very susceptible to frost damage. Because they start so late, however, they must grow unusually fast when the weather finally warms up, or the fruit won't have time to ripen. In cold, wet soils, growth begins so slowly that the vines may not get going until midsummer.

If the soil is not naturally light and sandy, sometimes gardeners build up a small, terracelike raised bed of sandy soil, 3 or 4 feet in diameter, for their grape roots.

In addition to abundant sun and warm, light soil, grapes need enough fertilizer available to make fast growth during the long days of early summer. Three or four pounds of dried cow or sheep manure worked into the top 2 or 3 inches of soil in a circle extending 3 feet in radius from the vine will help to provide these nutrients. The fertilizer should be applied just before the soil freezes in the fall, or in the spring just after the snow melts and the ground thaws, so it will be in a soluble form by early June when rapid growth should begin.

Sometimes gardeners use manure tea or a liquid chemical fertilizer such as Rapid-Gro or Miracle-Gro on their vegetables in midsummer to give them a shot of late growth and to help mature the corn, cabbage, and tomatoes. Grape growers in the North must *not* apply liquid or any other kind of fast-acting fertilizer after mid-June. They would not help to ripen the fruit; but they would most certainly stimulate a lot of late summer growth of new vines that could not harden before winter and would thus be winter-killed.

Treat your grape vines just as you do your tomatoes, and skip them when you are spreading mulch in the spring. Grapes don't grow well in a cool soil. Some growers put a layer of dark-colored crushed rocks or peastone around them to help attract more heat. Others use clear or black plastic for the same purpose.

PRUNING

Grape vines produce the most fruit when they are kept compact. They grow vigorously, however, and thus require more pruning than most other fruits. The more you prune, the more regrowth you encourage, which sets up a vicious cycle. A great amount of new growth is particularly bad for grapes, because it will quite likely have difficulty "hardening up" before the first frost in the fall.

Grapes trailing over arbors or trellises are beautiful, but if it is fruit you want, the Kniffen system of growing grapes works best for northern growers. Build the fence running north and south, or northeast to southwest, to give the vines maximum sunlight most of the day. They should be planted about 8 feet apart, with a post midway between each plant and one at each end. String two strands of smooth 10-gauge wire to the posts, stapling the first wire 2 feet above the ground, and the second about 3 feet higher.

During the second year after planting, allow four side branches to grow, two in each direction, and train them to grow along the wires. Pinch off any buds that try to grow in other directions. By the end of the second year, if growth has been good, the space along the wires should be filled. These vines should bloom and produce a few grapes the third year.

The third year, four more canes, and only four, should be allowed

Vines that grew last summer and are bearing this year (*A*) should be pruned off next spring. Current year's growth (*B*) which will bear next summer, should be trained to grow to replace canes now bearing.

to grow from the main stem. These should parallel the first four and replace them for fruiting the following year.

As you can see, the vines are treated as biennials, similar to raspberry canes. They are allowed to grow one season, overwinter, produce their fruit the following summer, and are then cut away. Only by pinching and snipping throughout the season, however, will you get them to grow from the main stem at the proper place and in the right direction.

Don't allow the vines to overbear. A vigorous, mature grapevine should produce no more than 10 to 15 pounds of fruit each year in the North, which means 17 to 20 bunches of grapes per branch. If your vines set more blossom clusters than that, snip off enough blooms to get the number down to 20 or less. A vine cannot safely support the maturing of more fruit, and will be weakened if it overbears.

If a grapevine has made good growth, it will be as large when it is four or five years old as it should ever get, although the main stem will continue to get heavier. Grapevines that cover an entire backyard and trail over fences and trees may be impressive but they are generally unproductive, and the fruit seldom ripens well. Furthermore, someone eventually must face the problem of what to do with the monstrosity.

CONTROLLING LATE SUMMER GROWTH

Like peaches, apricots, sweet cherries, and many plums, grapes are accustomed to a long growing season. Even the hardiest ones may find it difficult to stop growing in late summer if there is ade-

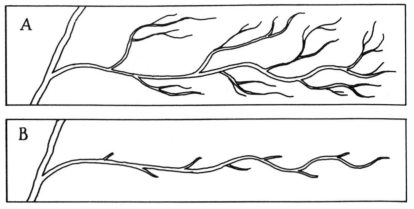

Unpruned grape vines (*A*) often suffer winter injury, bear sparingly, and shade fruit so it ripens poorly. Vine *B* has been kept in shape by frequent late-summer pinching, so wood can harden properly before winter.

quate moisture, fertility, and warm weather. Late growth is likely to be more of a problem in years when June and July are dry, and rains begin in August and September. If the temperature stays high during late summer, growth can be tremendous and, consequently, winter injury will be heavy.

You can help avoid late growth by giving each grapevine a full pail of water at least twice a week during dry periods in June and July, which will encourage normal growth.

Another way to help prevent possible frost injury is to prune off all late summer growth as soon as it starts. I select a cutoff date, about three to four weeks before the first frost is likely. After that time I don't allow any new growth to develop on the vines. I observe them carefully, and every three or four days pinch or snip off any new sprouts.

Although this pinch-pruning takes time and careful attention, if you live in a severe climate it may be the only way you can successfully grow grapes.

Some growers have had good luck with another method of checking unwanted growth—root-pruning. In midsummer they cut a circle about 3 feet in diameter all around the vine with a sharp, long-bladed spade, just as if they plan to lift it out of the ground. They don't dig it up; but the cutting off of part of the small feeder roots checks a great deal of late summer growth without harm to the vine.

LENGTHENING THE SEASON

Unlike pears, apples, and strawberries, grapes do not continue to ripen after they are picked. Since they must ripen on the vines, you can't pick your crop the day before the first frost and ripen them in the kitchen like tomatoes.

Although the first frosts of autumn may be hard, "white" ones, they are easy to overcome. Because the earth is still full of summer's warmth, grape growers can take advantage of that stored heat to keep the vines alive and protect the fruit from freezing. The easiest way is to throw a heavy, old blanket, canvas, or quilt over the whole vine, pinning or tucking in the edges over the wires so they won't gape open. Spread the covering out over the ground somewhat to take advantage of the ground heat. For a light frost it may be adequate to use cotton sheets, large pieces of paper, or sheets of plastic; but if you expect a hard frost, use heavier cloths or double thicknesses of plastic with air space between. On extra-hard frost nights, you may add extra heat by placing a light bulb or a string of Christmas tree lights under the covering.

Usually, after the first frost or two in the fall the weather warms up and may stay warm for two or three weeks. Getting the grapes through the first cold snap safely can often add many extra days to the growing and ripening season, making the difference between a good crop or none at all.

Even some of the wine-type grapes can be grown in the North by planting them in a plastic-covered greenhouse. The plastic can be removed for the summer after all danger of spring frosts is over, and put back on as days and nights begin to cool in late summer; and it should be left on all winter. A plastic house modifies the temperatures so much that only a light covering of the vines is necessary to get them through the winter. A ventilation opening must be provided, however, that can be used on early spring days. Without it the extra warmth would cause growth to start too early, and the tender new vines would be killed as the temperature fell at night.

WINTER PROTECTION

We've found that the *Beta* grape is the hardiest we have ever tried—nearly as hardy, in fact, as the wild fox grape. We grew the *Alpha* for many years, and found it has hardy as *Beta;* but we lost it, unfortunately, when trying to move it one year, and found that nurseries no longer carry it, so we have never been able to replace it. Even after a cold winter with little snow, both grapes suffered little injury and produced well, in spite of the fact that they were not covered.

Most other varieties of grapes must be laid down and covered after a few hard frosts, but before the ground freezes; and in the spring they should not be uncovered until all hard frosts are over.

As I said before, I've found that evergreen boughs are one of the best materials to use as a covering for most plants for the winter, and this includes grapes. They are excellent insulators, yet do not smother the vine, mat down, and make it rot or mold as leaves and hay often do; nor do they support mice or encourage weeds, as straw and hay do.

Avoid any pruning on grapevines before covering them up, unless it is absolutely necessary to untangle them or get them off the fence. There will probably be some winter injury, no matter how careful you are. It is best to cut off the injured wood in the spring when you uncover the vines and you can repair the winter damage as you do the regular pruning.

VARIETIES

As I said, *Alpha* and *Beta* are the hardiest grapes we have grown. Other varieties that are moderately hardy and ripen early enough in the North most years are: *Aurora, Brighton, Buffalo, Edelweiss, Fredonia, Hungarian, Interlaken, Jonesville, Moore's Early, Ontario, Seneca, Swensen's Red, Van Buren,* and *Worden.* Most of these varieties, with the exception of *Alpha,* are available from mail order nurseries in the northern and north central states. *Beta* and *Riding Mountain* are suggested for trial for the prairie provinces. The latter is not generally available in the U.S.

CHAPTER EIGHT

GROWING NUTS IN THE NORTH

Like most inexperienced northern gardeners, years ago I wasted a lot of time and money trying to grow nut trees that the catalogs promised were "hardy in the North." Some copywriters didn't indicate whether they had in mind northern Ohio or North Carolina, but others definitely claimed that their trees were hardy to −25° F. I've seen pecans, filberts, chestnuts, and walnuts described in such a way that you wouldn't dream there was a chance of failure if you planted them in zone 3.

What the catalogs didn't say, and quite likely the southern growers didn't know, is that, although some nuts can stand short durations of occasional low temperatures, they, like peaches and most grapes, cannot mature their new growth in a short growing season.

So, sadly, after years of testing and talking with other experimenters in the colder zones, I've had to conclude that our nut-growing prospects are limited mostly to the butternut; the wild native filbert, or American hazelnut; and the hardier strains of the black walnut. There are some oaks that produce edible acorns, but only a few of these are native to the North, such as the white oak. One choice white oak variety named *Link* produces small but sweet acorns. The American beech is another native tree, and it bears an abundance of tiny, sweet nuts—mostly consumed by wildlife. Little work has been done to improve it, although one selection, the *Jenner*, produces larger than normal nuts and is currently being tested in different regions.

One of the most exciting arrivals on the nut scene has been the Carpathian walnut brought here from Poland in the 1930's. They are almost identical to the English walnuts and have the same botanic name, *Juglans regia*. Since they grew so well in such a cold part of Europe, growers were hopeful that nut-growing possibilities of North America could be greatly expanded.

Those of us in zones 3 and 4 were disappointed to find that the trees resembled the peach in needing a long growing season. Each fall they were "winter-killed" by the first frosts rather than by low winter temperatures. Many experts feel that the full growing range of these nuts has not yet been met, so eventually even those of us who live in the glow of the northern lights may be able to grow them.

The late Fred Ashworth of northern New York State, one of the great pioneers in nut and fruit growing, collected and tested many different Carpathian walnuts and promoted the following that he considered moderately hardy: *Ashworth, Hansen, Himalaya,* and *Somers.*

Each year nut fanciers comb the woods looking for those special trees that produce nuts that are larger, tastier, and easier to crack than the ordinary ones. They have met with some success, and, by crossing some of these superior strains with each other, nut breeders have produced even better varieties. Many of these introduced varieties have been named and are being offered for sale.

Unfortunately, almost all of the new varieties that have been discovered or developed come from zones much warmer than ours, and efforts to get the improved butternuts and hazelnuts to live in cold areas have not yet been successful. There is a chance that some will become acclimated over a period of time, but for now the nut selection for northern growers is still limited pretty much to what the earliest settlers found growing when they arrived. Even the American chestnuts that were nearly wiped out in the great blight in the early 1900's never grew in the northern tier of the country.

Although all the nut trees we bought died over their first winter in our area, we finally found a few black walnut trees growing in a region with weather similar to our own. The nuts that we brought home and planted grew well.

Like some people, nuts seem to become so "acclimated" or attached to the environment where they live that they are unable to adjust to a new climate, especially one colder than their own. Butternuts are one of the hardiest nuts, and they grow even in zone 2, far north in Quebec. Yet we have brought dozens of nuts from the Albany, N.Y., area (zone 5) to northern Vermont (zone 3), seen them sprout well and grow well the first year; then, during the winter, they died. Even those grown in southern Vermont did not grow vigorously when moved to our northern section near the Canadian border.

BUTTERNUTS (Juglans cinerea)

We think that maple butternut fudge is one of the finest treats the North can provide, and for years northern cooks have made reputations with butternut cakes and pies. Although most people gather wild nuts from hedgerows, more and more northerners are growing them close to their homes. They take eight to ten years from the planting of the nut until they bear their first crop, so if they are part of your plans, put them in with that in mind. The first crop is usually a big one, however, and worth the wait.

Butternuts, like many nut trees, do not bear every year, and sometimes they bear heavily only once in three or four years. Luckily, if you store them in a dry place like an attic, they will keep for years and still be fresh and tasty when you crack them. Be sure that your storage is squirrel-proof, however, because the furry little thieves will stop at practically nothing to get back what they feel is rightfully theirs.

Years ago there was no need to plant butternuts, so many were available in the woods. Most of these beautiful trees were cut for their fine lumber. Disease and old age took their toll, as did the encroachment of farms and towns, although a few spreading giants may still be found dropping their nuts along country roads in September.

The best way to start your own butternut planting is to seek out an old tree and gather some of the best nuts. Choose those that have grown in an area as cold or colder than your own, and plant them immediately, the way the squirrels do, by burying them an inch or two deep. I usually plant extras, in case the squirrels find them, and, as an added precaution, sprinkle mothballs or wood ashes over the planting to discourage squirrel prospecting.

You may either plant the nuts in a bed and transplant them later or plant them directly where you want them to grow. Because butternut seedlings sometimes have trouble competing with heavy grass if they've been planted in a field, I prefer to plant the seeds in an especially prepared bed where they can get a good start for a couple of years. I spade up a small area quite deep and plant the nuts about 2 inches deep and about 3 inches apart, marking the place well to make sure nothing will disturb them before they sprout the following summer.

If you choose to plant them in a bed, let them grow only two or three years before planting them where they will ultimately grow. Butternuts form a long, deep taproot that makes them difficult to move as they get larger, because it should never be bent or broken in your transplanting operation. Transplant them in early spring before the buds begin to swell.

Butternut seeds planted in the fall usually begin to grow about midsummer, then shoot up rapidly, sometimes as much as a foot or two. Don't fertilize your planting the first year because it would stimulate too much growth that might not harden, and the nut has plenty of nourishment in it to feed the seedling for the first summer.

Butternuts may also be planted in the spring, but they should be frozen first if you choose to do it then. Place each nut in a half cup of water and let it freeze. Then pour in more water, filling the cup nearly full, and let that freeze. Keep it frozen at least a week, then plant it, ice and all. The large ice cube will help soften the shell and germinate the seed.

Not every nut will grow, but don't get discouraged. Any nuts that don't start the first summer should not be abandoned; some may grow the second year.

Nuts are often frozen before planting so they will sprout faster. Nut is placed in half cup of water and frozen solid in freezer (A). Cup is then filled with more water and frozen again, leaving the nut frozen in the center of the ice cube (B). It is then planted, ice and all.

If you are lucky enough to find any small, wild butternut trees, they can be dug up and moved in early spring. Just as with your own transplants, be careful not to bend or break the long taproots. Occasionally you may find seedlings where a neighbor's tree has dropped nuts into his flower bed, or along a roadside near a large butternut tree. Examine the trees carefully, because, with the leaves off, they are sometimes difficult to tell from ash trees. The buds of the butternut alternate along its branch and trunk, but those of the various kinds of ash are always directly opposite each other on the trunk, as are buds of the maple.

Planting the Butternut

By mulching the newly planted trees to suppress grass and weeds for the first year or two, you will help them get off to a fast start. Newspapers and magazines covered with hay or shavings make a fine mulch. Lay them out in a radius of about two feet all around the tree trunk. If you plant the tree in your lawn, you need not mulch it so long as you keep the grass mowed. Old butternut trees do not make beautiful lawn trees, however, and the fallen nuts are hard on bare feet and lawn mowers.

Butternut roots give out a mysterious substance that kills many evergreens and other plants, so don't plant them near flowering shrubs, ornamental evergreens, hedges, or flower and vegetable gardens. They do not kill off grass, fortunately.

Although I have not yet heard any northern gardeners relating success stories about growing the new, larger, easier-to-crack butternut hybrids, there are always those who want to try. Nut nurseries offer *Ayres, Beckwith, Chamberlin, George Elmer, Johnson, Weschcke,* and others. *George Elmer, Chamberlin,* and *Weschcke* are considered the most hardy.

Both butternuts and black walnuts are ready to gather as soon as they begin to fall from the tree. Be ready to pick them up, because chances are good that the squirrels have been watching them for weeks. The nuts all ripen at once, and any still clinging to the tree may be shaken loose—if the squirrels seem to be getting ahead of you. Dry all those you don't plant by spreading them out one deep in a warm, airy attic, greenhouse, or shed. Quick, thorough drying is important, or the nut meats will blacken and spoil.

Butternuts are easy to crack if you pour boiling water over them, and let them stand until the water cools. It saves a lot of smashed thumbs.

BLACK WALNUTS (Juglans nigra)

Black walnut trees are so similar to the butternut that the same growing directions apply to them. When they are young, it is very difficult to tell the trees apart, since bark, twigs, and leaves are so similar. But as they grow older, the bark of the black walnut becomes rougher.

Since the native growing range of the black walnut (not to be confused with the "English" walnut *Juglans regia*) is Pennsylvania, Ohio, Indiana, Illinois, Iowa and southward, it is not easy to find hardy strains; but throughout the North, from Maine to the Dakotas, black walnuts are growing and producing. The University of New Hampshire has done extensive work with developing hardy

Butternut and black walnut trees tend to grow into strange shapes when grown in the open (*A*). The resulting limb structure is weak. Prune young nut trees to grow with a straight central stem and good branch structure (*B*) for strong growth and best appearance.

strains. Consult garden clubs, extension services, and knowledge-able gardeners in your area, and advertise in local papers if you can't find them any other way. Plant only nuts from trees grown in an area similar to yours.

If you find you must buy black walnut trees from a mail order nursery, it is better to avoid the named varieties. Although the nuts are larger, I have yet to hear of any hybrid trees that have survived for more than a few years in the northern areas. It's a pity, because the wild black walnuts are so hard to crack. *Bicentennial, Burns, Cochrane, Patten, Patterson, Thomas,* and *Weschcke* are some of the not-so-hardy hybrids.

Black walnuts require a slightly longer growing season to ripen their nuts than butternuts, so you may have trouble when frosts come early. Luckily, the first autumn frosts are usually close to the ground, and the walnuts high on the tree often escape.

Although it is tempting to grow whatever nuts will grow in the North, you may want to consider carefully whether you should plant black walnuts. As an investment in fine lumber, they are hard to beat, but many people who have access to plenty of the nuts never eat them. They are hard to crack, and the flavor of the raw nuts is a bit strong for most palates. They are used mostly to flavor cakes, candy, ice cream, and other desserts.

HAZELNUTS (FILBERTS) *(Corylus)*

Wild hazelnuts grow throughout the colder sections of the country, and every rural child knows them well. Although the nuts are small, and the squirrels usually harvest most of them the day they are ready, they are so tasty that we always sought them out as a special treat.

Because American hazelnuts are small and hard to crack without wrecking their meats, experimenters have crossed many of them with the large European filberts. As a result, many new hybrids have been named and introduced, although most nurseries do not yet carry them. Some of these new trees produce nuts nearly as large as their European parent, and a few are almost as hardy as the American, but as yet none of the offspring seems to have the advantages of both.

Some European filberts and their hybrids that have proven moderately hardy are *Dropmore Hazel, Graham, Italian Red, Potomac, Rush, Skinner,* and *Winkler.* If by chance you discover a hardy variety, you can propagate it very easily by layering. Bend over one of the lower limbs, bury the middle portion in soil, and in a year or so roots will form where you bent it. When it gets well rooted, probably by the following spring, you can sever it from the parent plant, and you'll have a new filbert tree.

CHAPTER NINE

PERENNIAL FOODS AND HERBS

Like many of our northern neighbors, we like to get part of our food from the wild. We cut dandelion greens, gather butternuts and hazelnuts, make a bit of maple syrup, and pick wild berries. Recently we have learned from some of the newer homesteaders about how to add fiddlehead ferns, cattails, and lamb's-quarters to our diet. Most of the "living off the land" diet, however, we leave for people with more time and different tastes. It always seems more reliable to raise vegetables, berries, and fruits than to hunt for them, and we especially like those perennial foods that grow easily year after year without replanting. Asparagus, horseradish, rhubarb, Jerusalem artichokes, and herbs do well in the North.

ASPARAGUS

Most people we know who grow asparagus feel it is one of their most successful projects. For only a small monetary investment and surprisingly little work our small patch gives us a good meal of fresh asparagus nearly every day for six to eight weeks each spring, in addition to extra for freezing.

I ate one time at a friend's apartment in the city, and the hostess announced excitedly, "We're having fresh asparagus!" I could hardly wait. When it appeared, however, I realized that it was already at least two days old; these poor folks had never tasted really fresh asparagus.

Ours is rarely more than ten minutes old, but even we are not as fanatic as a relative who built his garden on a side hill so that he could quickly cut his prize stalks and race downhill as soon as his wife signaled from the kitchen window that the water was boiling.

Asparagus grows to perfection in the North. Like rhubarb, it thrives on lots of organic material and does not like an acid soil. Several varieties are offered for sale, either seeds or plants. We have

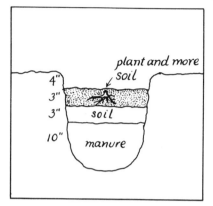 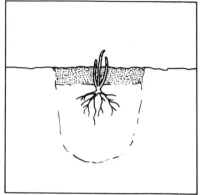

When *asparagus* is planted by the trench method, the roots are set several inches deep, and the trench is filled in during the summer as the plants grow.

tried *Mary Washington, Martha Washington, Paradise,* and *Waltham.* They all seem to be good, and we've found very little difference among them.

Planting asparagus in the North is not different from planting it in other areas. Although we don't use the deep trench method for our beds, I have seen some excellent beds resulting from it. I like to put the plants in beds rather than in garden rows, and keep the beds narrow enough to reach across. We use a lot of manure, mix it thoroughly with the soil, then add a little sand to lighten our heavy loam. We set the roots about 15 inches apart each way, and plant them 4 or 5 inches deep so that when we begin to cut the stalks, we won't cut into the roots.

After you stop picking, let the plants grow tall for the rest of the summer. The female plants will produce pods that turn red in late fall, open, and drop seed all over the bed. Cut them off before this happens or they will grow, and your planting may become a mass of small worthless plants rather than a few large productive ones. Cut down all the plants as soon as they turn yellow and before putting on the fall mulch.

We like to use a heavy mulch to help cut down on grass and weed growth, and it helps to add a continuous supply of fertilizer and humus to the soil as well. Each fall, after the yellowing stalks have been cut down, we put a heavy layer of farm manure or a thin layer of dried manure over the bed. Then we add a thicker layer of partly composted leaves, and, finally, cover it all with a layer of partly rotted, shredded bark from a nearby sawmill. Many other materials may be used instead, such as peanut shells, salt hay, spoiled farm ensilage, rotted shavings, or lawn clippings. Hay is often used, but it is likely to be full of weed seeds. Sawdust packs too hard and robs nitrogen from the soil.

Mulch keeps the asparagus bed cool late in the spring, so usually our neighbors are eating from their unmulched beds long before we are each year. However, we enjoy a longer picking season than they do, and our mulched plants produce lots of good eating until the fresh peas are ready. We could, of course, pull the mulch away from a few of the plants and also enjoy early asparagus, but we seldom remember to do it.

If you don't mulch and still don't like to hand weed, asparagus is tolerant of certain herbicides, and some of them may be used safely to prevent weed and grass growth. Princeps and Dacthyl are two of those most commonly used, but directions must be carefully followed or you may damage the plants.

HORSERADISH

We wouldn't want to be without our horseradish bed. Like the lilac bush, it has probably been here almost as long as the house, growing and producing with no care whatsoever. The earliest settlers to the North learned the value of horseradish and understood that, like the limes the British sailors sucked on their long ocean voyages, it prevented scurvy during the winter months. It is a health food in every way, rich in vitamin C and stimulating to lazy appetites.

Like artichokes and rhubarb, horseradish grows with little fuss. You can buy the roots from most mail order nurseries or garden centers, and plant them about 2 feet apart in good garden soil. Plant them well away from other plants and in a spot where they can be contained by mowing or cultivation, because they are vigorous growers and can spread far beyond the area you have in mind for them.

After your bed is well established, you may dig the roots extravagantly, but when it is still young, it is better not to deplete the bed too heavily. You may dig part of the plants, cut off their roots, but leave a piece attached to each top. Replant this to grow more roots so your bed keeps producing. You may dig horseradish at any time, though it tastes best when dug in late fall or early spring. We like to gather a lot of roots in late fall, store them in a plastic bag with a little soil, and grind a few now and then throughout the winter, tossing them in the blender with a little vinegar.

ARTICHOKES

In 1816 northern New England suffered an infamous summer that later became known as "eighteen hundred and froze to death." It froze and snowed intermittently all spring, summer, and fall. Most crops failed, and in those days of no government-declared disaster areas, people and animals were in dire straits. After that summer my family and many of the other pioneers regarded artichokes as an emergency or starvation food—available even if wheat and potatoes failed.

Over the years we have always eaten them occasionally, but no one in my family was ever too excited about them. They are rather bland, even when garnished with sauces and herbs. Our vegetable crops never failed, at least completely, so artichokes were never necessary, even during the Depression. They were like our tiny bank account—for emergency only—and a novelty food.

Jerusalem artichokes bear no resemblance to the supermarket variety of artichoke, which is usually grown in California. The name "Jerusalem" is also misleading, because they are a North American native and actually related to the sunflower. Described as a "starchless potato," their small tubers may be cooked like potatoes, or sliced and eaten raw like radishes, used in salads, or pickled in vinegar. They are very low in calories—an added bonus.

The top growth resembles that of the sunflower, and it occasionally has sunflowerlike blooms. The stalks have been tried for silage, and are now being used experimentally as a source of alcohol for fuel.

The plants are so vigorous that they often become rank weeds and take over whole fields, so be careful where you plant them. Plant the tubers 2 to 3 feet apart in an area you can mow around to keep them under control. Dig them in early spring or late fall only, and store them for winter in the root cellar if you want.

Many busy gardeners like a crop they don't need to plant every spring, cultivate, spray, and fertilize. Some even let their poultry live among them. The birds enjoy the shade, keep out the grass, and add some fertility to the planting.

RHUBARB

Rhubarb is another wonderful cool-weather plant that is a natural for the North. It was introduced to England from Turkey in the mid-1600's and reached New England in the early 1800's. The plant became an immediate success, and was a welcome addition to the limited country fare. For over a century the pie plant, as it is sometimes called, was THE spring tonic, and credited, as one old medical book stated, with "cleansing the blood and purifying the humours."

It certainly tastes good. In addition to the fact that it supplies generous amounts of vitamins A, C, B_1, and B_2, calcium, iron, and phosphorus, we like its reliability. Frost may hit the plum and strawberry blooms, and birds may eat the raspberries, but we can always count on rhubarb. Even the deer, racoons, and woodchucks don't bother it.

In setting out your new rhubarb bed, for best results choose a location where the plants will be in sun for at least half of each day. They like good garden soil that's rich in manure, leaf mold, and compost, and not too acid. Although they thrive on moisture, don't plant them on heavy, swampy, clay soils. Don't plant them, either, near shrubs, trees, berry beds, horseradish, asparagus, artichokes, or other competing plants.

Early spring, before rhubarb begins to grow, is a good time to plant it. You can either buy new plants or roots, or split divisions off old clumps, with downward thrusts of a sharp spade. Plant them 3 to 5 feet apart, and water them thoroughly. Set the dormant roots deep enough so that they are covered with 2 inches of soil. If potted plants are used, set them deep, too; otherwise they may come out of the ground when you begin to pull rhubarb stalks in a year or so. Put a few shovelfuls of farm manure or a pint of dried manure around each new plant.

Rhubarb is a heavy feeder, so use a generous amount of fertilizer on it each fall. A quarter bushel of farm manure on a large, established clump is not overdoing it. A thick mulch of leaves, hay, shredded bark, or similar material helps keep the soil moist, full of earthworms, and fertile. Scatter a cup of lime or a pint of wood ashes around the plant every two or three years, too.

You can begin a light harvesting of the crop the following year if the plants grow really well, but it is better to wait until they are firmly established. Pick it by pulling the stalks from the plant with a twisting motion rather than cutting them off. Never strip the plant completely, but always leave four or five leaves to feed it; and stop picking before midsummer to let the plant set lots of buds for the next year's crop. Cut the leaves from the stalks you harvest, and leave them on the ground around the plant for a mulch.

To keep your bed from getting overgrown and unproductive, split up each clump into three or four pieces every eight or ten years. You might add these to your planting or give them away.

There are several new varieties of all-red rhubarb on the market: *Valentine* and *Canada Red* are two good choices. Our favorites are still *Strawberry,* an older kind that produces enormous, tender, red-skinned stalks, and *MacDonald,* which bears all-pink, very tender, smaller stalks. Both taste wonderful and may be used over a much longer season than the fancier, but much less productive, all-red kinds. None of the named varieties are as stringy as the old-fashioned skinny, green kinds found around old cellar holes.

Only the stalks are edible, so resist any temptation to cook the leaves. Rhubarb leaves are deadly poison and are sometimes stewed to make an effective garden insecticide.

Most people plant four or five roots for a small family, but I think six or eight make more sense, since rhubarb also freezes beautifully. We use it for pies, sauce, puddings, cakes, jam, and juice. It tastes good, and less sweetening is required when it is combined with naturally sweet fruit, such as raisins, strawberries, raspberries, bananas, pineapple, apples, or oranges.

HERBS

Growing and using a variety of herbs is a fairly new thing in our household. When I was young, we grew only sage for flavoring homemade sausage, gathered wild mint for peppermint tea, and wild caraway for cookies. Like a lot of New Englanders, I felt that if food was well grown, properly cooked, and generously garnished with pepper, salt, butter and cream, it didn't need any extras, and other seasonings were probably added only to cover up the cook's mistakes.

My wife lived in several different countries and traveled around a lot before we were married, and she likes to use a variety of herbs and spices in her cooking. Although we still use them much more sparingly than our Latin friends, they have added a new and delightful dimension to our eating . . . and gardening.

Since many annual herbs become mature only late in the summer season when they have been sown directly in the garden, we like to start a few seeds indoors as well. As soon as the frosts are over, when we set out the tomatoes, we also put in started plants of basil, borage, dill, marjoram, parsley, and summer savory. It's nice to have sprigs of fresh dill for the early peas, fresh basil for the first tomatoes, and parsley for garnish early in the summer season.

Some perennial herbs need special treatment in order to survive the winter well in zones 3 and 4. Rosemary, for example, is too tender to overwinter outside, so we usually dig up a plant or two in the fall and bring them into the house for an aromatic winter houseplant, and to use for cuttings to start new little plants for spring. Lavender will "winter" outdoors, but should be planted in a sheltered spot out of the wind.

A heavy mulch helps all the perennial herbs come through the winter better. Although most will survive without it, some of the more tender herbs need mulching, especially when they are young and not yet fully established. Lavender, tarragon, lemon balm, pennyroyal, and sage do better when they're protected. Remove the mulch as soon as threat of frost is over in the spring.

Some growers in zones 3 and 4 have noticed that, just as with fruit and nut trees, perennial herbs that have been grown in the North seem to be better adjusted to our climate. So, if it is possible, find local sources for perennial herb plants, especially those that are semihardy. Friends who are dividing their beds are usually happy to share and swap them.

Some gardeners like to pot up and bring herb plants inside in the fall to use the fresh snips all winter. Parsley, chives, marjoram, and thymes all make nice window-garden plants. Because we have lim-

Rank-growing herbs may be planted in square or round tiles to keep them looking nice and in their place.

ited space and too many houseplants, however, we've given up bringing most of them inside. (Rosemary is the exception.) Instead, we use those that tolerate cold weather, like chives and parsley, from the garden until they are covered with snow.

In deep winter we use herbs from the freezer and find they taste almost as good as fresh ones. On a dry day in midsummer, with kitchen scissors we cut lots of chives into small pieces and freeze them quickly on cookie sheets. We then put them into plastic bags or small cartons with tight covers (small yogurt containers work well), to be scooped out by the teaspoon whenever they're needed for a salad, soup, or sauce. We cut dill and parsley, and freeze them in the same way. We know others who always freeze basil, fennel, and tarragon, as well, for winter use.

·Herbs dry quickly in a warm attic. We tie clumps together and hang them with string from the rafters. Paper bags inverted over them keep out light and dust. When they are thoroughly dry, we "skin" the leaves from the stalks, crush them with a small mortar and pestle, and place them in tight, opaque containers on the pantry shelves: peppermint and spearmint for teas, lovage leaves for soups, sage for the Thanksgiving turkey, caraway for cookies, and plenty of catnip to help the cat survive her winter doldrums.

If you want to save seeds from dill, caraway, anise, or other seed-producing plants, watch them carefully in late summer, and when the seeds are dry enough to drop off, pick the stalks, place them in a paper bag, and shake them vigorously until the seeds fall free.

The common, mostly culinary herbs mentioned in the following list are only an introduction to the variety that may be grown in the North. There are many others—medicinal and aromatic. Some are grown for their dyes, others to repel insects, and many simply for their beauty in the garden and in bouquets, both fresh and dried. There are excellent guides available on their lore, cultivation and use (see appendix).

Good Annual Herbs for the North

All annuals are started from seed. Some will reseed themselves and surprise you by popping up the following year. All thrive in full sun.

ANISE—1 to 2 feet.* Space approx. 8″ apart. Likes good garden soil. Use ripe seeds in pastry, cookies, soups, candy, meat; and leaves in salads.

BASIL—1 to 2 feet. Space 10″ apart. Grow out of the wind in good garden soil. Harvest leaves just as the plants begin to blossom. Use them in meats, salads, omelets, sauces, soups, stews.

BORAGE—1 to 2 feet. Space 1′ apart. Large hairy leaves and attractive blue flowers. Attracts bees. Use leaves in salads, soup, stews.

CARAWAY—1 to 2 feet. Space 8″ apart. Carrotlike plant. Use the seeds dried in breads, cakes, cookies, soups, salads.

CHERVIL—1 foot. Space 6″ to 8″ apart. Grow and use like parsley. Anise flavor. Harvest leaves. Freezes well.

CORIANDER—1 to 2 feet. Space 12″ apart. Needs full sun. Large, coarse plant. Crush mature seeds for pastries, pickles, beans, liqueurs, sauces.

DILL—2 to 3 feet. Space 10″ apart. Fragrant, feathery leafed with seeds that grow in umbrellalike heads. Use sprigs or seeds—for pickles, vinegar, meats, fish, salads, and dressings.

* Height of mature plant.

FENNEL—1 to 3 feet. Space 12″ apart. Florence fennel produces a large bulb, which is used as a vegetable, especially by Italians. When plants are half grown, pile earth around them to blanch them. Use sprigs for garnish, soups, fish.

PARSLEY—5 to 6 inches. Space 6″ apart. Plant seeds early, because they often take a long time to germinate. (Soaking them for 24 hours will help germination.) Both the curly (French) and plain-leaf (Italian) varieties are well-known garnishes, used in salads, soups, and for many other uses.

SUMMER SAVORY—18 to 24 inches. Space 8″ apart. Sow seeds as early as possible, but not until all frost danger is over. Use leaves for salads, soups, beans, dressings, poultry.

SWEET MARJORAM—12 inches. Space 10″ apart. A "perennial" that is an annual in the North. Similar to oregano in looks and aroma when young. Use leaves for dressings, salads, soups.

Perennial Herbs

CATNIP—1 to 3 feet. (Seeds, cuttings, or divisions) Vigorous-growing, bushy, fragrant plant, valued as a tonic for cats and tranquilizer for people. Very hardy. Use leaves either fresh or dried. Usually steeped for tea.

CHIVES—12 to 15 inches. (Seeds or divisions) Hardy, small, onion-like plant that may be grown inside as a pot plant. Leaves flavor salads, soups, cheese, and egg dishes.

COMFREY—2 to 3 feet. (Cuttings or divisions) Very hardy. Large leaves with blue/pink flowers. Leaves and roots used in tea, and early leaves as salad greens. Considered by some a healing, medicinal food; but recent findings indicate that in large dosages it may be harmful to health.

COSTMARY—2 to 4 feet. (Division) Large, sweet-scented leaves. Used as garnish and in tea . . . and as a bookmark in Bibles of Early American colonists.

HOREHOUND—2 feet. (Seeds, cuttings, division) Bushy, woolly leaves, covered with white hairs. Odd, musky medicinal flavor. Dried for tea, and used fresh for candy and to make cough syrup.

LAVENDER—1 to 2 feet (Seeds and cuttings) Fragrant, bushy, semi-woody plant. Needs winter protection. Dry leaves or use fresh—for sachets and perfumes.

LEMON BALM—1 to 2 feet. (Cuttings and division) Vigorous-growing, hardy plant. Mulch for winter for best results. Dry, or use fresh for teas, jelly, and flavoring.

LOVAGE—2 to 3 feet. (Seeds) Vigorous-growing, hardy plant. Leaves and stalks taste like celery and are used in a similar manner.

MINTS—18 inches to 3 feet. (Division) Vigorous-growing plants that should be kept separate from other perennials or you'll need to pull them forever out of your beds. They like a rich, moist soil. Leaves may be used dried or fresh for teas, jellies, juleps and for other flavorings. Peppermint, Spearmint, Apple Mint, Orange Mint each have distinctive flavors. English pennyroyal is a low-growing, ground cover with somewhat bitter-tasting leaves often used as an insect repellent.

OREGANO—2 feet. (Seeds, cuttings, divisions) Vigorous, productive. Use leaves for flavoring soups, salads, meat.

ROSEMARY—2 to 3 feet. (Cuttings) Tender perennial that must be taken inside for the winter in the North. Makes a good winter houseplant. Fragrant flavoring for sauces, soups, teas, and meats, especially lamb.

SAGE—18 inches. (Seeds and cuttings) Easily grown from seed. Use fresh or dried leaves for flavoring meats, fowl, stews, fish, and stuffings.

SORREL—2 to 3 feet. (Seeds and division) French sorrel has long leaves with a somewhat sour flavor. Well known for flavoring soups and salads.

TANSY—3 feet. (Seeds and division) Rank growing. Used in clumps as a fly and ant repellent. Young leaves used for tea, but mostly its yellow foliage is used for bouquets and dried. Medicinally, said to cause abortions.

TARRAGON—2 feet. (Division and cuttings) Choose French only, for fine flavoring, not to be confused with the Russian variety. Likes good garden soil. Aniselike flavor. Leaves used for salads, eggs, vegetables, and vinegar.

THYME—2 to 12 inches. (Seeds, cuttings, division) Many different kinds and uses. Aromatic and ornamental, as well as culinary. Use leaves for soups, salads, dressings, omelets, bread, sauces, and vegetables.

WORMWOOD—2 to 4 feet. (Seeds, cuttings, division) Strong-smelling, bitter, medicinal herb. Attractive foliage. Useful in keeping wood-chucks and other animals out of the garden. Very vigorous, and may become a pest.

CHAPTER TEN

GRAINS

In the summer one of our favorite walks is along our brook. We always linger by the clearly visible foundation, outlined in stone, where my great-grandfather operated his gristmill 180 years ago. There was a lot of grain grown in the North right after the Revolutionary War. Villages were often built near fast-running streams that could be easily dammed for gristmills and sawmills, two indispensable industries.

Although a lot of grain was grown, not every farmer grew it, for the pioneers learned quickly where it grew best, and those with the right location and proper soil grew most of it to barter with others who could better grow other crops. Those in our area soon found that it was more practical to buy their grain from the Champlain Valley rather than to grow it in the northern mountains. Today nearly all of it comes from the Midwest.

Farmers in the northern hills had difficulty not so much in growing the grain crop, but in getting it dried thoroughly so that it would keep after it had been harvested in late summer. Short, cool days, foggy nights, and fall rains made field-drying difficult, and combining, as done in the West, was nearly impossible.

Although the same problem still exists in much of the North, homesteaders who are willing to spend the time can usually grow successfully a small patch of grain for their own use. In fact, by cutting and stacking it in the old-fashioned way, many are growing grain for eating as well as a bit extra for farm animals and sometimes even to sell to a local food co-op. It takes a great deal of time, however, and if you have a good source of grain, you may want to concentrate on raising something that is easier to grow and harvest.

Most northern farmers who raise grains use them mainly as soil builders, and for cover crops to keep the soil from being bare for long periods, as well as for animal feed.

WHEAT

A few years ago some of our friends decided to grow their own wheat. Although they had little knowledge of its culture or the varieties, luck was with them and they harvested a good crop the first season. The next year, however, the weather was bad, and they barely got their seed back. They persisted, however, and after several more failures they are now successfully growing several bushels of wheat each year, all they need, on a small plot of ground. They use a small, home grain grinder and are enjoying wholesome, fresh-ground wholewheat breads and cereals. Now that they have found a variety that does well in their locality, they save some seed each year for planting the next spring.

Although there are special new varieties of hybrid wheat available, most home growers choose the more common kinds and save their own seed, to lessen their dependence on suppliers far away. Buy your initial seed locally, if possible, because there are many advantages in planting acclimated seed. Choose disease-resistant varieties, and if you use seed from a neighbor, make certain he has had no disease problems.

Wheat is usually planted in the spring in the North, 120 pounds, or two bushels, to the acre. This comes to about three pounds for 1,000 square feet, or about a 32-foot-square plot. Wheat yields vary widely, but 20 bushels (1,200 pounds) per acre is about average. This would amount to a 30-pound yield on the 32-foot-square plot.

Wheat needs a balanced fertilizer. Three or four tons of farm manure, or 600 pounds of 5-10-10 commercial fertilizer per acre, well harrowed into the soil, are needed for a good crop.

The soil for wheat should be carefully prepared to eliminate as much weed and grass competition as possible. Because wheat is not as vigorous-growing as many other crops, often mustard (kale), quack grass, and other weeds can be a real problem. Plant the wheat early to give it a fast start, which will help it battle the weeds more easily.

Wheat is sometimes rotated with cultivated crops, such as corn or potatoes, for weed control. Some farmers use herbicides, but these must be carefully applied or the wheat as well as the weeds may be damaged. Limit your wheat field, just as you do your vegetable garden, to a size you can easily manage.

Sow it by hand or with a hand-cranked spreader, making sure the area is evenly covered with seed. Rake or harrow it lightly to cover it with soil.

Lodging is one of the biggest problems for grain growers. The heavy wheat kernels easily cause the stalk to fall over in late summer and early autumn in a strong wind or rain. Lodging makes harvesting, even hand-harvesting, difficult; and this difficulty is shared by large and small growers alike. Some new varieties have been developed with shorter, sturdier stems, especially to resist lodging.

Five basic types of wheat are grown in North America. Hard, red-seeded winter wheat and hard, red-seeded spring wheat are both grown mostly west of the Mississippi. They are used primarily for making bread and do best where the climate is not too wet. Soft red winter wheat is grown mostly in the East and is used for pastries. Durum is grown in the North Central Plains and is used for making spaghetti and macaroni. Soft white wheat is grown mostly in the Pacific Northwest and the Northeast, and is used for making bread.

Each wheat variety is grown in limited amounts in the North. Spring wheat is usually considered the best kind to grow here, because cold winters with little snow can kill off the tender seedlings of winter wheat, which is sown in the fall to be harvested midsummer.

Era, Lark, Opal, Nepawa, Manitou, and *Justin* are some hardy spring wheat varieties being planted in the North. However, there are over 300 different kinds currently being raised in the United States and Canada, and new ones are being introduced annually, so check with your local farm seed store to see what is available and recommended for your area.

One reason that wheat is more commonly grown throughout the world than oats and barley is because it is much easier to separate its kernels from the hulls. Although large plantings should be harvested by machine, anyone can grow a year's supply of grain in a small area and harvest, thresh, and clean it in the ancient way, without too much trouble.

Wheat must be harvested at the right time. If you begin too early, it will not be hard enough and cannot dry properly. If you wait until too late, it will shatter, fall on the ground, and be lost. So check it often and begin to cut as soon as it is ready to separate easily from the stalk.

Wheat may be mowed by hand with a scythe or small sickle mower. Tie it into sheaves and lean them against each other to form shocks or stooks in the time-honored way, as this allows the grain to continue drying. Four sheaves are usually piled together to make a sturdy shock, and it works out well if two people work together to lean one sheaf against the other.

Wheat growers pray for dry weather at harvest time. A week of rain when the wheat is ready to be cut is disastrous to the crop. Wheat must dry thoroughly for days if it is to store well, and small amounts may be dried in barns or greenhouses.

The threshing should be done as soon as the grain is dry, before mice, rats, and birds find it. A threshing machine, flails, clubs, or other instruments may be used to separate the kernels from the stalks. A clean barn or garage floor, or a heavy plastic sheet or canvas spread on the ground is a good place to do home threshing.

The wheat may be cleaned by winnowing the grain in the wind, or in front of an electric fan. Pour the grain from one bucket to another in a mild breeze, and the heavy wheat will flow easily, but the lighter chaff will be blown free.

Wheat should be stored in a cool, dry place that is completely protected from mice, rats, and other vermin. It tastes best when it is ground fresh for each use.

Two tied sheaves of wheat are leaned against each other with heads up (A). Two more are placed on the other corners so the four make a shock or stook that stands by itself (B). With this method, the grain dries easily with little shattering.

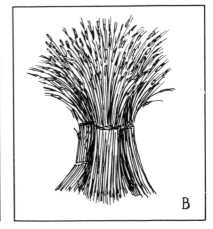

O A T S

When I was a child, a bowl of hot oatmeal was on the table for each member of our family every morning except Sunday, when we usually ate cornmeal porridge. Although I smothered the oatmeal with maple syrup, I got very sick of it and resolved never to eat another bit of the stuff when I became a grown-up. Now, years later, even though no one makes me eat it, I often do. It is one of the most nutritious grains, in some respects more nutritious than wheat, as the expression "feeling one's oats" implies.

Oats have long been grown for animal feed in the North and are excellent for horse, poultry, or cattle. The Scots, who came early to our town, had high regard for the grain as food for humans as well, and an oat mill was an important part of many little northern villages in the early days.

Oats are easy to grow nearly everywhere, and they dry much faster at harvest time than wheat. They are good soil builders, so they fit well into a crop rotation program. Planting methods are similar to those for wheat, and the amount to sow per acre is the same. There are not as many varieties as there are of wheat, and you should find out what is available and grows well in your area. *Orbit, Astro,* and *Dal* are three kinds being grown currently in the North.

A rich soil is required in order for oats to produce well. Five to 7 tons of manure per acre, or 300 to 400 pounds of 10-10-10 commercial fertilizer, well harrowed in before planting should be adequate. Yields vary from 60 to 100 bushels per acre, depending on the soil and weather conditions. As sufficient moisture is necessary for a good crop, oats should be planted as soon after hard frosts are over as possible. By planting early, as soon as the soil is dried out, you will be able to take advantage of the early summer rains.

Harvesting may be done by hand, but teaming up with a neighbor who has a combine would make it a lot easier. Like all grains, it needs to be stored in a dry place and carefully protected from mice and rats.

It is very difficult to separate the grain from the hulls, and, unfortunately, no small, home-type dehuller is yet available. Some growers have found that heating the grain to about 180° F in the

oven aids somewhat in the separation, but most of us find it easier
to buy the rolled or steel-cut oats than to mill them.

BUCKWHEAT

Buckwheat cakes and syrup were standard fare on many western
frontier farms, and often cowboys started long, difficult days after
such a breakfast. Buckwheat is a rich source of nutrition, and
northern homesteading families are discovering that it is delicious,
as well.

Buckwheat is vigorous and quite a dependable crop, even in the
North. It is often grown as a cover to kill off weeds and grass before
other crops are planted. Because it grows and matures rapidly—it
needs only ten to twelve weeks to grow and ripen—unlike most
grains it may be planted late, even after mid-June, and still be
ready to harvest before hard frosts in the fall.

It has its drawbacks, however. It lodges easily in rain and wind,
making it difficult to cut. The seed shatters easily, and, since it
ripens irregularly, it is difficult to determine when to harvest the
crop. Some of its grains will be ripe while others are just blossoming.

When planted as a weed-killing crop, it should be harvested before it begins to go to seed, even slightly, or the buckwheat seedlings may become a serious weed in that area the following year.

Soil preparation and planting instructions for buckwheat are
similar to those for wheat; however, grass and weeds are not a
serious problem. Sow 1½ pounds per 1,000 square feet, and plant
the seed deeper than most grains, about 1 to 1½ inches deep.

Common Japanese and *Pennquad* are both recommended when
planting for eating purposes. *Tartary* is fine for soil improvement,
but somewhat bitter for eating. Other varieties may be available
and recommended where you live. If you plan to raise buckwheat
every year, save some of your own grain to plant. If you buy seed,
however, be sure to order it early, because small lots of grain seed
are sometimes difficult to locate at the last minute.

MILLET

Although millet has been an important part of many diets in the
Orient for centuries, in North America it has been grown mostly

for wild bird feed and farm animal forage. Recently those who are searching for healthy foods have been using it for cooked cereal, breads, stews, casseroles, and sauces, either by itself or in combination with wheat and other grains. Nutritiously, it rates well with wheat, and is an important part of the diet of the healthy, long-lived Hunzas.

Millet grows well in the North, even on poor soil, and it ripens early, fortunately, in the heat of the summer when we can use summer's heat to dry it. Even in dry summers it thrives, and it is as easy to grow as buckwheat. The culture and harvest are about the same, although millet is somewhat more difficult to dry. The birds love it, so you must cut the stalks before the seeds are dead ripe, and dry them in a drying shed or some other place where the birds won't steal them all.

"Foxtail" millets, particularly the Hungarian strain, have been used for many years as quick-growing forage crops to feed cattle when the graze in dry summer pastures is scarce. Although this and other varieties can be used as food for humans, the "proso" millets are better for that purpose. Originally from Japan and China, they have been greatly improved and are sold under the names of *Early Fortune, Turghai, Crown,* and *White.*

Since millet, unlike oats, doesn't have to be milled to remove the hulls, it is, like wheat and buckwheat, a good grain for the home gardener.

CORN

Corn was grown in North America by the Indians for centuries before the early settlers came, and it provided a reliable source of nutrition for both natives and newcomers. It is still one of the best grains for northern homesteaders to grow, as it needs no special harvesting or threshing equipment, it dries and stores well, and can be used in a wide variety of ways, including cereals, rolls, breads, and cakes.

Although sweet corn and even popcorn may be ground for cornmeal, field corn is a much better choice. Choose a kind that produces large, hard kernels rather than the kind that grows husky stalks, which are used mostly for farm ensilage. *Early Northern Flint* is commonly grown in the North, and your farm supply store and extension service can probably suggest other varieties that may be better suited for your particular location.

Corn needs a lot of fertilizer to produce well. Twenty tons of manure are recommended for each acre, or 1,000 pounds of 10-15-10 commercial fertilizer, unless a soil test indicates otherwise. Like sweet corn, field corn grows best on well-prepared soil that is cultivated occasionally to eradicate weeds and grass. In the North the corn should be hilled up during its early development. Hilling provides a sun-soaked, well-aerated soil that corn roots like. Many growers treat the soil with an herbicide called Atrazine (Aatrex) that suppresses grass and weed growth, lessening the need for cultivation.

Corn can be predried by "shocking" it up, that is, by cutting the stalks and standing them on end in big bunches in the field for a couple of weeks. Then the ears can be picked from the stalk and further dried, after husking, by spreading them loosely on a dry, well-ventilated barn or attic floor and turning them occasionally; or they may be stored in bins built of hardware cloth or chicken wire to allow a free movement of air around them.

OTHER GRAINS

Other grains were also once widely grown in the North. Barley and rye were raised mostly for animal feeds or for making whisky. Today they are grown here more for soil-building purposes. *Tetra-Petkus* and *Balboa* are winter rye varieties often planted in late summer for covering soil and adding humus to it. *Eire* is a northern variety of barley, and is planted in spring, often in combination with oats and wheat.

Flax used to be grown both for its fibers, which were used to make linen, and its seeds, which were used for a variety of things, including medicine. It is seldom grown at all in the North these days.

Rice is strictly a warm weather grain, and is not likely to be adapted to the North, at least until there is another major climatic change. Soybeans are a legume, but are often regarded as a grain. When they are grown in the North at all, they are usually planted to improve the soil, because the beans seldom ripen in a climate as cool as ours.

PART THREE

Landscaping in the North

A short distance from our home in northern Vermont is a beautifully landscaped farmhouse with trees, hedges, flowering shrubs, perennials, and a manicured lawn. All the hedges are neatly sheared, the evergreens trimmed, and the flowering bushes well pruned. At any time of year it looks nice, but it is not showy or offensive.

Last year the couple who owned the farm and worked so hard on it sold it for a vacation home. There is no way of knowing how much their landscaping added to the value of the place, but it was certainly a great deal, probably many thousands of dollars.

How much did the planting cost originally? Of the hundreds of trees and plants around their home, probably fewer than a dozen were purchased. The rest they dug up on their farm. It was their skill in selecting the right plants, setting them in the proper spots, and keeping them fed, pruned, and healthy that made them so attractive. It took time, but I'm sure they enjoyed their gardening, and they inspired others to dress up their homes as well, so it benefited the entire neighborhood.

CHAPTER ELEVEN

PLANNING AND PLANTING

Those of us who decide to live or spend long vacations in this bewildering climate too often forget all the wonderful trees and shrubs that abound locally, and never realize their potential. Native plants, besides having the advantages of being more likely to survive and lower in cost, are fresh. Often they can be dug and planted the same day instead of being stored for months in refrigerated cellars, shipped long distances, and held for extended periods in shopping centers or post offices.

Colorful photos in nursery catalogs tempt us to send off for plants or visit garden centers where we spend lots of money on yews, azaleas, rhododendrons, forsythias, redbuds, junipers, dogwoods, crepe myrtle, tea roses, and other exotic plants that were bred to grow hundreds of miles away.

Unfortunately, most nursery catalogs are of little help in selecting northern home landscape plants. I once looked carefully through the large catalog of a nationally known nursery, checking off the plants and trees offered that would grow well in zones 3 and 4. It was a pitifully short list, yet a novice gardener in this region could easily have felt that he could order everything he wanted, plant it on a windswept northern mountainside, and successfully transform his home into a replica of one in the suburbs of Washington, D.C.

Each part of the world obviously has native plants that grow best there. For each region there are specific flowering bushes and trees, berry-producing shrubs, shade trees, evergreens, ground covers, and hedge materials.

Although we don't all own pastures, roadsides, and woods where we can dig up the plants we want, there are, in nearly every region, individuals and nurseries who sell wild trees; or you may find an agreeable farmer who doesn't mind selling a few trees from his pasture. In any case, don't help yourself to wild trees without an agreement. No matter how abundant they may be, or how worthless they appear, both the landowner and the law are likely to be quite unforgiving about stolen trees.

Most of us want to have a few plantings around our grounds that are not native, to make the landscape more interesting. Luckily, many shrubs and trees that are native to other regions will thrive in the North as well. Early settlers brought many plants from northern Europe, and missionaries and other travelers have brought back hardy specimen plants from China, Japan, Korea, Siberia, and Manchuria. Lilacs, hydrangeas, honeysuckles, flowering crabapples, Lombardy poplars, Norway spruce, and mugho pines are some of the "exotics" that have become so comfortable in northern gardens that they seem almost native.

In addition to the foreign imports, plant life has also been moved around this country a great deal. Hardy junipers, blue spruce, hemlocks, firs, pines—both the tall-growing kinds and dwarfs—have been traded between the cold regions of New England, the Appalachian Mountains, the North Central states, and the Prairie states and provinces. The concolor fir, from Oregon, now grows in Maine; and eastern white cedars form windbreaks in the West.

We have learned to use perennials in our landscaping, as have many other gardeners in the nippy North. Because they die down and are out of the way for the winter months, they are especially useful under eaves, where ice and snow from a roof might crush evergreens or flowering shrubs. We use peonies, ferns, bleeding hearts, daylilies, hosta, hollyhocks, and other perennials quite successfully in these and other difficult places. Maintenance is low, since plants need little care and last for many years. Near our front doorstep we have a large pink peony with shiny leaves that people sometimes mistake for a rhododendron from a distance.

We also use plants like dahlias, large geraniums, and chrysanthemums instead of small bushes; and sometimes plant rows of zinnias, marigolds, or Mexican firebush to replace low-growing hedges where snow plowed from roads or paths would be hard on woody plants.

Before you put in trees and shrubs at random around your property, keep in mind that landscaping should have a purpose. Plunking a few green bushes with pretty flowers in front of your house is not really good landscaping. The plantings should tie your house to the surrounding land and make it look like a lived-in home. Shade

Good landscaping should appear natural and provide an attractive setting for the buildings.

trees should frame the house; evergreens and shrubs must relate nicely and in proportion to the windows, doors, paths, and other features of the house as well as to each other, and never be showy or gaudy. If the first thing you notice about a house is its landscaping, there is probably something wrong with it. Try to think of your home as a diamond, and the plantings as a lovely setting for it.

CEMETERY PLANTINGS

Which plants to use in a cemetery may be a hard decision in the North. Since the plants are not likely to get much care, choose those that don't need careful pruning, special fertilizer, spraying, or covering for the winter. Also, select varieties that don't grow too big.

If the lot is large, however, and regulations permit that kind of planting, the old-fashioned and French lilacs are good choices, as are the medium-sized Canadian lilacs, such as *James MacFarlane*.

Mock orange, honeysuckle, and hydrangea, both the pink and white kinds, may also be suitable.

On a small lot, potentilla, spirea *Anthony Waterer,* bridal wreath, and dwarf cranberry are all good choices. We like potentilla, especially, because it blooms throughout the summer. In sheltered places the hardy daphne and hardier weigelas may be satisfactory.

Bird's-nest spruce, dwarf mugho pine, and dwarf globe arborvitae are good evergreens for cemeteries because they stay small and need little trimming. Peonies, daylilies, bleeding heart, and daffodils are rugged, long-lived perennial plants that are often used, and look good.

PLANTING IN THE NORTH

In the North almost everything should be planted in the spring—those plants purchased through the mail and at garden centers and nurseries, and those you dig and move yourself. Since spring, in this case, means the interval between the time that the ground gets bare and thaws out to the time when everything starts growing, it can be a very short period. Sometimes it lasts only two or three weeks in our area.

A few tough, native, deciduous trees can be moved in the fall in the North if the trees are small and they are moved with care. Maples, oaks, tamaracks, beeches, and ash can be moved successfully after their leaves have come off in October if you dig them carefully with a big rootball. Birches, poplars, and willows, however, should be dug only in the spring before their leaf buds begin to grow. Evergreens may be dug and moved in September if the weather is not dry and a large ball of earth is left undisturbed around the roots.

Since wild trees and bushes often grow on poor soil, their roots roam all over the area searching for nutrients. When you dig them up, you must break off many of their roots. The trees suffer badly and will take a long time to recover.

This planting shock can be minimized for a wild tree, or a domesticated one that you wish to move, by treating the tree as a nurseryman would, and root-prune it. With a sharp spade, cut a circle around the tree you want to move in early spring. The diameter

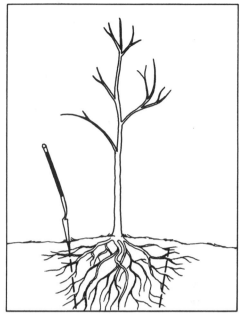

Root pruning a tree a *year* before moving it makes it easier to dig up; and it will be more likely to survive.

and depth you cut depend on the size of the tree. For a 3-foot evergreen or an 8-foot maple, a diameter of about 30 inches and a depth of 20 inches should be about right. It's best not to attempt to move wild trees much larger than that, since big trees will grow more slowly for the next few years than the smaller ones.

Be very careful not to miss any roots as you encircle the tree. You will hear the roots snap as you cut. Dig as if you planned to lift the tree out of the ground; but don't do it. Instead, leave it there until the following spring.

The idea behind root-pruning is to force the tree to grow new, **small fibrous feeder roots inside the rootball you have cut. Enough** new roots will grow, hopefully, to support the tree when it is moved to its new location. By sprinkling a cupful of plant food all over the cut circle, you can encourage this new root growth even more.

The next spring, while the soil is wet, carefully dig out the tree, **wrap up the rootball so it won't dry out, and move it to its new** location. There should be very little setback, and new growth should start soon.

If you must move a tree at a time other than early spring, soak it well before you dig it. Moving it in a rain is best. Dig the tree with a ball of soil as big as possible, and wrap the top in a white sheet or burlap for several days to prevent evaporation through the needles or leaves. Professional growers, and sometimes amateurs as well, spray the tops with a chemical called Wilt-Pruf to prevent evaporation. It is a liquid plastic that seals leaf pores for several weeks, long enough, usually, for the tree to recover from the transplanting shock. Naturally, the tree must be heavily watered each day until it shows signs of recovery and is making new growth.

If you buy trees or shrubs from a nursery, follow carefully the planting directions that come with them. Many nurseries sell their plants in large pots, or with the roots wrapped in a ball of soil. These may be planted all summer, until the middle of September.

FERTILIZING IN THE NORTH

It is tempting, whenever you see a tree or shrub that is doing poorly, to give it a shot of chemical fertilizer. Feeding a tree at the wrong time in any part of the world is risky, but especially so in the North, where an overdose of plant food may be fatal. For the best growth, dry chemical fertilizer should be applied only before the tree starts to grow in very early spring. If organic fertilizers are used, they may be applied either in early spring or late fall.

Most evergreens make a fast growth in early summer, and the tops grow little or none after that period, though the roots keep growing all season. Hemlocks, yews, and arborvitae are exceptions and continue to grow in midsummer. Deciduous trees grow over a longer season, and some of the less hardy ones, catalpa, many oaks, and some willows, for instance, grow quite late in the summer, which may cause winter injury.

Unless newly planted trees receive special attention not only their first year but for several years, they may grow very little in the short growing season and poor soil of the North. They may need to be watered heavily two or three times a week the first month after planting if the weather is at all dry. Not only will they respond to a thick mulch of old hay, rotting leaves, shredded bark, or similar materials, but they should also receive some additional fertilizer. I prefer to avoid strong, dry chemical fertilizers completely the first year, and feed a new tree, instead, with manure tea. Some people prefer to use liquid chemical fertilizer. If you choose to do so, follow directions on the container carefully. Stop all liquid feeding —whether manure tea or chemical—by July 1, so the tree will cease growing before the first frosts.

Maples do well in a very rich soil, and grow rapidly when they are well fertilized, as do birches, and mountain ash. Pines, on the other hand, may grow crooked if they are overfertilized when they are young, so if you use chemical fertilizers, be very stingy when feeding them.

The soil pH is usually not an important factor in the growth of your trees, since most hardy trees grow over a wide range of soils. A few are fussy about acidity, however. Oaks, most pines, red spruce, and all broadleaf evergreens like acid soils (4.5 to 6 pH). Arborvitae, white spruce, balsam fir, and lilacs prefer soil that is more alkaline (6 to 7 pH). For best growth try to provide the type of acidity that these trees prefer.

TREES AS ENERGY SAVERS

We've always recommended plantings of trees and shrubs around the home for beauty, to block out unpleasant views and street noises, and to increase privacy. Now, with the increased costs of home heating and air conditioning, we often suggest plantings for the purpose of slowing down cold winds, and for shade from the hot summer sun.

We have friends who lived in an old colonial house at the edge of the woods on a southern slope. Five years ago they felt they were missing a great deal by not taking advantage of the view at the top of their hill, so they built a low ranch house where they could enjoy the sunset as well as the sunrise. They insulated the new house heavily and installed thermopane glass.

To their astonishment the new house was far colder on windy days than their old, uninsulated farmhouse in its sheltered spot. The hill and trees apparently offered better protection than today's insulation. Now they are busy trying to shut off their spectacular northern and western view with a grove of evergreen trees.

I'm sure that when our own house was first built at the edge of a woods it was snug and warm; but my ancestors, like all the early pioneers, regarded a tree as something to cut down so that they

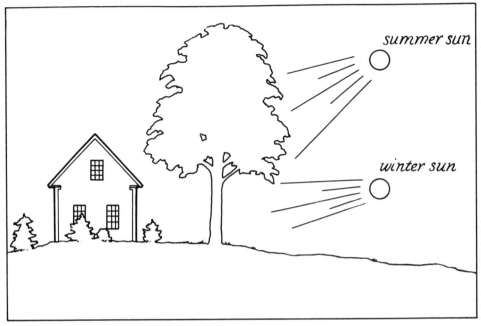

A large *shade tree* can have a much appreciated *cooling* effect on the house in summer. Remove the lower limbs to let the low-angled winter sun shine in the windows.

could plant a more valuable crop. Eventually, all the nearby trees were gone. A few years ago I planted a tall, tight cedar hedge, hoping to stop the cold north winds that whistle through the house for much of the year.

The hedge is now about 15 feet tall and still growing. Not only is the house warmer, but the backyard has become a pleasant summer outdoor living area. We can have a cooking fire safely, and the food no longer blows off the picnic table when we eat there. The flowers in the perennial border stand erect instead of blowing over, and even the birds are happy. There are no whitecaps on the bird-bath.

We have learned to plant shade trees in the right location to cast a cooling shadow on the house or outdoor play area during the heat of a summer day, but let the sun shine beneath their limbs and enter the house windows when we most want it—during the spring, fall, and winter months.

TREES AND SALT

Salt damage to trees was once a problem only for those who gardened near the seashore—but not any more. Trees and shrubs planted near paved highways, driveways, and parking areas often suffer severe damage from the salt used to melt ice in the winter. The primary damage is caused by the action of salt on the roots, so those trees growing in areas lower than the salted area or near drainage ditches are most affected. Trees on banks higher than the road are less bothered.

But salt sprayed by vehicles can cause damage to the tops of plants and trees, too, particularly to evergreens. The spray is caused when cars drive fast through melting ice, kicking up the spray, which is then carried for great distances by the wind. Damage is always worse on the side of the highway that gets the most wind. Much of the noticeable browning of evergreens that we see each spring near highways is caused by sprayed salt, although the damage from windburn is similar. Either salt burn or windburn may show up as a temporary discoloration, or in some cases it may be serious enough to kill the tree.

Plantings must be positioned carefully wherever snowplows and road salt may leave their marks.

TREES' TOLERANCE TO SALT

Trees Most Susceptible to Salt Damage on Their Roots

Alder, speckled
Basswood
Beech, American
Birch, White
Elm, American
Fir, Balsam
Hemlock, Canadian
Hornbeam, American
Larch (Tamarack)
Linden, Littleleaf
Maple, Red
Maple, Sugar
Poplar, Lombardy
Serviceberry (Shadbush)
Spruce, Norway

Trees Moderately Susceptible to Salt on Their Roots

Ash, Green
Ash, White
Aspen, Quaking
Birch, European
Birch, Gray
Birch, Paper
Box Elder
Hawthorn, Cockspur
Maple, Norway
Maple, Silver

Trees Most Resistant to Salt Damage

Birch, Sweet
Birch, Yellow
Honey Locust
Horse Chestnut
Locust, Black

Trees Most Resistant to Salt Damage

Oak, Red
Oak, White
Olive, Russian
Poplar, Silver or White
Spruce, Blue
Willow, Weeping

Tolerance of Trees to Salt Spray on Their Foliage or Branches

MOST SUSCEPTIBLE	MODERATELY SUSCEPTIBLE
Arborvitae (Eastern white cedar)	Fir, Douglas
Hemlock, Canadian	Juniper
Pine, White	Pine, Scotch
Spruce, Red	Spruce, Norway

MOST RESISTANT
Pine, Austrian
Spruce, Blue
Spruce, White

CHAPTER TWELVE

SHADE TREES AND EVERGREEENS

·Visitors to the North frequently remark about the beautiful trees. Thousands ride buses or drive north each fall to view the brilliant foliage of the swamp and sugar maples, the birches, and other hardwood trees. Later, the larches (tamaracks) turn a feathery orange-yellow. In the springtime, soft, new greens cover the mountainsides; and apples, flowering crabs, shad, wild cherries, and others burst into bloom. Even in the winter, snow-covered evergreens and outlines of the deciduous trees offer a wide variety of interesting beauty. The white birches, silver-gray beeches, gnarled, limby silver maples, and countless others give us endless possibilities for home landscaping.

TREES FOR SHADE

We usually laugh at the thought of air conditioning in our part of northern New England, but when the thermometer occasionally reaches the high 80's, we're uncomfortable and can sympathize with people who live in those parts of the northern plains where it stays very hot throughout the summer. Shade trees placed in the right spots can increase summer comfort for everyone, and cut cooling costs for anyone who uses air conditioning.

To be most effective, a shade tree should be planted so the shade will fall on the house during midafternoon in July and August. The tree should be of the spreading type, like a maple, and not compact-growing, like a Lombardy poplar. Its lower limbs should be cut off as the tree grows so that the low winter sun can better shine into the house windows when it is most needed and be blocked out effectively by the leaves in the summer when the sun is high.

Trees that have heavy foliage, such as maples, beech, and oaks, are better than birch or ash, which have less leaf density. The light

Shade trees that are allowed to grow with bad crotches near the ground (*A*) will eventually split. Train your shade tree to grow with one main trunk for at least the first 15 feet (*B*).

shade trees are good to plant where you want less shade, perhaps near a flower bed, picnic spot, or outdoor living area.

GRAFTED TREES

In recent years a great many named varieties of grafted, deciduous shade trees have been introduced. Each has something special about it—red leaves, perhaps, weeping branches, variegated foliage, or an unusual shape. Most of them, unfortunately, have not proven suitable for much of the North.

The beautiful Crimson King maple, probably the best known of the new trees, has been only partially successful, and most of the thousands of Crimson Kings that have been planted in our area over the last two decades have died. Since the named trees are practically always grafted on wild trees, it is sometimes hard to determine whether the new variety itself or the graft union is unable to stand our northern climates. Crimson King maples cloned on their own roots have proven more successful than the grafted trees, but these are not widely available. We have had good luck growing the Canada cherry as a substitute for the Crimson King. It is a smaller tree, better suited for small lots, and much more certain to live.

Although it may be fun to experiment with one or two, you may not want to order large numbers of new grafted shade trees until they have been grown successfully in your area for six or seven years. In that length of time they should have experienced most of the likely weather conditions in the North.

DECIDUOUS TREES YOU MAY WISH TO CONSIDER AS LAWN TREES

ALDER, SPECKLED *(Alnus incana)*—This tree grows to 50 feet and is of little value except that it will grow in soil too wet for better trees.

ASH, GREEN *(Fraxinus pennsylvanica)*—One of the most widely planted ash trees. It produces a light shade, and there are few leaves to rake up in the fall. Its many seeds, however, may grow where you don't want them, and it "leafs out" rather late in the spring. There is no fall color. By pruning off the lower branches, it makes a tall-growing, elmlike tree.

ASH, WHITE *(Fraxinus americana)*—A native tree of the northern woods, the white ash has fernlike foliage and growth habits like the green ash. It can often be dug from the woods. The wood is very hard. In fact, tool handles are often made from it. Grows quite fast and is very hardy.

BALM OF GILEAD *(Populus candicans)*—This is probably the best poplar for northern gardens. It is longer-lived than most of the poplars, yet grows quickly and develops into a giant spreading tree. It does drop its cottony seeds all over the lawn, suckers badly, and its big roots are often close to the surface, where they interfere with walking and mowing.

BASSWOOD *(Tilia americana)*—This big-leaf native linden of the North Woods is a beautiful tree with fragrant flowers so high up you seldom see or smell them, but bees love them. The wood is prized by carvers and whittlers.

BEECH *(Fagus grandifolia)*—A slow-growing native tree that is most attractive in winter with its silver gray bark and much hardier than the European varieties with colored leaves.

BIRCH, EUROPEAN *(Betula pendula)*—The European birch with white bark is widely planted, but it often has trouble and looks less attractive than the native paper and gray birches as it grows older. Although the European birch grows faster, the natives are better choices for the North.

BIRCH, GRAY *(Betula populifolia)*—A native tree that is often collected and sold as "white" birch. The bark is white and clings tight to the tree. It tends to grow in attractive clumps. Usually it requires spraying to keep the birch leaf minors from turning the leaves brown in late summer.

BIRCH, PAPER *(Betula papyrifera)*—Sometimes called "canoe birch," this is the best choice if you want to grow birch trees in the North. It is more resistant to birch leaf minor than the gray birch. It is hardy, but slow-growing. It gives a filtered shade and is ideal for background plantings. Don't let people pull off its loose-hanging bark, or it will permanently disfigure the tree.

BIRCH, SILVER *(Betula lutea)*—Not one of the best shade trees, but it is hardy and grows well. Gives filtered shade, and its leaves are little problem in the fall.

BOX ELDER *(Acer negunda)*—This is a good, shrubby tree to grow where other trees don't do well—in cities, dry areas, and as a lawn tree where there isn't enough room for a large tree. It is not nearly as attractive as most other maples, however.

CHERRY *(Prunus)*—Each area of the North has wild cherry trees that may be dug and planted as lawn trees. All flower early in the spring and most have fruit that is good for jelly and birds. Many do not grow very large. Most of those in catalogs with red and pink blooms are not hardy in the North.

CHERRY, CANADA RED *(Prunus virginiana)*—Sometimes called Schubert's cherry. New foliage growth is green, but then turns a pretty red that stays colorful all summer and fall. The chokecherry-like fruit is good for birds. It grows 15 to 20 feet tall.

ELM, AMERICAN *(Ulmus americana)*—This fine, stately old tree is fast disappearing from the scene, having been attacked by Dutch Elm disease; but there are some survivors, and some are still being planted.

FLOWERING CRABAPPLE *(Malus)*—One of the best flowering trees. These burst into bloom—pink, red, or white in spring, then produce attractive fruits in early fall. Many varieties of these beauties are perfectly hardy. Among them are *Hopa, Dolgo, Royalty, Red Radiant,* and *Mary Potter.*

HORNBEAM *(Carpinus caroliniana)*—This slow-growing, tough, strong, wiry little tree is a natural for northern landscapes. Not particularly beautiful or even interesting, but reliable, tough, hardy, and long-lived.

JAPANESE TREE LILAC *(Syringa amurensis)*—Tall-growing, long-lived lilac with creamy white blooms in early summer. 20 to 25 feet tall.

LARCH OR EASTERN TAMARACK *(Larix laricina)*—The native variety of larch is usually more satisfactory than the more commonly sold Japanese or European kinds. These deciduous conifers are beautiful in spring with their soft, new green growth, small pink blooms later on, and tiny cones in the fall. Their yellow-orange foliage provides bright fall color after the maple and birch leaves are gone. Grows well anywhere, but is especially good in places too wet for other trees.

LOCUST, BLACK *(Robinia pseudoacacia)*—A thorny native tree that is becoming more popular because it resists road salt better than other trees. It is not a particularly good shade tree, though, and leaf minors and borers sometimes make it even less attractive.

MAPLE, RED *(Acer rubra)*—This native maple is sometimes called swamp maple or soft maple. The foliage turns the brightest red in the autumn. It is often confused with the red leaf maples such as Crimson King whose leaves stay red all summer. Red maples grow well nearly everywhere, but their leaves are less dense and less attractive than those of the sugar maple. It does well in moist spots.

MAPLE, SILVER *(Acer saccharinum)*—This large-growing tree is often confused with the smaller-growing "maple leaf" or white poplar that has grayer leaves. Both have leaves that are nearly white underneath. The true silver maple grows into weird shapes, becomes very large, spreading, and has huge crotches. It grows fast and is long-lived in the North.

MAPLE, SUGAR *(Acer saccharum)*—One of the best of all shade trees. It responds well to fertilizer, and grows fast only when well fed. Maple forest lands were sought after by the early settlers because they always indicated the best soil, and the trees were valued as a source for maple sugar.

MOUNTAIN ASH *(Sorbus)*—Attractive small tree with orange-red berries. Called moosemissi by the Indians and early settlers, because the moose and deer love it. Both the American ash *(S. decora)* and the European *(S. aucuparia)* rowan tree are very hardy in the North. In fact, the American grows near the tree line of some of the highest eastern mountains. Both need spraying to control the sawfly.

OAK *(Quercus)*—"Hardy as an oak" does not mean quite what we'd like to think, since most oaks have trouble growing on exposed hillsides in zone 3. Red oak and swamp white oak are the hardiest and do well in zone 4.

PLUM, NEWPORT *(Prunus americana)*—This small tree or large bush is grown for its bright foliage, which stays red all summer. Like the Canada cherry, it needs to be in full sun to develop the best color. It is slightly less hardy, however, and is susceptible to winter injury on the ends of the branches. This injured growth needs to be pruned off each spring, which keeps the tree at a fairly dwarf (4'–6') size in the North; but the attractive, bushy shape and vivid color merits it a place in northern gardens. It is hardier than the more popular Thundercloud plum.

POPLAR *(Populus)*—Most of the poplars are hardy in the North, but some are more useful than others. Almost all of them are fast-growing, but are short-lived, sucker badly, and are brittle. The white poplar *(Populus alba)* is a small tree that has gray-green leaves with white undersides. It is sometimes called silver maple because of the shape of the leaves. The tall Lombardy poplar from Europe is one of the most beautiful, and is particularly attractive along country lanes, or for accent points in the landscape.

WILLOW, GOLDEN BARK *(Salix niobe)*—The massive weeping willows that grow along southern streams are not hardy in the North. The Niobe is the best choice here. Unlike the southern varieties, it does best where it is not wet. It should not be fertilized, since it grows too fast anyway, and moist soil and overfeeding are very likely to cause winter damage. Where it is successful, the Niobe is a beautiful tree, but even under the best conditions it is likely to be short-lived.

TREES THAT SHOULD BE CONSIDERED EXPERIMENTAL IN ZONES 3 AND 4

BEECH, COPPER *(Fagus sylvatica)*—This hasn't been proven suitable for most areas in the North.

BIRCH, WEEPING *(Betula pendula gracilis)*—These grafted trees seem to have trouble in cold, exposed areas.

CATALPA *(Catalpa speciosa)*—Needs a sheltered spot on lower elevations, and even there may suffer some winter dieback.

CUCUMBER TREE *(Magnolia acuminata)*—These survive occasionally in favored mini-climates in the North, although they seldom grow to full size.

GINKO *(Ginko biloba)*—Oriental tree that succeeds only when planted in really sheltered spots.

HAWTHORN *(Crataegus)*—Most need favorable growing conditions. Cockspur *(crusgalli)* is one of the hardier ones.

HICKORY, SHAGBARK *(Carya ovata)*—Needs a longer growing season than most northern areas provide.

HONEY LOCUST *(Gleditsia)*—Most of the named varieties, *Moraine, Skyline,* and *Sunburst,* for instance, have trouble growing in exposed location.

HORSE CHESTNUT *(Hippocastanum)*—Needs a long growing season, and has little to recommend it as a desirable tree, anyway.

LINDEN, SILVER *(Tilia tormentosa)* and LITTLELEAF *(Tilia cordata)*—These European trees are moderately hardy, but the native linden (basswood) is a better tree for the North.

MAPLE, NORWAY *(Acer platanoides)*—An excellent small street tree in sheltered villages, but not good on exposed mountain areas in zone 3.

MOUNTAIN ASH, KOREAN *(Sorbus alnifolia)*—Tall-growing mountain ash. Choose the hardier American and European strains for zone 3 and most of zone 4.

PHELLODENDRON *(Phellodendron amurense)*—Many books rate this cork tree as hardy nearly everywhere, but it hasn't proved to be so on our northern hillside. Grows well in sheltered areas, however, in zones 3 and 4.

REDBUD *(Cercis)*—Very successful in milder parts of the North, but even the hardiest strains have trouble in the colder regions and in the mountains.

RUSSIAN OLIVE *(Elaeagnus angustifolia)*—Does well in the valleys and areas where frosts come late. Winter-kills badly in zone 3. The autumn olive is slightly hardier, but not much.

SERVICEBERRY, JUNEBERRY, OR SHADBUSH *(Amelanchier)*—The different strains of shad vary widely as to hardiness. Choose the native kinds when possible.

SYCAMORE *(Platanus occidentalis)*—Hardy only in favorable spots, and susceptible to twig blight.

TULIP TREE *(Liriodendron tulipifera)*—This large-growing, flowering tree needs a more sheltered location than much of the North offers.

YELLOWWOOD *(Cladrastis lutea)*—A flowering tree with wisteria-type blooms. It succeeds only in the warmest pockets of the North.

Trees for Wet Places
Alder *(Alnus)*
Cedar, white *(Thuja occidentalis)*
Larch, Tamarack *(Larix laricina)*
Pussy Willow *(Salix discolor)*
Red or Swamp Maple *(Acer rubra)*

Trees for Dry Places and Poor Soils
Box Elder *(Acer negundo)*
Birch, gray *(Betula popufolia)*
White Poplar *(Populus alba)*, sometimes called "silver maple."

EVERGREENS

The term "North Woods" conjures up an image of acres of majestic evergreens—pines, spruce, balsam fir, white cedars, and Canadian hemlock. They grow to perfection in the cold North, and look very nice in the home landscape. In a region where the leaves are off the deciduous trees for seven or eight months of the year, the green adds a great deal of color, and helps break up the bleak grays of winter.

Some evergreens not native to the North also thrive here. Colorado blue spruce, Englemann's spruce, Austrian pine, and Norway spruce, for example, all grow well on our windy mountain. Many of the Northwest trees, however, such as the Alberta spruce and the Douglas, Concolor, and Noble firs, must be planted in favorable locations if they're to thrive. The redwoods, cypress, and Japanese jack pine seldom make it, even in sheltered spots.

The pines do best on slightly acid soils, as do red and black spruce. White spruce, the firs, and white cedar grow better on sweeter soils. In fact, arborvitae (white cedar) hedges are unhappy in many locations unless lime is added to the soil.

Windburn

Frequently the needles of evergreens become severely dried out, or windburned, in late winter in the North. This condition is especially common in windy locations during cold winters when there is little snow. Small or newly planted trees are especially susceptible to windburn, since their shallow roots are unable to supply moisture during late winter, either because the ground has frozen deeply or because of prolonged fall droughts.

Large trees with deep roots sometimes become windburned, too, however, even when the ground doesn't freeze. The needles of evergreens sometimes turn brown or reddish brown, often looking worse on the side that gets the most wind.

Windburn is most common on those trees and shrubs that are exotic to the area. In our section Japanese yews are hardy, and usually overwinter well in protected areas where there is little wind, although temperatures may drop to −45° F. If they are planted in windy spots, however, they may have lost every bit of their green color by spring, and it usually takes all summer for them to recover if they survive at all. Many pines, junipers, concolor firs, and other imported trees are also affected in the same manner.

Surprisingly, some native trees also occasionally suffer windburn unless they are protected by buildings, hills, or woods. Hemlock and red spruce are very hardy native trees and grow to great heights

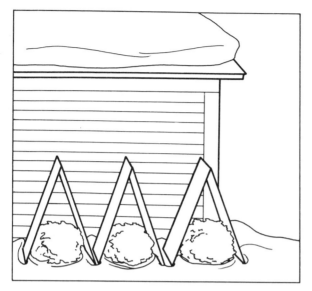

Evergreens and *shrubs* growing under eaves should be protected before winter from falling ice and snow.

in the forest, yet both can suffer severe windburn when isolated trees are grown unprotected in windswept locations.

Home gardeners who have no good way to grow evergreens out of the wind sometimes wrap the plants in black plastic or burlap, or they build wooden shelters around them. The snow itself is the best protection against windburn, so these types of shelters sometimes do more harm than good. Wooden shelters, however, may help protect fragile evergreens from being broken under heavy snow loads.

Some gardeners spray their evergreens in the late fall with a liquid plastic such as Wilt-Pruf, the same material sprayed on trees to prevent their wilting when they are moved during the summer. The plastic seals the pores of the needles, preventing moisture loss during the winter and early spring, yet it weathers off enough so that new growth is not restricted. Aerosol cans are available for treating a few small trees, or the material can be bought in gallon jugs and mixed with water to protect large plantings. A second dosage may be necessary in late winter whenever winds are severe and the snow cover is light. A better way to protect any tender yews, hemlocks, and junipers, is to plant them close to a building on the east side, where they will be protected from winter winds.

Shearing

Evergreens used in landscaping need some shearing or cutting back of their new growth occasionally to help them look their best and to keep them from getting too large. Even the low-growing dwarf evergreens usually must be sheared to keep them from getting too wide.

Blue and white spruce, balsam fir, Canadian hemlock, mugho pine, and eastern arborvitae (cedar) and yews are all good subjects for shearing. Red, white, Scotch and Austrian pine are vigorous growers with long needles, and although they too may be sheared tightly, I have found that sooner or later they manage to get away from me. On the other hand, we have several white spruce around our home that are forty to fifty years old and only 3 feet tall. If they had not been clipped tightly each year, they would be 30 or 40 feet tall now.

Start clipping your tree when it is small. Some people feel they should wait until the tree gets to the size they want it to be ultimately, and then start shearing. This procedure results in a tree that will never be compact and tight.

Usually there won't be much new growth on a new tree the first summer after planting, but by the second season shearing should begin. In the North the shearing period is not long, because it should be done only when the trees are growing. Yews, firs, spruce, and pines, including mugho pines, grow only during three or four weeks in late spring, usually from the last of May until the last

Wild evergreens can be sheared in a natural way to make them tighter by one light annual clipping (*A*); or they can be kept in a small compact form by several tight shearings in early summer (*B*).

Evergreens need *regular shearing* so that upward and outward growth will be slowed and redirected inward to make the bush grow thicker.

of June where we live. Hemlocks, cedars, and juniper grow later, in late June and July.

Do the first shearing as soon as the tree begins to grow so that upward and outward growth will be slowed and redirected inward to make the bush grow thicker. When you cut off the tips of the new growth, you stimulate the buds along the inside, older branches to grow. In other words, the purpose of shearing is not so much to remove new growth, but to keep the tree from growing where you don't want it. Growth then takes place where it ordinarily would not, and the result is a smaller but thicker tree. If you were to wait until the end of the growing season to cut off all the new growth each year, the tree would stay small but never become thick.

When you shear, be careful to shear all around the sides as well as the top to have a tree that is well shaped instead of a short, squatty shrub. Always stop shearing before the tree stops growing entirely; then the buds for the next year will form and the tree will not look "shorn" and unsightly.

If you want to "tighten up" a tree but still would like it to grow somewhat larger, wait until the new spring growth is about 3 inches long, then snip only an inch off the ends of that new growth. This will tighten up the tree, yet let it grow larger. It takes a few years to achieve a "tight" look, so don't get discouraged. If you want your tree to look bushy but still natural, continue to shear it once each year in the same way. Eventually it will probably get too big, but you can keep it under control for many years.

If you want, instead, a very tight, formal effect, you can prevent a tree from ever growing any larger. As soon as it gets as large as you want it to be, shear it as usual in late spring as soon as the new growth is about an inch long. Clip off all the new growth, "carving" the tree into the shape you want it to be. Clip tightly several more times during the next three or four weeks, whenever the tree starts to grow out of shape.

As with any evergreen pruning, keep your tree wider at the bottom than at the top so that sunlight will be able to reach the lower branches and keep them alive. Make the top pointed or rounded rather than wide and flat. This will prevent heavy layers of snow and ice from crushing it.

Shear boldly. Many new gardeners prune too timidly, apparently afraid of hurting the tree, which is only too eager to take advantage

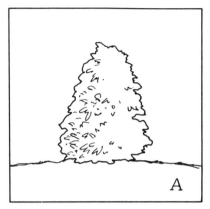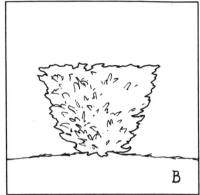

Shear evergreens narrow and with pointed and rounded tops (*A*). Plants sheared to grow wide and flat (*B*) collect heavy loads of snow that break the branches.

of such a situation and grow too big. Be firm, and clip closer than seems necessary. You'll like the results, and the tree won't suffer a bit.

Once you start to shear, be sure to continue it each year. If you miss even one trimming, it will be extremely difficult to get the tree into shape again.

Topiary

Northern gardeners often envy the way evergreens are sculpted into animals and geometric forms in England, Disneyland, and formal gardens further south. Although the heavy snows are hard on delicate topiary, and most plants commonly used for plant sculpture are not hardy here, I have seen some beautiful shaping of native white cedar and white spruce in northern gardens. Fancy shearing even of hemlock and the upright form of Japanese yew is possible in northern landscapes that are sheltered from the wind.

Hardy Evergreen Varieties

ARBORVITAE, AMERICAN *(Thuja occidentalis)*—Eastern white cedar of the northern swamps. Good for windbreaks, hedges, screens. Fast-growing and hardy, but needs additional lime unless soil is sweet.

FIR, BALSAM *(Abies balsamea)*—This fast-growing, beautiful conifer with its fragrant, rich, green foliage is at its prime only in the cold North. Looks best when sheared; otherwise it grows more loose and tends to lose its lower branches. Excellent Christmas tree.

HEMLOCK, CANADIAN *(Tsuga canadensis)*—A hardy tree, but it tends to windburn badly when planted where it is exposed to cold, drying north and western winds. Needs slightly acid soil for best growth and color.

JUNIPER, COMMON PASTURE *(Juniperus communis)*—The wild native shrubby pasture juniper varies widely in size and texture. Choose ones that look nice and shear them lightly for the best effect. Prefers a slightly acid soil.

PINE, SCOTCH *(Pinus sylvestris)*—Strains from various European countries and the United States vary widely in color and needle length. Nice tree, but its wood is brittle, and it is subject to scleroderris canker. Looks best when young.

PINE, SWISS STONE *(Pinus cembra)*—Thick-growing, attractive pine, but slow-growing. Good for formal gardens when sheared. Light green color.

PINE, WHITE *(Pinus strobus)*—Magnificent native pine tree with light green needles. Keep them several hundred feet away from currants or gooseberries. Like all pines, it does best on an acid soil.

SPRUCE, BLUE *(Picea pungens)*—Colorado spruce in green to blue-white color. Hardy, prickly, and a vigorous grower. Englemann's spruce is similar, but not as attractive. Holds branches to ground well in later life.

SPRUCE, NORWAY *(Picea abies)*—Dark green, short needles. Looks best sheared, since it is too fast and loose-growing to be attractive naturally. The dwarf varieties are best for home landscaping. Its large slender cones are widely used for Christmas decorations.

SPRUCE, RED *(Picea rubra)*—Dark-colored, native spruce. Less attractive than the white spruce, but it is one of the longest-lived trees. Very hardy, and yields spruce gum. Grows best on slightly acid soils.

SPRUCE, WHITE *(Picea glauca)*—Grows best in the cold climates and likes a slightly sweet soil. Beautiful blue-green color. Prickly, holds needles to the ground well, so is good for screens, windbreaks, Christmas trees and hedges.

Evergreens Worth a Try in Milder Sections

DOUGLAS FIR *(Pseudotsuga)*—Christmas tree growers have tried for a long time to grow this beautiful western tree in the Northeast with only fair success. Apparently a well-fertilized soil, as well as a sheltered spot, is necessary.

FALSE CYPRESS *(Chamaecyparis)*—Comes in many varieties and sizes, but only a few will grow in the North, and then only in sheltered locations.

FIR, WHITE *(Abies concolor)*—This blue-white western fir is a beauty and does well in a sheltered spot. Best when kept sheared, it is sometimes difficult to make it grow with a single top.

HEMLOCK, CAROLINA *(Tsuga carolina)*—Needs a sheltered area. The native (Canadian) kind is a better bet for the North, but both kinds tend to windburn badly.

JUNIPER *(Juniperus)*—Most junipers have trouble in zone 3 and the colder parts of zone 4. *Virginiana* is worth a try in zone 4.

PINE, AUSTRIAN *(Pinus nigra)*—Grows best in a valley or other sheltered location. One of the best of all the pines because of its dark color and majestic beauty, and because it holds its branches to the ground better than most pines.

SPRUCE, ALBERTA *(Picea albertiana)*—For some reason, this attractive, tight-growing spruce does well in western Canada, but thrives only in a sheltered spot in the Northeast.

SPRUCE, SERBIAN *(Picea omorika)*—One of the better ornamentals, with glossy green needles that are white underneath. It, also, has trouble except in protected locations. Some of the dwarf varieties are more satisfactory because they get snow cover protection.

Dwarf Evergreens

When people move to the North from a warmer climate, often they want to plant dwarf evergreens similar to the ones they enjoyed at their former home. But they soon discover that the North is rather limiting in its choice of dwarf landscape plants.

Mugho pine *(Pinus mugo)* is one of the hardiest and best dwarf evergreens for the North. A native of Austria and Switzerland, it grows well on cold, windswept mountain slopes and in poor soil. We've found that it stands dry summers, heavy snow loads, animal activity, and neglect better than any other attractive evergreen.

There are many strains, so you should pick the mugho pine that best fits your needs. Various varieties may grow from a few inches to 20 feet tall or more. For most modern homes, choose the low-growing kinds; but Colonial houses, A-frames, and chalets look better with varieties that grow at least 3 feet tall. Windbreaks, tall hedges, and large lodges call for the giant-growing types. Even the taller-growing kinds can be kept low by shearing.

Yews and junipers are tender, and only a few are really successful in cold areas. Of the many yews, the Japanese *(Taxus cuspidata)* variety is the most hardy. They come in many sizes, in

spreading and upright shapes, and produce red berries instead of cones. The English yew (*Taxus baccata*) is far less hardy, and most of the hybrids of the two, *Taxus media,* for instance, are not reliable either.

Even though they are fairly hardy, as I mentioned, the Japanese yews must be planted out of the wind. Every spring throughout the North they look brown and ugly unless they are growing in a sheltered spot. Even the native American yew (*T. canadensis*), which grows throughout the North Woods and is often called "ground hemlock," browns badly when moved from the shelter of the woods to an exposed location.

Of the junipers, the creeping varieties *(Juniperus horizontalis),* such as *Bar Harbor,* are the hardiest. The spreading kinds, *Andorra,* for instance, are moderately hardy, and the larger *Pfitzer* types are considerably less hardy. The slim, upright-growing kinds like the Irish juniper are the least hardy of all, although the Swedish strain does fairly well in sheltered spots.

Bristlecone pine, a western dwarf, lives for centuries in the high, cold mountains of California, but does well in the Northeast only when protected. It is an excellent tree for bonsai and for enclosed Japanese-type gardens.

Hardy Dwarf Evergreens

A surprising number of newly introduced, miniature-type evergreens do well in northern gardens. Many of these are freak forms of tall-growing, native evergreens—spruce, pine, cedar, fir, and hemlock. Others are cultured from the tangled growths called "witches' brooms," or northern mistletoe, that are often found on native trees.

Many of these evergreens are now available. Bird's-nest spruce, weeping pines and hemlocks, firs in all forms, creeping junipers and globe arborvitae have been introduced in such numbers and under so many names that the nomenclature of the tree world is hopelessly confused.

Most of the dwarf pines, arborvitae, and spruces have proven hardy in zone 3. The dwarf hemlocks, yews, junipers, and firs do well only when sheltered from the north and west winds.

Some of the most hardy dwarf evergreens commonly offered for sale are:

ARBORVITAE, PYRAMID *(Thuja occidentalis pyramidalis)*—A narrow, upright-growing white cedar, 12 to 14 feet high.

ARBORVITAE, GLOBE—*(Thuja occ. globosa)*—Round-shaped, in sizes that vary from 10 inches to 4 feet tall.

FIR, DWARF HUDSON BALSAM *(Abies balsamea hedsonia)*—Low-growing, compact balsam fir, about 2 feet tall. Slow grower.

FIR, KOREAN PROSTRATE *(Abies koreana)*—Creeping, flat-growing fir with foliage that is silvery colored underneath.

HEMLOCK, DWARF *(Tsuga canadensis nana)*—Low-growing hemlock with short needles. Slow grower.

HEMLOCK, SARGENT'S WEEPING *(Tsuga can. pendula)*—Weeping form of hemlock. Short, compact growth.

PINE, DWARF WHITE *(Pinus strobus nana)*—Compact-growing dwarf, spreading white pine with beautiful light green foliage.

PINE, SCOTCH UPRIGHT *(Pinus sylvestris fastigiata)*—Tall (to 12 feet), slender form of Scotch pine.

PINE, WEEPING WHITE *(Pinus strobus pendula)*—Impressive, slender-growing pine with graceful drooping branches.

SPRUCE, BIRD'S-NEST *(Picea abies nidiformis)*—Tight-growing, symmetrical evergreen, about 18 inches tall.

SPRUCE, CREEPING *(Picea abies procumbens)*—Low-growing, spreading type. Good for rockeries.

SPRUCE, WEEPING *(Picea abies pendula)*—Dwarf, slow-growing, drooping form.

SPRUCE, KOSTER WEEPING BLUE *(Picea pungens pendens)*—Tight-growing, weeping type with very blue foliage.

CHAPTER THIRTEEN

ORNAMENTAL SHRUBS

During the spring and summer the North Country is layered with rich green. After a long winter, this lush color seems a welcome blessing, and the flowers that add to it red, pink, lavender, yellow, orange, and white blooms in ever changing variety, give a whole new dimension to the landscape.

Although many of the beautiful shrubs from farther south are stubborn about setting up residency in the colder zones, there are many flowering shrubs that thrive here. Gardeners moving to zones 3 and 4 are likely to miss forsythia, dogwood, azalea, weigela, and laurel; but they soon learn that lilacs, flowering crabs, hydrangeas, honeysuckles, mock orange, viburnums, and shrub roses are lovely too. Sometimes newcomers are surprised to discover that certain plants behave differently in the North. Flowering quince gets only about a foot tall on our hilltop, and bridal wreath stops growing at about 3 feet; yet each blooms profusely and often for a longer period than where spring temperatures are warmer.

In addition to the beauty of the flowering shrubs, they provide berries and nesting places for birds, serve as hedges and snow fences, block out street noises or unpleasant views, and steer trespassers off lawns. Whether you're looking for a foundation planting that's perfect for a low, ranch-style house or a tall Victorian mansion, their wide range of heights—from a few inches to 20 feet or more—offer a variety of choice.

A wide range of blooming time ensures that if you plant only a few different kinds, one variety or another will be in blossom all summer. Some, such as roses and potentilla, actually bloom for most of the growing season, and others produce colorful blossoms in the spring and attractive berries or fruits later.

Because of wide variations of growing conditions in the North, it is difficult to say what will be entirely successful in each area, but the following lists and brief descriptions may be helpful.

SPECIAL SHRUBS FOR SPECIAL PURPOSES

For Wet Places
Arrowwood
Elderberry
Red Osier
Shadbush
Winterberry

For Dry Spots
Alpine Currant
Barberry
Buckthorn
Potentilla
Rugosa Rose

For Light Shade Spots
Shadbush (Juneberry)
Barberry
Privet
Mock Orange
Flowering Raspberry
Red Elder
Nannyberry

For Spots with Acid Soil
Azalea
Blueberry
Heath, heather
Holly
Rhodora
Rhododendron
Shadbush

Shrubs for Birds
Arrowwood
Barberry
Chokecherry
Cotoneaster
Elderberry
Highbush Cranberry
Honeysuckle
Nannyberry
Red Osier
Shadbush (Juneberry)

LILACS (Syringa)

No flowering shrub is more at home in the North than the lilac, which was one of the few ornamental bushes planted by the early settlers. The fact that many of these same lilacs are still blooming a century or two later speaks well for their hardiness and endurance, for they were seldom pruned, fed, or sprayed.

BLOOM SUCCESSION OF NORTHERN FLOWERING ORNAMENTALS

Spring

Shadbush
Flowering Crab
Old-fashioned Lilac
Beauty Bush
Honeysuckle
Daphne

Summer

Hydrangea A.G.
Anthony Waterer Spirea
Smokebush
Elderberry
Ninebark
Cranberry (Viburnum)

Early Summer

Lilacs
Mock Orange
Roses (continue for most
   of summer)
Potentilla (continue for
   most of summer)
Japanese Lilac
Bridal Wreath
Flowering Quince
Snowball

Late Summer—Fall

Hydrangea P.G.

If you have one of these old-fashioned lilac bushes that is looking somewhat past its prime, you can get it in shape again by spending a few hours cutting out the old wood in very early spring and spreading two or three pints of a complete fertilizer such as 5–10–10, or a few bushels of manure, around it.

All lilacs need sun, so if yours is not blooming well, it may be that shade trees have grown up and are crowding it, or a newly built structure is shading it. For the best blossoms in the North, nearly full sun is a requirement. Apply a few pounds of lime or wood ashes, too, if your soil is at all acid. To ensure annual bloom-ing, cut off the faded flower blooms soon after they've gone by.

Varieties

The old-fashioned, common lavender lilac is still one of the best. It is hardy, and the most fragrant of all varieties. Although it be-comes infected with leaf minor and mildew occasionally, Malathion can control the former, and Ben-Late, the latter.

French lilacs are grown throughout the North. They are less hardy than the old-fashioned, and some kinds suffer winter damage at higher elevations. Many are slow-growing and take longer to bloom than other lilacs, but their deep, rich colors are gorgeous and add much to the spring landscape. Most of these, too, are very fragrant.

The French lilacs are sometimes propagated by being grafted on privet or ash roots. When they are, they are quite unsatisfactory for the North, so make sure those you buy are on their own roots. Catalogs that sell own-rooted lilacs nearly always say so.

The late-blooming lilacs, many of which are of Canadian origin, are relatively new additions to the lilac scene and, while the color range is not as wide as that of the French lilac varieties, they are more hardy, more vigorous, and bloom even when they are only a few inches tall. They bloom heavily nearly every year, and the blossoms form all over the tree rather than only on top, as is the habit of many kinds of lilacs. Their fragrance is lighter than either the French or old-fashioned, but it is still pleasing and definitely "lilac." Most bloom at least a week or two later than the other lilacs, and on our hill they are often still in bloom on the Fourth of July.

The Japanese lilac is a hardy, blooming tree that does well in the North. It looks like a very large hydrangea in early to mid-summer, and, although its white blooms are showy, they are not fragrant. The tree is much the same size and shape as a full-sized apple tree, and it takes several years to bloom. The wood is rather brittle, however, and may break easily, so if you plant one, give it room to grow in a spot that's not too windy. It will, no doubt, thrive there for a century or more.

SOME LILAC VARIETIES WORTH PLANTING IN THE NORTH

Old-fashioned (Syringa vulgaris)

PURPLE or LAVENDER—The familiar country lilac with the sweetest scent of all.

WHITE—Very tall, with little fragrance.

French Hybrids

BELLE DE NANCY—Rose with white center. Double blooms.

CHARLES X—Red blooms. Single.

CONGO—Red, single blooms.

LUDWIG SPAETH—Deep purple, single blooms.

MADAME CASIMER PERIER—White. Double.

MONGE—Purple. Single.

PRESIDENT LINCOLN—Blue. Single blooms.

Dwarf Lilacs

DWARF KOREAN—Lavender blooms. Fragrant. About 3 feet tall.

MISS KIM—Bluish-pink. Very late bloomer. About 3 feet tall.

Late Blooming

AGNES SMITH—Clear white, large flower trusses. Outstanding.

HIAWATHA—Lavender.

JAMES MACFARLANE—Clear, true pink. Compact and heavy blooming.

NOCTURNE—Dark purple buds, maroon-red blooms.

POCAHONTAS—Pale lavender.

ROYALTY—Dark purple. One of the darkest Canadian lilacs.

RUTILANT—Light maroon-red. One of the tallest growing. 16 feet or more.

Tree Lilacs

JAPANESE—White, tall-growing, long-lived tree.

SHRUB ROSES

In recent years shrub roses have become very popular in the North. They resemble the wild or half-wild roses the early settlers used to grow, being hardy and fairly tall-growing. Most are pleasantly fragrant, and are also disease- and insect-resistant. They have some characteristics that make them even better than the older kinds. Their blooms, which are often double or semidouble, are larger, and they blossom throughout most of the summer and early fall.

Like all roses, they should be planted in good garden soil in a location where they receive full sun, and they must be given enough room to develop well. Since some grow 5 or 6 feet tall, they can get floppy, so a severe cutback should be done each year, either in late fall or very early spring, when the plant is dormant. Cut each stem to about a foot from the ground in order to get bushy, stocky plants with heavy blooms.

Shrub Rose Varieties

AGNES—Large, yellow, double blooms.

AMELIA GRAVIEUX—Bright red, double flowers.

BELLE POITEVINE—Large, pink, semidouble, with great fragrance. Vigorous, heavy-blooming bush. Often produces lots of rose hips.

GROOTENDORST—Clusters of very double, small, carnationlike blooms of great beauty. Not very fragrant, and only medium vigor.

GROOTENDORST PINK—Like the above, except a lovely pink. Not as vigorous or as long-lived as most shrub roses.

HANSA—One of the most vigorous of the shrub roses. Prolific bloomer with large, very fragrant, semidouble wine-red blooms over a long season. Also produces rose hips.

HARRISON'S YELLOW—An old-time variety that seems to live forever and is much beloved. Light fragrance, clear yellow semidouble blooms. Blossoms heavily, but only over a three-week period.

LILLIAN GIBSON—Tall-growing, vigorous bush, producing large, double, rose-pink blooms. Early, fragrant, and prolific.

MAGNIFICA—Quite similar to Hansa, but not as tall-growing.

NEARLY WILD—Beautiful apple-blossom pink, single roses in large numbers throughout the season. Makes a nice bush rose and is excellent for a hedge.

PERSIAN YELLOW—Yellow rose with clear, semidouble blooms. Moderately vigorous, but takes awhile to get established.

ROBIN HOOD—Red, single rose. Bush is vigorous, fairly hardy. Good for hedges where winters are not too severe.

RUGOSA—Old favorite rose, often grown from seed. Red or pink fragrant blooms, usually single or semidouble. The bush is vigorous, and the hips are valued for their vitamin C.

SIR THOMAS LIPTON—Clear white, large, semidouble blooms with a spicy fragrance. Bush is vigorous, tall-growing, and blooms heavily.

THERESA BUGNET—Fragrant rose-pink, double blooms of good form. Prolific, ever blooming, and grows tall. New and worthwhile.

ORNAMENTAL SHRUBS GENERALLY HARDY IN THE NORTH

ARROWWOOD *(Viburnum denatum)*—Medium-sized shrub that produces lots of dark-colored berries enjoyed by birds and animals. Grows well in moist places.

BARBERRY *(Berberis)*—Thorny plant that makes a useful barrier, but tends to get messy as it gets older. Needs hard pruning, and the deadwood should be removed often to keep it looking well. Good in dry, poor soils.

BEACH PLUM *(Prunus maritima)*—Attractive, small tree that produces an abundance of small, tasty fruits for preserves and wildlife. Seems to do best near the seashore.

BEAUTY BUSH *(Kolkwitzia amabilis)*—Tall bush with attractive pink flowers in spring.

BLUEBERRY, LOWBUSH *(Vaccinium augustifolium)*—Attractive covering for dry banks where the soil is acid.

BUCKTHORN *(Rhamnus frangula)*—Tall, slender-growing plant useful for hedges and borders. Needs careful pruning, or it gets thin at the bottom. Tolerant of salt, and produces an abundance of berries for birds.

BURNING BUSH *(Euonymus alatus)*—Tall bush with foliage that turns a brilliant pink-red in fall, making the plant look as if it were in full bloom. The dwarf *(E. alatus compacta)* grows only 2 to 3 feet tall. Both need a sheltered place in zone 3.

CHOKEBERRY *(Aronia)*—A medium-sized bush that produces wild cherrylike fruit suitable for birds.

CORALBERRY *(Symphoricarpos)*—A berry-producing, medium-low shrub. Useful where other shrubs do poorly.

CRANBERRY, AMERICAN (*Viburnum trilobum*) and EUROPEAN (*V. opulus*)—American and European cranberry are both beautiful border plants. The American grows taller and is the one to choose if berries are wanted for jelly. The European is more showy, but the fruits are bitter, and they stay on the bush all winter. Both are very susceptible to road salt. Dwarf kinds are grown mostly for foliage and rarely produce fruit.

CURRANT, ALPINE (*Ribes alpinum*)—An upright-growing, ornamental that produces attractive berries and is suitable for untrimmed hedges. Good for dry places.

DOGWOOD (*Cornus*)—Although flowering dogwood is not hardy, several of the native dogwoods are useful. The red-twigged variety (red osier, *Cornus stolonifera*) is quite ornamental, produces berries for the birds, and grows where it is too wet for other shrubs.

ELDERBERRY (*Sorbus*)—A good bird attractor and delicious for people as well. Grows well in moist places, but may become too rank for general home landscaping.

HONEYSUCKLE (*Lonicera*)—Tall-growing berry producer, with white, pink, or red blooms in the spring. *Zabeli* is a red-blooming variety that stays compact and neat. Susceptible to salt injury, however.

HYDRANGEA (*Hydrangea arborescens grandiflora* and *H. paniculata grandiflora*)—Both the tall-blooming P.G. and the medium-growing A.G. are excellent landscaping plants in the North. The former has pink-bronze flowers, and the latter, pure white blossoms that are often called "Hills of Snow." Both need a sweet soil and are susceptible to salt injury. One A.G., *Annabelle,* is a new variety with heavier blooms. The pink and blue hydrangeas are not hardy in the North.

MAPLE (*Acer*)—Several dwarf maples make ideal shrubs for the North. *Acer ginnala,* or *Amur maple,* grows 6 to 9 feet, has small leaves, and an excellent fall color. Mountain maple (*Acer spicatum*) and striped maple (*Acer pennsylvanicum*) are both native trees that grow well in light shade.

MOCK ORANGE (*Philadelphus*)—The old-fashioned sweet mock orange *(P. coronaris),* sometimes called syringa, is among the hardiest and best, but this may suffer light injury in exposed spots. The new doubles and dwarfs must be placed in favored spots only, but *Sylvia,* a new variety, is quite hardy and worth a trial.

NANNYBERRY (*Viburnum lentago*)—This native Viburnum has dark-colored berries and is good for a partly shaded border. Birds and wildlife both enjoy the fruit.

NINEBARK (*Physocarpus opulifolius*)—The dwarf-growing ninebarks are well shaped, upright-growing, flowering bushes that grow to 4 feet high. They make ideal hedges, either sheared or unsheared. Yellow-leaved varieties are also available.

POTENTILLA (*Potentilla*)—This low growing shrub is a favorite of northern gardeners because it is so easy to grow and blooms all summer.

QUINCE, FLOWERING (*Chaenomeles*)—Farther south this beautiful plant reaches a good size, but in the North it stays low because it dies back so much each year. It is very attractive, even so, and makes a good, spreading low bush or ground cover, with bright orange blooms over a long season.

RASPBERRY, FLOWERING (*Rubrus odoratus*)—Interesting and different, it grows native in many areas. Has purplish-pink flowers in midsummer, huge leaves, and edible fruits. Likes moisture and partial shade.

RHODORA (*Rhododendron canadensis*)—Small shrub that needs an acid soil, and is useful in semiwild plantings. Grows 3 feet tall, with rosy-purple flowers and bluish leaves. Very hardy.

SNOWBALL (*Viburnum opulus sterile*)—Tall bush with abundant blooms resembling popcorn balls in early summer. Hardy, but susceptible to aphids and other insects, so may need spraying.

SNOWBERRY (*Symphoricarpos albus laevigatus*)—A medium-sized bush producing white berries in late fall. Not particularly beautiful, but hardy, and grows in shady places and poor soil.

SPIREA (*Spiraea*)—The low-growing, pink-flowering Anthony Waterer and the taller-growing, white-blooming Bridal Wreath, and others do well in the North. The latter grows to its full height only in a sheltered spot. Both make nice flowering hedges and need little care.

SUMAC (*Rhus glabra*)—The native sumac is a tall-growing, attractive plant with brilliant red fall color.

WILLOW, ARCTIC (*Salix purpurea nana*)—This dwarf-growing shrub with tiny blue-gray leaves is good for edging beds and walks, and for rock gardens. Shear it to keep it neat.

ONLY IN SHELTERED PLACES

ALMOND, FLOWERING (*Prunus triloba*)—Beautiful, double pink flowers cover this bush in early spring. Needs a sheltered spot, and kills back badly, seldom getting more than 2 to 3 feet tall in the North.

ANDROMEDA (*Pieris floribunda*)—Mountain andromeda is one of the hardiest of the broad-leafed evergreens, but needs a warm spot and an acid soil. Keep out of wind and winter sun.

APPLE SERVICEBERRY (*Amelanchier grandiflora*)—Hybrid shadbush produces better flowers and larger fruits than common shad.

BUTTERFLY BUSH (*Buddlea*)—Hardy only in sheltered locations, but may die to the ground each winter even there. Blooms on new wood, however, so it still comes up and blooms each year.

COTONEASTER (*Cotoneaster*)—The spreading (*horizontalis*) kinds are the hardiest, but *C. acutifolia* is also quite hardy. All need a sheltered location, and seldom bloom and fruit heavily in zones 3 and 4.

DAPHNE (*Daphne*)—Both the February daphne and garland flower need an acid soil and a sheltered spot in the North. The Somerset daphne and the Somerset variegated daphne are both hardier and more tolerant of alkaline soils, but not as attractive or as readily available.

FORSYTHIA (*Forsythia*)—"Vermont Sun." is a new variety that looks promising in sheltered places in the North, but it is not yet available everywhere. The most common varieties grow well in the North, but suffer blossom bud injury during the winter and seldom bloom.

HEATHS (*Erica*) and HEATHERS (*Calluna*)—These do well only in an acid soil, sheltered from the wind, and with a good snow cover or heavy mulch all winter.

HOBBLEBUSH (*Viburnum alnifolium*)—Grows in protected, moist, shady areas. White flowers in spring.

HYPERICUM (*Hypericum*)—Low-growing plants with a variety of yellow blooms. Good in sheltered rock gardens.

LAVENDER (*Lavendula*)—Fragrant, herblike shrub that grows well even in cold places if sheltered from wind. Likes an acid soil.

OREGON HOLLYGRAPE (*Mahonia aquifolium*)—Hollylike plant that survives in sheltered valleys in the warmer spots of the North. Needs an acid soil.

PRIVET (*Ligustrum*)—None of the privets are perfectly hardy, but *Cheyenne* does fairly well in protected spots. *Amur* is hardy only in sheltered valleys in zone 4.

ROSES, TEA *(Rosa)*—Nearly all the tea roses, floribundas, polyan-
thus, and similar roses need protection throughout zones 3 and 4.
Hybrid perpetual roses are somewhat more hardy than tea roses,
however. Even the subzero types seem unable to survive without
being completely covered most winters. Most roses are grafted, so
make sure they are planted with the graft 2 inches under the soil.

Most gardeners feel it is a mistake to allow tea roses to bloom
unless the bush is growing well. If it is still weak and straggly, they
pinch off all forming buds until it becomes husky enough to support them.

ROSES, CLIMBING *(Rosa)*—Climbing roses need to be taken off
the trellis and covered up for the winter throughout the North.
Some rambler roses, such as *Excelsa,* are hardy and often survive
when merely laid on the ground and covered by the snow.

SMOKEBUSH *(Cotinus coggygria)*—Needs a sheltered location and
may suffer winter injury even then, during severe years. Blooms in
mid-to-late summer.

SNOWBALL, FRAGRANT *(Viburnum carlesii)*—This is somewhat tender
for northern gardens, but I see it now and then in sheltered spots.
Sweet, pink-white flowers in the spring.

WEIGELA *(Weigela)*—There are many hardy varieties of this plant,
but all need a sheltered spot. *Bristol Ruby, Rosalie,* and *Pink
Princess* seem to be among the hardiest, and *Vaniceki* is worth a
trial too.

WINTERING TEA ROSES IN THE NORTH

In spite of the difficulties, many gardeners persist in trying to grow
the spectacular tea roses in zones 3 and 4. Over the years I've met
a few northern growers who have had excellent success, but I believe
that Stanley Osborne gets the best results in overwintering them.
His rose bed is one of the most successful in northern New England.

Although it is protected from the north and west winds by the house and trees, and gets sun most of the day, it is, nevertheless, high in the mountains of northern Vermont where a short growing season and temperatures that plunge to —45° F make all gardening a challenge.

The Osborne Method

1. Just before the ground begins to freeze in the fall, cut back the tops to 2 or 3 inches above the ground. Pile soil over them to completely cover them.

2. Scatter a few mothballs every few feet to discourage mice.

3. Place a layer of straw several inches thick on top of the soil.

4. Cover the straw layer with several inches of boughs—spruce, pine, or fir.

5. In the spring uncover the plants carefully only after all danger of hard frosts is past. Do it in late afternoon, or, better yet, on a cloudy or rainy day so that any new, tender shoots that have sprouted on the roses will not be damaged by strong sunlight.

Styrofoam buckets are often used to cover up roses and other tender shrubs, but other methods are often more successful.

BROADLEAF EVERGREENS

Although I personally have had no success in growing azaleas and rhododendrons, some do grow well in the North. Many have been living in rather exposed spots for decades, and often no one remembers where they originated. The University of Vermont horticulturists are currently attempting to collect and propagate some of the more rugged specimens, since they seem much more hardy than the named varieties usually offered by the nursery trade.

Some azaleas being sold are fairly hardy, however, and they are being grown in sheltered spots all around the North Country. The Exbury hybrids are considered among the hardiest, and many have survived and still bloom after several winters of −30° F temperatures. The key to their success is probably the fact that they are sheltered from the wind and protected by a heavy snow cover.

Friends of ours who live near the 2,000-foot level in northern Vermont have a thriving azalea bed on the west side of their home, sheltered by a steep hill that is close to the building. The snowdrifts there are 7 or 8 feet deep most winters, and snow often lasts well into May—optimum conditions for northern azaleas.

Both commercial and hobby gardeners are doing experimental work with rhododendrons and azaleas, and some new, apparently hardy strains are being tested. Check with your local experiment station for their recommendations.

Hollies are somewhat tender, even in southern New England, and do best south of New York State. Although some new varieties have been developed in recent years, and a few have been grown successfully in sheltered spots in New Hampshire and Vermont, most northern gardeners have had disappointing results with them.

HIGHWAY SALT

Cold temperatures, wind, ice, and snow have always taken their toll of shrubbery. But northern gardeners must be aware of a more recent killer—the melting salt that is used on highways, driveways, paths, and parking areas.

Buckthorn, cotoneaster, elderberry, honeysuckle, lilac, potentilla, shrub roses, and spirea are fairly tolerant of salt if they are well established, but new plantings of these shrubs may suffer badly. Try to have your plantings situated well above the road or driveway if possible so that melting snow won't run on them in the spring or during winter thaws, and place them far away from the road—enough so snowplows won't pile layers of salt-soaked snow on them.

CHAPTER FOURTEEN

GROWING FLOWERS IN
THE NORTH

One couple, newcomers to our region, got so excited about the way their flowers flourished in the North that the entire village soon shared their enthusiasm. Although they were accustomed to gardening in a much longer growing season near Providence, R.I., their planting skill, combined with the North's cool days and dewy nights, helped them create a flower garden that was the envy of the community. Their plants grew so well that they had a tremendous surplus to give away, and, in addition, planted a large flower border at the village church. Those of us who had been grumbling about June frosts and September snowstorms began to wonder. Did we have something going for us in the North after all?

I am convinced that we have. From the first crocus and daffodils of spring to the chrysanthemums of fall, a wide variety of bulbs, annuals, and perennials flourish in zones 3 and 4.

ANNUALS

A small packet of annual flowering seeds is one of the best bargains left in the world. It contains, if you do everything right, an entire summer of colorful blossoms in the garden and many fresh bouquets as well. Small wonder the seed catalogs are so welcome when they arrive soon after New Year's Day!

Although annuals must be planted each year, they provide more continuous bloom than perennials, and once they begin to flower, will keep on throughout the summer. Since different varieties of many annuals, such as asters and zinnias, vary widely in the length of time from planting until blossoming, we read the seed catalogs carefully to get our money's worth. We choose only those kinds that promise early blooming.

Because the summer season is so short, we must start the seeds of many plants inside if we're to see their blossoms before frosts threaten. We start begonias and double petunias in January. In February we put in the regular petunias, giant marigolds, impatiens, ageratum, coleus, seed geraniums, snapdragons, vinca, and pansies; and in March or early April we plant most of the other annuals, such as asters, salvia, dwarf marigolds, alyssum, and dwarf dahlias.

We usually plant poppies, nasturtiums, four-o'clocks, sweet peas, and morning glories directly in the garden because they don't transplant well, and they grow fast and bloom early. Cosmos, zinnias, calendulas, and bachelor buttons also seem to do better if we plant them directly in the garden rather than start them inside. When they're grown in an indoor environment, cosmos and bachelor buttons become sprawly and leggy, and zinnias get disease easily if the days are cloudy and cool. These plants bloom somewhat later, of course, when the seed is planted directly outside, but if we choose early varieties, they still bloom through most of August, and can be covered up for the first frosts.

The seeds of most annuals should not be planted in the ground until the soil warms up and all hard frosts are over. Sweet peas are an exception, and should be planted early, practically as soon as the ground thaws, because their hard-coated seed takes some time to soften up. Soaking it for twenty-four hours before planting will help to speed up germination.

Help Them Grow Fast

Annuals need lots of encouragement if they are to grow fast and bloom early. Try to provide ideal growing conditions, just as you do for your vegetable plants. Give each variety the exposure it prefers. Most do best in a warm, sunny location that is sheltered from chilling winds. Impatiens, coleus, and begonias grow better in light shade, however, and they don't like cold, windy spots.

Annuals need a well-prepared, loose soil rich in well-rotted manure or compost if they are to grow fast and bloom heavily. Even if your soil is well enriched, you may want to add small amounts of liquid chemical fertilizer or manure dissolved in water to speed up growth, if the plants appear a bit sluggish. A friend of ours who has one of the most successful gardens anywhere around swears that manure tea is his secret. He applies it frequently and generously to all his plantings, and they respond magnificently.

Give each plant plenty of room to grow, whether you're putting in transplants or planting seeds directly in the ground. Space the transplants and thin the seedlings sufficiently so that they'll be able to grow quickly, to their full size, without being crowded by their companions. An impatiens plant may grow 15 inches or more in diameter, and a cleome or flowering cabbage even larger.

Keep the plants free from weeds and grass, because if they must compete, the flowers usually suffer badly in the battle. Even if the weeds grow for only a short time and are removed later in the season, much of the damage will already have been done. They will be straggly, weak, and never quite catch up.

Annuals need moisture to grow, not only when they are first set out, but whenever nature doesn't provide enough rain. They must grow very fast in the first part of the summer if they're to get in two or three months of blooming before frost.

Spend a few minutes every day picking off the faded annual blooms, so the flowers always look fresh. They want to go to seed, but if you let them, they will have accomplished their purpose in life and won't bloom any more. If you keep the flowers picked, they will reward you with blossoms all season. Experienced gardeners usually can't stand the sight of faded blossoms. If they're anywhere in the vicinity of one, they have an uncontrollable urge to pinch it off, whether they're in their own garden or a public park.

Frosts

Years ago, early June was the time to set out tomatoes, annuals, geraniums, and everything else that hadn't been planted out earlier. Most years, flowers could be planted in the cemetery on Memorial Day without fear that they would be frosted. The weather patterns seem to be changing in our part of the North, and now we often have cool, even freezing, weather in late May and early June, and occasionally a sizable snowstorm.

Although springs seem to arrive later, the time comes when we must transplant our flowers into the garden, or they won't begin to bloom well before they are frozen in September. Usually we treat annuals like the tender vegetables and plant them out sometime in early June when it "feels" right. Then we pessimistically stand by to cover them with pasteboard cartons and paper bags if the thermometer dips low on a clear night.

If a frost was unexpected and you didn't get things covered, you can often wash it off the following morning if the freeze was not too hard. Sprinkle all the new transplants and seedlings with cool, not cold, water before the sun hits them. Some plants, such as marigolds, are very tender to frost, and it may be hard to save them by using this method, but water often revives many that would otherwise be defunct.

Water may also be used to revive tender flowers that get a light frosting in the fall. Covering is a safer bet than trying to wash the frost off the next morning, however, so gardeners in the far North listen intently to the weather forecasts in late summer and discuss their plan of action if freezing weather should occur. Everyone gets busy when a frost seems certain, because an extra month can often be added to the flower season by covering up the plants.

Knowledgeable gardeners, when they're planting in the spring, sometimes group together those flowers that will need covering, such as marigolds, asters, and zinnias. Impatiens, geraniums, petunias, and snapdragons, however, are among those that are somewhat tougher and can stand a light frost unscathed.

Just as when you cover vegetables, utilize the heat accumulated in the ground to help keep your flowers from freezing, and cover them in such a way that you include patches of ground under the covers. This ground heat can often help the flowers get through the first two or three early frosts and enable them to flower during the three or four warm weeks that follow, if we're lucky.

To get the full benefit of ground heat, don't mulch any annuals that may be especially sensitive to fall frosts. Just as with beans, a layer of mulch serves as insulation, holding the heat in the ground and keeping it away from the plant tops.

When you cover your plants, be sure to uncover them the next morning, even if you expect another frost the following night. Plants don't appreciate the daytime cover.

In the North we must watch for sudden weather changes, some of them rather frustrating. We've carefully covered up our tender annuals on a clear, frosty night, only to have it rain heavily after midnight. Naturally, the soaked covers weighed down the plants and broke them all, causing far more damage than a frost would have!

Potted "Gift" Plants

Gardeners who receive chrysanthemums, poinsettias, azaleas, Easter lilies, cinerarias, and other gift plants often ask if they can save them after they have finished blooming and help them to bloom again. Although it is certainly possible to save chrysanthemums, poinsettias, and lilies, it is often not practical.

Poinsettias and potted chrysanthemums may be kept inside year round, or planted out for the summer, repotted in the fall before a frost, and taken inside. They will seldom bloom outdoors, since hard frosts always come in the North before their blooming season. They may bloom again as houseplants if given the proper amount of light. Both flower only as days get shorter, so they must get no artificial light or they will blossom much later, if at all.

Easter lilies may also be planted outdoors for the summer, dug in the fall, potted, and stored in a cool root cellar until January, when they should be brought into the light in a warm room. By giving them varying amounts of light, you may be able to speed up or delay them enough to get a few blooms for Easter, but it is unlikely that they will be as spectacular as the original.

Cinerarias blossom only once, and may as well be thrown out when they've finished their period of lovely blooms.

Most of these flowering plants are greenhouse specialties and not at all like geraniums, begonias, African violets, and gloxinias. Usually they should be treated as a one-time delight, like a bouquet of fresh flowers. Of course, if you're sentimental about the plant and have time to fuss, it's always fun to try for repeated blooms.

PERENNIALS AND BIENNIALS

Sometimes customers say, "I want to plant some perennials so I won't have to keep putting in annual plants." The implication is that, once they've planted the perennials, they can sit back for many years to come and simply enjoy their colorful garden.

Of course it's not that way at all. Gardeners who tend large perennial beds can easily make their gardening chores a full-time

occupation, with weeding, fertilizing, mulching, watering, removing the fading flowers, dividing plants, planting new acquisitions, and putting the garden to bed for the winter.

The results of all this work are well worth the effort, however. Hardy, flowering perennials are naturals for the North, and reward the gardener with a long season of colorful blossoms. From the early primroses and Virginia bluebells, to the fall asters and chrysanthemums, there are always a great many perennials in bloom.

Most, like the Oriental poppies and delphinium, have a short blooming period; but a few, the fernleaf bleeding heart and pansies, for example, bloom nearly all summer. Some, like the peony plants, live for many decades. Others—pansies, Sweet William, hollyhocks, foxglove, rudbeckia, and canterbury bells, although they are biennials, sometimes survive for several years. Daylilies come in so many different varieties that it is possible to have one kind or another in flower all summer.

Many perennials grow better in the North than they do further south. The delphiniums in our vicinity, for instance, often grow 8 to 12 feet tall, and hillsides become covered with lupin gone wild. Many alpine plants that couldn't possibly grow where it's warm grow beautifully in the mountains of the northern states and southern Canada. We notice during rare hot summers how quickly the blossoms fade and go by, and are thankful that usually the cool season keeps them blossoming for longer periods. The plants live years longer, also, where seasons are short and climates are cool.

Many perennials have a sun-shade preference and do best if planted under those conditions. Most like a sunny spot, but many others, such as hosta, lily of the valley, myrtle, primoses, daylilies and most ferns, do well in light shade. These shade-lovers, however, may also grow well in full sun in many cool mountain areas.

Unlike annuals, there is no need to get perennials to grow faster to see them bloom before frost. Their blooming patterns are already well established, although their blossoming season may differ from year to year as a result of varying temperatures. The fall-bloomers— anemones, asters, torch lily, white turtlehead, and most chrysanthemums, may bloom too late to be useful where seasons are extremely short.

On the other hand, a light frost doesn't hurt some perennials.

Delphinium grows to mammoth size in the cool northern climate.

Perennial flowers are usually cut down before winter.

Azure monkshood (*Aconitum fischeri*), Japanese anemone, Tatarian aster, chrysanthemum, coneflower, blanket flower, phlox, sage, viola, and others continue to bloom after several light frosts, even if they are not covered.

Fading flowers should be removed almost daily, for the sake of neatness and for other reasons as well. Some, such as pansies and canterbury bells, can be kept blooming for a much longer season when regularly picked. The blossoms of certain plants, such as phlox, lupin, and Oriental poppies, must always be removed promptly, before they go to seed, because their seedlings will usually be of inferior color, yet so vigorous they will crowd out the good, original plants.

You may want to let certain plants mature and drop some of their seeds, so new plants will continue to come up each year. Short-lived perennials and biennials, such as Sweet William and hollyhocks, are in this category. But be careful. Some heavy seed producers, like the forget-me-nots, lupins, and foxglove, can sow a whole garden and produce a bumper crop of colorful "weeds" that will crowd out the good plants. Whenever we forget to behead the foxgloves, we devote many hours the following summer weeding it out of the garden.

Northern gardeners sometimes disagree on whether or not to cut back their perennials for winter, and those who do cut them back don't always agree on how much. We compromise between cutting plants to the ground and removing only the fading flowers by cutting them to about 4 to 6 inches from the ground. The short stalks collect drifting snow, much as a snow fence would, and thus help protect the plants over the winter.

Cut perennial plants back severely only after their leaves begin to lose their green color and their energy returns to the roots. When you prune off a huge, bushy perennial that is still green and growing, it is weakened tremendously.

Winter Protection

Most perennials need no winter protection, but some gardeners like to cover their bed with rotted manure and compost, and then dump leaves over it after the perennials have been cut back in the fall. The leaves insulate the soil and roots from frost if the snow cover is light and the temperatures low. In spring the leaves can either be removed or left for a mulch that will gradually be converted to rich fertilizer by the earthworms and night crawlers. Year-round mulch doesn't hurt perennials a bit; in fact, we've found they flourish under it.

Many North Country gardeners live in chalets or homes on windy hillsides that have exquisite views, but lots of cold weather and wind. It is important, if you garden on such a hill, to choose only the most rugged varieties for your perennial plantings, and to buy them from nearby growers if possible. Hibiscus (mallow), lavender, many primroses, heaths and heathers are on the list of perennials that can't tolerate a cold, windy location, yet each grows well in a sheltered nook.

Because perennials depend on the soil for their insulation during the winter, planting them in raised beds, planters, and urns may not be wise. Even growing them on steep, exposed terraces or rock gardens that get a lot of wind often leads to excessive winterkill if there is insufficient snow cover.

Perennial Division

Winter often gets the blame for killing off plants that have actually been weakened by overcrowding. If perennial plants get too "uptight," they deteriorate and soon die. Shasta daisies and chrysanthemums must be divided practically every spring to keep them healthy. Daylilies, coral bells, phlox, primroses, iris, and most others should be divided every three or four years. Peonies, on the other hand, may need this attention only once every decade, or perhaps not even that often.

Like transplanting, dividing is best done early in the spring, before much new growth has started. Oriental poppies and peonies are the exception, and should be divided in August when they have finished blooming.

Chrysanthemums

One of my great joys, when traveling to southern New England during the autumn many years ago, was seeing huge masses of chrysanthemums in bloom. Only a generation or two ago, growing mums in the North was nearly impossible because most of the plants were not hardy enough to stand a northern winter, and almost none would bloom well before the onset of hard frosts.

Today, thanks to work done at experiment stations in short-season states, there are hundreds of varieties that will bloom in the North before the killing frosts, and we no longer must take a trip south to see the colorful mums. Many new varieties are hardy enough to overwinter if they are mulched with leaves, evergreen boughs, or similar insulation, and divided each spring so that the clump doesn't become too large. Even the choice, more tender kinds may be saved by potting and storing them in a cool, dark basement, cold frame, or unheated greenhouse.

Northern gardeners should choose only those varieties that bloom in August or, at the latest, the first week in September. Chrysanthemums bloom, as do poinsettias and Christmas cactus, only when the days get shorter, so don't plant them near an outdoor light. In fact, if you want to hustle up the blooms somewhat, you may put a heavy box or a black cloth over them every day at four o'clock in the afternoon, and remove it about eight in the morning. The unsuspecting mum will think it is autumn and begin blossoming even in late July if you wish.

Pinching, usually considered a necessary part of chrysanthemum culture if you want bushy, well-developed plants, must be done differently in the North. By pinching off the buds on the end of each stem, you encourage side branching and the development of a full-blooming plant.

Directions usually advise you to pinch several times about two weeks apart, ending about July 15. Northern gardeners have found, however, that July 15 is much too late. In the North, June 21, the longest day, is the cutoff time for all pinching. Any pinching or pruning after that date delays blooming, and some say that if you pinch late, each day after June 21 delays the blooming by several days.

A few northern growers claim that a lush garden plant can be produced by good spacing and adequate fertilizer and moisture. They maintain that mums bloom better and look nicer if they are not pinched at all. So "you pays yer money and you takes yer choice."

Bulbs

Most spring bulbs do very well in the North. The pretty little snowdrops and the yellow and purple crocuses are harbingers of spring, followed soon by daffodils, hyacinths, and tulips. They stand the winter cold well and bloom prolifically, even when they start early in the spring and get covered with snow.

Daffodils (narcissus) are among the most durable bulbs and, once planted, last almost indefinitely. You can renew the clumps and keep them blooming better by digging them up every eight or ten years, splitting up the bulbs, and planting them again 5 or 6 inches deep.

Tulips and hyacinths grow well, too, but northern growers sometimes have trouble overwintering the more tender hybrids, including the double varieties and parrot types of tulips. Crocus grows wonderfully in the North, as do snowdrops and grape hyacinths, and these are long-lived, too.

Although some tulips come up several times after planting, as a rule they don't hold up for as many years as daffodils. If you want to save them for another year, take them up after the stalks have died down, spread them out and dry them, and replant in the fall.

Summer flowering bulbs vary widely in hardiness. Some, such as gladioli corms, tuberous begonias, and dahlia tubers, are not really bulbs and are not at all hardy. They must be planted each spring and taken indoors each fall before hard frosts.

When planting the tender corms and tubers, choose those varieties that will bloom before the first frost. Some gladioli and dahlias bloom so late that they are impractical to grow in the North unless they are started early in a greenhouse or hotbed. The best way to get varieties that are suited for your climate is to buy your stock from a local grower. Bartering with a successful gardening neighbor may be an even better way, if his plants are disease- and insect-free. Both glads and dahlias multiply rapidly, and gardeners are usually eager to dispose of their extras.

Most lilies are winter-hardy and seem to thrive in a northern climate. We have had very good luck growing them, and were surprised to find that such beautiful flowers are so easy to grow. The tall-growing *Imperial* strains are hardy and especially beautiful, as are the *Mid-Century Hybrids, Regals, Olympics,* and *Fiestas.*

The popular *Madonna Lily,* which must be planted quite shallow, is one variety that often doesn't overwinter well. A few tropical hybrids are somewhat tender, too, even though they are planted deeper. Plant lilies in well-drained, sandy garden soil at the depth suggested in the planting directions, and mulch the bed with leaves, composted bark, or evergreen boughs each fall, as an extra precaution.

Cannas, the showy plant that blooms in late fall, although it is widely planted in parks in southern New England, blossoms too late to be practical in the North. Some gardeners occasionally plant a few of the tall varieties that have mammoth, rusty-red leaves for an impressive background, and they don't much care whether they bloom or not. Others start the tubers inside in late winter in order to get flowers.

Tender Perennials

Many long-lived, tender perennials are grown in the North. Geraniums, fuchsias, tuberous begonias, and ivies are all popular plants for beds, window boxes, planters, hanging baskets, and similar landscaping. Some people treat them as annuals, allowing them to be killed by frost in the fall. They grow or buy new plants each spring. Others take them inside before freezing weather and keep them as houseplants in the winter, then put them outside again each summer. This isn't a bad idea, since the expense of buying new plants each year is considerable.

Overwintering the plants in sunny windows or under grow lights is ideal, but very few places have enough warm, sunny windows, and grow lights are expensive to buy and operate for the entire winter. Farm families sometimes keep geraniums and other plants in barn windows where the livestock can keep them warm.

The traditional way works well for overwintering geraniums, begonias, and other houseplant types that you want to save. Let the plants nearly dry out, then store them in a basement or a cool, but not cold, place. Placing them on a dirt floor seems to work best, but it is not necessary. The plants should be cut back when they're brought inside, both so that a new, bushy plant will result when it begins to grow in the spring, and also so that the resting plant will not dump a lot of messy leaves. Check the plants from time to time and water them sparingly whenever it is necessary. Never let them become completely dry.

When you take them out in the spring, don't move them into wind or direct sunlight too fast, since their pale new growth will be tender. Set them, instead, where they will get indirect lighting for a few days, and expose them to direct sun and outdoor weather only after all the leaves and sprouts have turned a rich green.

CHAPTER FIFTEEN

HEDGES FOR THE NORTH

Over the years I have planted a great many hedges for customers, for a wide variety of reasons. Some wanted them to slow the northern winds, or stop the drifting snow, or attract birds. Others wanted to block out noises or smells from a street, factory, or farm, or to shut off an unpleasant view. Some people simply liked hedges. Some wanted more privacy, and more than once I've been asked to plant a tall cedar hedge between people and their "unpleasant" neighbors. On one memorable day two neighbors argued violently as they measured the lot, read survey maps and deeds, and eventually both called their lawyers, who came and paced back and forth as I planted.

Usually, however, a hedge is a friendly barrier, and it always appears far less offensive than an iron spike fence. It may be started with small plants and gradually grown to an effective size without anyone being aware of it.

"Hedge" is an all-inclusive term for a wide range of borders. They may be sheared very tight, reminiscent of an English formal garden, sheared lightly to look natural, or left completely unsheared and informal, like a country hedgerow. They may be tall, short, flowering, fruit-producing, evergreen, deciduous, thorny; and they may be created of annual or perennial plants.

Since many common hedge plants are not hardy in the North, gardeners often get off to a bad start when they order plants from a catalog from further south. Boxwood, holly, and most privets are usually poor choices. Yews and some varieties of barberry suffer severe damage, too, in exposed places.

Better choices, instead, for gardeners in zones 3 and 4 are, for a sheared evergreen hedge, arborvitae (white cedar), white spruce, or balsam fir. For a deciduous hedge, good plants include ninebark, honeysuckle, potentilla, buckthorn, lilac, shrub roses, hydrangea, viburnum, and spirea. For sheltered places, hemlock and Japanese yew develop into beautiful evergreen hedges, and euonymus, flower-

A *hedge* serves as the boundary marker for the lawn, cuts off an unpleasant view, and blocks a great deal of wind and drifting snow.

ing quince, and Cheyenne privet make good deciduous hedges. Although the Scotch, white, red, and Austrian pines are sometimes used for hedges, their foliage is so coarse and they grow so fast, it is difficult to keep them looking nice.

It is important to choose the right planting material, not only to ensure the survival of a hedge, but also to get the results you want with the least maintenance. Some hedges require a great deal of pruning to keep them looking nice, but others need very little. Some grow all summer, while others grow only in June. Some get tall, others stay short, and some are inclined to get quite messy and die back a great deal as they become older.

Many northern hedges are made of plants dug from the wild. Spruce, balsam fir, and the native arborvitae (white cedar) are most commonly used. Although spring is the best time for planting a hedge, many evergreens can be planted in September, and the white cedar may be dug and moved during a rainy week practically any time all summer.

Usually it is better not to plant anything larger than 3 or 4 feet in height, since the smaller trees catch on faster and are easier to shape. White cedar is a notable exception. They may be moved, even though they've grown to 10 feet or more in height, since their fibrous roots make it easy to dig a good ball of soil. In fact, cedars of nearly any size can easily be sheared to a beautiful shape.

If you want a hedge that will always stay low, you must start with small plants, whether you dig your own or buy them. Plant them about 2 feet apart if you want a tight dwarf hedge.

If you want your hedge to grow six feet or more in height, on the other hand, set the plants 3 feet apart or perhaps more. Lilacs, for instance, may be planted 5 feet apart and still grow into a closely formed hedge. It will, no doubt, look a bit sparse for the first few years, but after that it will quickly become full.

Follow the directions for planting in chapter 11 and those for shearing in chapter 12, keeping in mind, especially, that all hedges must be kept narrow in snow country. Wide hedges collect tremendous loads of snow some winters, and the weight can crush and break them. Hedges with flat tops often suffer the same fate. Keep the tops rounded or slightly pointed so that snow loads will slip off easily. Never set the plants more than one tree wide, either. Narrow hedges are more practical, anyway, since they waste less land, and if an individual tree dies or gets broken off accidentally, it is much easier to replace it.

To force an evergreen hedge to grow tight, shear the trees just as they begin to make their most active growth. In northern New England this is likely to be sometime during late May and the month of June for yews, spruce, firs, and pines. Hemlocks and cedars grow a few weeks later, in late June and July. Although yews often make a second growth in late summer when they're grown farther south, they seldom do in the North.

For a tight-growing hedge, clip honeysuckle, ninebark, rose, barberry, and similar deciduous hedges throughout the summer whenever they need it. Lilacs, hydrangea, viburnum, and other tall-growing shrubs are usually grown as informal hedges, and may not need trimming for many years. Whenever they need pruning, do it just after they finish blooming, so they will have time to set new flower buds for the following year.

Although it is best to choose trees or shrubs that will create the effect you want with the least work, practically any tree may be used as hedge material and kept sheared to any size. Some may require much more work and patience than others, but even sugar maples can be sheared into a low, tight hedge if you are persistent.

WINDBREAKS

Evergreens make the best windbreaks and snow traps; and American arborvitae and spruce are two of the best trees for this purpose. They are most likely to hold their branches to the ground and grow thick and tight naturally. Pines grow faster, but tend to lose their lower branches as the trees grow older, as do balsam firs. Hemlock makes a good windbreak, but it is slower growing and becomes windburned when planted in an exposed place.

Windbreaks should be as tight as possible. Cut off the tops of young trees as soon as they are planted, and clip back the side branches a little for the first two or three years to help the hedgerow to grow tight. Plant them in a place where they will get full sun, if possible, for sunlight is necessary for their best growth and to make them grow tight. Screens and hedges that are shaded by other trees will be loose, and the wind will sneak through them.

Whenever a hedgerow windbreak is planted, it also acts as a snow fence, piling up a deep drift of snow on both sides of it. If the hedgerow is being hit by winds sweeping across a wide open area, a great deal of snow may accumulate at times; and until the trees grow quite tall, they may be covered with snow each winter. These deep drifts are not only hard on the hedgerow itself, but they can be tough on anything else in the area. Plant your windbreaks so that drifts won't form on paths you must keep open, on delicate trees and shrubs that can't stand the weight of the snow, or on small outbuildings that may get buried. The deep drifts are ideal, however, for covering strawberries, asparagus beds, perennial borders, and other nonwoody plants.

If having a hedgerow close enough to your house to be beneficial will result in a snow pile on valuable plantings or interfere in any other way, you may plant a second hedge 20 to 50 feet behind the windbreak to serve as a snow trap. This hedgerow doesn't need to be as tight as the windbreak. In fact, it can be quite loose, just as a wooden snow fence is. Tall-growing, deciduous shrubs and small trees are good for this purpose providing their growth habit is bushy and they don't break easily under snow loads. Wild plums, chokecherry, thorn apple, lilacs, honeysuckle bushes, and many wild trees, as well as most evergreens, make fast-growing, hardy

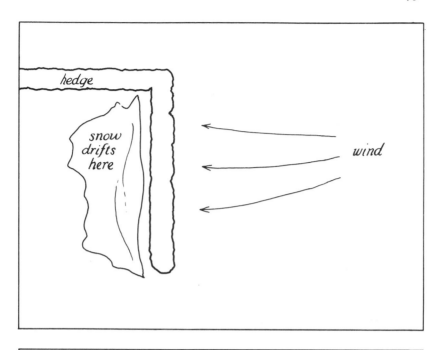

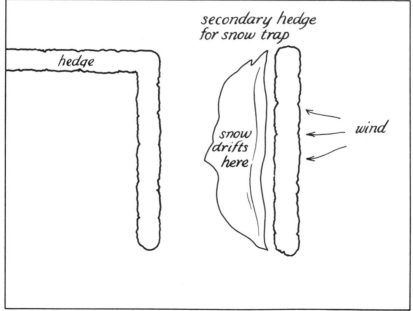

Position *windbreaks* and *snow traps* to protect buildings and plantings from north and west winds.

snow traps. Be sure to plant them in the path of the predominating wind and drifting snow you mean to slow down, so the snow will land exactly where you want it.

Windbreaks and snow traps not only provide comfort and protection for people where we live, work, and go to school, but they are also useful to shelter animal barns and yards, garages, machinery sheds, driveways, and as protection for tender plants and shrubs. Strategically placed, they can save a great deal of snow moving and shoveling. During the spring and summer, they also provide nesting places for hundreds of insect-eating songbirds that are a welcome addition to any home and garden.

EVERGREEN HEDGE PLANTS

ARBORVITAE *(Thuja occidentalis)*—The eastern white cedar is one of the best, fast-growing, tight hedges in the North. It may be a bit coarse for a formal planting, and often browns a bit during the winter, but it is easily sheared, and kept to any size you want. It needs a sweet soil to grow well, so if yours is at all acid, lime must be applied every few years. Responds beautifully to fertilizer and adequate watering. Grows later in the season than most evergreens, so shear it once or twice in midsummer.

BALSAM FIR *(Abies balsamea)*—The fragrant balsam tree shears well and shapes beautifully into a tight hedge that is not prickly. It grows well only where winters are very cold, so is ideal for zones 3 and 4. It may need a little lime on extremely acid soils. Give it one to three shearings in early summer when it is growing fast.

HEMLOCK, CANADIAN *(Tsuga canadensis)*—When left alone, the native hemlock will grow to a giant tree, but it can be shaped easily into a lacy, tight, beautiful hedge that will look nice year round. Unfortunately, it is apt to brown badly over the winter if exposed to wind. It grows fairly slowly and thrives on acid soils. Shear two or three times in midsummer, since it grows later than spruce, fir, and pine. It is one of the few hedge plants that still looks nice when it must be grown in light shade.

PINE, MUGHO *(Pinus mugo)*—The dark green, beautiful mugho pines are natives of Switzerland and Austria, so they feel perfectly happy in the northern mountains. Cold winds and poor soils don't distress them. They come in many varieties that grow from dwarf rock garden height to 20 feet or more tall, so choose the kind that will grow to the height best suited for your needs. Even the tall-growing ones can be kept low by hard pruning, and the dwarfs will need their sides sheared or they will eventually get too wide. Shear two or three times, early in the summer.

PINE, OTHER *(Pinus)*—Any hardy pines may be made into a hedge, but most are a bit coarse and grow so vigorously that it is difficult to keep them sheared indefinitely. The Austrian *(Pinus nigra)* is slower growing and therefore probably the best choice; but it sometimes has trouble growing on a cold, windy mountain top. Shear two or three times in early summer.

SPRUCE *(Picea)*—White spruce *(Picea glauca)* or Black Hills spruce *(Picea glauca densata)* are the best choices for hedges. Red spruce *(Picea rubra)* may also be used, but is less attractive. Colorado spruce *(Picea pungens)* is somewhat coarse and comes in so many different shades of green and blue that a hedge of it often looks mottled. For an impenetrable, prickly barrier, however, it is ideal. Shear two or three times in early summer.

Dwarf spruce, such as bird's-nest *(Picea abies nidiformis)*, can be used to make a very low hedge that needs only the sides sheared to look well. Since they are very expensive, they are often not practical for large plantings.

LOW AND MEDIUM DECIDUOUS HEDGES (to 8 feet tall)

BARBERRY *(Berberis)*—The thorny barberry was once planted a great deal in the North, but is not as common today because as the bushes get older they get very messy unless they are renewed by being cut to the ground every few years. It is still used as a thorny barrier, but there are better choices. Shear whenever it grows out of shape. The Japanese barberry *(B. thunbergii)* is the hardiest and best for the North. Many of the newer, better kinds have difficulty overwintering.

CRANBERRY, DWARF *(Viburnum opulus nana)*—There are many dwarf cranberries of various heights. This is the lowest-growing one. It is neat, has colorful red foliage in the fall, and is good for low edging. Shear only to keep it from getting too wide.

EUONYMUS, DWARF *(Euonymus alatus compactus)*—Good, low-growing shrub for an informal, untrimmed hedge. Excellent pink fall color. Shear only to keep it from getting too wide. Plant in a sheltered spot if you live at a high elevation.

HONEYSUCKLE *(Loncera claveyi)*—The dwarf bush honeysuckle can be grown naturally, or it may be sheared to a tight, formal hedge with persistent clipping.

HYDRANGEA, A. G. *(Hydrangea aborescens grandiflora)*—Excellent for an untrimmed, flowering hedge. May be kept shorter and more compact by cutting back heavily each fall. Clip to keep from getting too wide. Needs lime for best growth and the whitest blooms.

LILAC, DWARF *(Syringa)*—Several of the dwarf lilacs make neat, low-growing northern hedges. *Miss Kim,* a pink bloomer, is among the better ones. It blooms best in a slightly sheltered location. Since it is a slow grower, prune it as little as possible.

NINEBARK, DWARF *(Physocarpus)*—One of the best choices for a clipped, formal hedge in the North. It is widely used in Canada. Shears beautifully, and holds its foliage long into the fall when it becomes deep red. Shear every few weeks all summer.

POTENTILLA *(Potentilla)*—For informal, low-flowering hedges this is a neat beauty. It comes in various shades of yellow and white, and blooms profusely all summer until frost. We like *Klondike,* a rich, yellow, upright-growing one; but many of the newer varieties are also good. Cut back whenever necessary to keep it in a good shape; and cut back severely every five or six years to renew the bush.

QUINCE, FLOWERING *(Chaenomeles)*—A bit spreading for a good hedge plant, but it is so colorful and so long-blooming, it may be worthwhile to shear it into place. Prune off winter injury in spring, and clip sides to prevent its getting too wide.

ROSES, HARDY *(Rosa)*—Several of the hardy shrub roses, especially those of the rugosa family, make good hedges. I would avoid the notorious multiflora rose, because it is much too rank-growing; and I've found that the much-recommended *Nearly Wild* rose and *Robin Hood* both need sheltered locations.

Hansa, Belle Poitevine, Agnes, Grootendorst Red, Harrison's Yellow, Magnifica, and *Sir Thomas Lipton* all make good rose hedges, mixed or all one kind. Prune in early spring or late fall to keep them from getting too tall and flopping over.

SPIREA *(Spiraea)*—Many of the spireas make good flowering hedges. The white-flowering *Bridal Wreath* is a good one that reaches 3 to 6 feet tall. *Anthony Waterer,* especially the new, improved, red-blooming strains, make a colorful, low-growing hedge. Prune right after blooming for best results.

TALL-GROWING, DECIDUOUS HEDGES
(over 8 feet tall)

BUCKTHORN *(Rhamnus)*—This plant, especially the named variety, *Tallhedge,* has been recommended very much in recent years. Some of the hedges I have seen in the North looked rather spindly at the base and not very attractive, though even they were good producers of berries for birds. Prune hard in summer for tightest growth.

CRANBERRY, HIGHBUSH *(Viburnum)*—For purely ornamental reasons, the European cranberry *(V. opulus)* is the prettiest. For edible, though sour, fruit, choose the American Highbush *(Viburnum trilobum).* Both are vigorous, have large clusters of white flowers, and red berries that hang on all winter. Prune only in early spring to shape and to keep the height even.

EUONYMUS *(Euonymus alatus)*—Cork tree, or burning bush, is good as a specimen, and it also makes a showy hedge. The foliage turns a brilliant pink in the fall. It tends to winterkill at higher elevations, and needs a protected spot in zone 3. Prune early in the spring.

HONEYSUCKLE *(Lonicera)*—The bush honeysuckle is a hardy, color-ful bush that makes a good hedge, either sheared or unsheared. We like *Zabeli* best because it doesn't get as tall and straggly as many of the older kinds. The bush is showy, both with its small but abundant red blooms and red berries that are much loved by the birds. Prune directly after blooming, and continue to shear it all summer if you want a tight, formal hedge.

HYDRANGEA, P. G. *(Hydrangea paniculata grandiflora)*—The showy flowers of this bush brighten the landscape in late fall when few other bushes are in bloom. The white flowers turn first a rich pink, then a colorful bronze. It is effective as a tall, untrimmed hedge, but it may be cut back late each fall to keep it at a low or medium height if you like it better that way. Even if it's pruned hard at that time, it will still bloom heavily the following year. Needs lime on most soils for best bloom, and will do fairly well in light shade.

LILAC *(Syringa)*—Lilacs are a natural tall hedge for the North. The old-fashioned lavender pink *(S. vulgaris)* is still the favorite and the most fragrant. The Canadian varieties are the most vigorous. They bloom when they're very young, and all over the bush, even close to the ground. The pink *James MacFarlane* is our favorite for a hedge. All lilacs need full sun and a sweet soil well supplied with nutrients.

These plants are only a few of those that may be used for hedges. I have seen crabapples, peonies, thorn apples, dahlias, geraniums, Chinese elm, chrysanthemums, and many other plants shaped into useful and beautiful hedges and borders.

CHAPTER SIXTEEN

L A W N S

One of our friends, an avid golfer, became thoroughly tired of mowing the lawn every week when she wanted to be on the golf course, so she planted her whole lawn to low shrubs, wild flowers, ground covers, and ferns. Although the new lawn was not completely work-free, it certainly was a great time saver, and looked rather nice. She never felt quite comfortable with it, however. She missed being able to go barefoot, and sunbathing on the lawn and she always was a bit nervous about having wildlife, including snakes, so close to the house.

It used to be a status symbol in some places, to have the biggest and greenest lawn in the neighborhood. Now, with increased food and energy costs, many people are planting part of their lawn space to vegetable gardens, fruit orchards, and berry patches. Others, like our friend, who have become discouraged over the many valuable hours they spend each year mowing, trimming, raking, and tinkering with the lawn mower, are now planting shrubs, ground covers, and perennials.

Although lawns may shrink in size and grow fewer in number, they don't seem about to become obsolete, because they are a valuable addition to any landscape. They accentuate a house, furnish a place to play and relax, and give an "open" feeling, and, in keeping them looking nice, provide lots of good outdoor exercise. They also provide protection against creepy and crawly things.

Fortunately, grass thrives in cool climates, so growing and maintaining a lawn in the North is often easier than it is further south, where lawns tend to dry and get brown in the summer unless they are watered heavily. Cool, dewy nights and rains that are usually adequate and often overabundant ensure that dried-up lawns in August and September are, in most of the North, fairly rare.

But nothing is perfect, and lawns have other problems here. Heavy snow or layers of ice can encourage diseases that kill grass, as the keepers of golf greens well know. Moles work vigorously un-

285

der the cover of snow, in soil that often stays unfrozen all winter. Weed seeds blow freely for great distances and grow with vim and verve.

Vigorous-growing, deep-rooted grasses are a necessity in the North Country. Not only do they help ensure winter hardiness during years with little snow, but their roots are able to reach down for adequate moisture from the lower soil, even during dry summer seasons. They also offer the best competition against quack grass, crab grass, dandelions, and other weeds.

STARTING A NEW LAWN

New lawns may be started either by seeding or by planting mats of started turf. Turf is a great deal faster, but it is also more expensive. If you do it yourself, the labor for each is about the same, since the ground must be well prepared and smooth whether you plant seeds or put in turf.

In much of the North successful lawns can be planted any time from spring until fall. It is possible to seed a lawn even during droughts if sprinklers are operated for most of the day. The best months to plant lawns, however, are April, as soon as the ground thaws, May, early June, and September. Grass seed germinated after October 1 may not root deeply enough to stand a hard winter.

The area to be planted or sodded should be tilled thoroughly enough to get rid of all the dirt clods. If clay or rocks present a problem, enough topsoil should be added to give the grass a good chance to grow well. Rake or grade the entire spot to eliminate any depressions that will collect water and freeze. Snow is a good insulator for lawn grasses, but ice is not. A gentle slope away from the house is best. If the earth heaves up where you shovel the snow from a path during the winter, it won't catch a puddle of water to freeze if the lawn is properly graded.

GRASS VARIETIES

Buying grass seed can be a puzzling chore. Many lawn mixtures are completely unsuited for the North. Some of the cheaper ones contain mostly annual grasses that look nice the first season, but die

over the winter. Perennial grasses are necessary for a lawn anywhere, and hardy perennial grasses are essential for the North. So
avoid all the bargain mixes and choose only those from reliable
companies.

The most common grasses recommended for good lawns are the
various bluegrass varieties, red fescue, and perennial ryegrass. Good
lawn seed mixtures usually contain various quantities of these
grasses, plus small amounts of annual rye and other fast-growing
annual grasses that will give the lawn a quick start. Choose the
mixtures that contain a high proportion of bluegrass and fescues if
you can find them, because even the perennial ryegrass is not re-
liably hardy in the North.

Clover is added to some mixtures. We like it because it makes a
tough, sturdy lawn, but some people object to the white blooms
and the bees they attract, the patchy look of clover during droughts,
and the stain it leaves on clothes.

Bent grass is found in some mixtures. It is low growing, unattractive, and has a lot of winter injury. Although it is often chosen
as a cover for closely mown putting greens, it is a good one to avoid
for the northern home lawn. Meadow bluegrass *(Poa trivialis)* is
usually chosen for lawns that are in shade for much of the day. Although it tolerates shade, its growth is weak, and it doesn't hold
up well under heavy use. Mixed with red fescue, it produces a
passable-looking lawn, however, especially if the spot is not too
dry.

Plugs (clumps) of zoysia grass are often advertised in garden
magazines and newspapers. This grass does well in the warmer
parts of the country, but is completely unsuited for northern lawns.
Zoysia grows very slowly and turns brown for the winter, even in
the South. It must be started from plugs, an expensive and laborious
project, and it is almost certain to be winter-killed in most of the
North.

PLANTING A LAWN OF WILD GRASS

Our own lawn and the lawns belonging to most of our neighbors
were started in quite a different way. We planted no seed. Instead,
the wild hay already growing was simply mowed closely for a year
or two. Small amounts of fertilizer were added each spring and

late summer, and the weeds were kept sprayed with an herbicide. The close mowing controlled the coarse, tall-growing hay; the herbicide spray eliminated the dandelions, thistles, plantain, and other weeds; and the feeding encouraged the short, soft grasses to take the place of the more weedlike varieties. The resulting lawns are not only winter-hardy, but they also stand heavy use and dry weather.

We think our lawn looks as nice as any that's been planted. It is now over forty years old, it never gets additional watering, and it burns slightly only under the most extreme drought conditions, which come very rarely in the North.

If you want a similar lawn around a newly built home, you may want to plant wild grass seed instead of lawn seed. Rototill and rake the soil smooth, and persuade some neighboring farmer to part with a few bushels of chaff from his haybarn floor. Scatter this mixture of seeds, chaff, and bits of hay over the lawn area.

Then, unless it rains right away, water the area heavily so the seed will not blow away. In the cool weather of early spring or fall you won't even need to rake in the seed, but in late springs that are dry, cover the area with hay or straw.

After the lawn is well established, it should be mown closely to get rid of the hay grasses, and sprayed with an herbicide suitable for lawns.

Although wild grasses are more vigorous and grow better than exotic varieties, no grass will do well on clay, subsoil, sand, gravel, or rock. If your lawn must be grown on any of these, spread several inches of good topsoil first, rototill or harrow, and rake it smooth, just as you would if you were using the most expensive mixture.

LAWN CARE

Both old and new lawns need occasional care. We spend very little time or money on our lawn, however. We mow whenever it needs it—twice a week when it starts to grow in the spring, once a week the rest of the summer, and even less often if the weather is dry. Fertilizers come in many kinds and prices, but we usually choose an inexpensive mix that contains 5 percent nitrogen and 10 percent each of phosphorus and potash. We spread it every spring just as the grass begins to grow vigorously, at the rate of about 20 to 25 pounds every 2,500 square feet (50 feet by 50 feet). The application is repeated during a rainy week in late August or early September only if the lawn isn't looking good. Overfeeding means faster growth and more lawn mowing, and I certainly don't need that.

Spreaders made especially for that purpose are the best way to apply fertilizer, but I still use the old-fashioned way of flinging it off the tips of the fingers, the same way that grain is planted by hand—and it works fine. Be sure to put on extra amounts of plant food around trees, hedges, and shrubs so that the heavy feeding needed by these trees won't make the lawn look thin in those areas. Feed as evenly as possible, however; you don't want to leave globs of fertilizer that may burn the grass or other plantings.

Rake up the needles under pine trees whenever they accumulate enough to be obvious, and cut the lower branches of large trees if they shade the lawn too much. Northern lawns need at least a half day of sun to look really nice.

Many northern soils are rather acid, so, unless a soil test shows otherwise, it is a good policy to add lime to your soil every three or four years. Fifty to 80 pounds of ground limestone every 1,000 square feet (20 feet by 50 feet) may be applied any time during the summer. Wait for one good rain before putting on the lime after you have applied fertilizer, however, or the lime may prevent the fertilizer from working.

If you burn wood, you may use those ashes on your lawn instead of lime. Scatter one or two buckets over each 1,000 square feet every winter.

Cut lower branches off large, dense-leaved shade trees so sunlight can reach lawn grass for at least part of the day. Most lawn grass does poorly in heavy shade.

We try to keep the mower sharp and mow the lawn when the grass is dry, clipping it close enough to look nice, but not so tight that it looks as if it has been lathered and shaved. We leave clippings on the lawn after each mowing, unless they are unusually heavy, because they help fertilize the lawn.

The soil may pack so hard that rains don't penetrate well, and grass roots grow poorly on lawns tramped down with heavy traffic or where there is a lot of clay in the soil, especially if chemical fertilizers are used exclusively. Aeration with a roller studded with sharp spikes usually remedies this situation. Organic gardeners firmly believe that leaving the lawn clippings and spreading shredded leaves, compost, manure, or peat moss on the lawn each fall encourages a multitude of earthworms that take care of the aeration adequately.

FALL CARE

The subject of when to stop mowing in the fall always gets a discussion going among northern gardeners. We always used to stop mowing about Labor Day; we felt that in our cold climate a good layer of grassy mulch helped to protect the sod over the winter. Watching our neighbors merrily mow through September with no bad consequences changed our ways, however. The lawn not only looks better when it is kept mowed later in the fall, but it needs far less raking in the spring. Although we no longer stop mowing on Labor Day, we still don't mow too late in the fall. A couple of inches of top growth is good protection for winter.

We've learned to remove carefully as many maple and other leaves in the fall as possible. Heavy mats of leaves may smother the grass and kill it. We add some leaves to the compost pile, but leave a few on the ground and run over them with the mower. It is easier than raking them, and, when they've been shredded, they rot quickly and add valuable fertilizer to the lawn.

REVITALIZING AN OLD LAWN

Old lawns are sometimes rebuilt and reseeded with much labor and great expense, when a little lime, fertilizer, aeration, proper mowing, and weed spraying would give better results. If your lawn is in poor condition, you may need to give it more than the usual amount of fertilizer. Do not increase the amount used, however, but give it an extra application about a month after the first. Be sure to water it thoroughly after applying chemical fertilizers if it doesn't rain. Chemical fertilizer demands moisture to dissolve, and if none is available, it will pull water from the soil around the grass roots and burn the plants.

LAWN PESTS

When the snow melts in spring, gardeners are often distressed to find holes and underground tunnels, sometimes of extensive size and in large numbers. Both the tunneling moles and the skunks that dig holes are after large insects, particularly the white grubs that live in turf most of the year. These emerge in early summer as May beetles, or June beetles, depending on where you live, and bang on screens and windows on hot summer nights.

Cats, mole traps, and poison baits may be used effectively against the moles. Mothballs and similar repellents are somewhat effective against skunks. Getting rid of the grubs is the most effective control, but easier said than done. Lead arsenate and DDT were the old remedies, but both are forbidden today, with good reason; and chlordane, the most recommended chemical in recent years, is so severely restricted that it is now difficult to buy. Imidan, malathion, methoxychlor and pyrethrum have all been used with some success, but none remain effective for long.

Snow mold is a severe disease in some areas, and shows up as pink or gray mold over dead patches of grass when the snow melts in the spring. It is particularly bad on golf courses because it strikes bent grass. It can affect other grasses, also, especially those that have been mown too close in late fall. Snow mold can be controlled if you avoid planting bent grass initially, and don't make the last cutting too late in the fall or cut the grass too short the last time.

Control of insects and disease on lawns has been more difficult in recent years because many of the chemicals that gardeners used previously are now illegal. Check with your extension service to see what is now being recommended for your problem.

CHAPTER SEVENTEEN

GROUND COVERS AND VINES

Because it grows so well in the North, grass is probably the best ground cover for most spots, and many gardeners are perfectly happy with it. There are some places, however, where grass won't grow well. The area may be too shady, too rocky, or too steep; or it may be impractical for other reasons. Perhaps you simply don't wish to mow the lawn, or you want to add some color or variety.

Gardeners who have moved to northern New England from areas only a hundred miles farther south are often surprised at how different the growing situation is. Heavy snows and cool summers make a rich variety of alpine plants possible in the North that would have trouble farther south; and some plants that were horrible weeds in the more southern regions behave beautifully farther north. Others that were good garden or ground cover plants in Connecticut take over whole hillsides in Maine. Some shrubs that ordinarily grow 4 or 5 feet tall on Long Island remain a few inches tall in zone 3.

Consequently, transplanted gardeners must sometimes give up preconceived notions of what a ground cover should be. In most windy spots in the North, those that are common elsewhere do poorly: pachysandra, candytuft, ivy, heathers and heaths, euonymus, cotoneaster, and many other spreading dwarf shrubs.

Fortunately vinca (myrtle or periwinkle) thrives in the North, as do ajuga and crown vetch. Many other plants not usually thought of as ground covers offer northerners further choice. Some of the same plants that nature uses to cover bare spots work well. Abandoned northern pastures, for instance, are often covered with pasture juniper *(Juniperus communis)* or potentilla. Roadside banks sometimes bloom profusely in July with lupins escaped from flower borders. Many cemeteries are surrounded by either escaped myrtle or daylily plants.

Because cool weather encourages rank weed and grass growth, it is difficult for noncompetitive ground covers to become established.

Winds that continue to blow from the dandelion season until fall are full of weed and grass seed of one kind or another; and most will outgrow a newly planted ground cover if they have a chance. Northern gardeners who plan elaborate rock gardens often decide to abandon the idea when they see the amount of hand weeding it involves.

It's important to choose the right ground cover for your specific location—a variety that is hardy and will grow well without too much work and expense, yet is not so pushy that it will pose a problem in later years.

Some covers—woodbine, for instance—may be planted among grass and weeds and will still compete successfully; but most plants need a good chance to become established. It is usually best to clear out the competition by tilling the topsoil very well or by using an herbicide such as Round-up. Then fertilize and add humus if the soil is poor. Mulch the new plants with shredded bark or other weed-free material to prevent the soil from washing if the area is a slope.

Some weeding will probably be necessary the first year to keep the planting clean until the ground cover takes over. Some land-scapers use an herbicide, Princeps (Simazine), to keep grass out of myrtle beds. Although Princeps is safe to use on myrtle after the plants have been established a couple of months, it is not safe to use with many other ground covers, and even with myrtle, mugho pine, and juniper, directions must be carefully followed.

Ground covers are not like lawn grass, and are not suitable for walking, so provide paths if there is likely to be foot traffic through your plantings.

You may not be able to buy all of the ground covers listed here

Most ground covers winter best on slopes (A), because flat areas and pockets (B) may collect water and ice that will kill the plants.

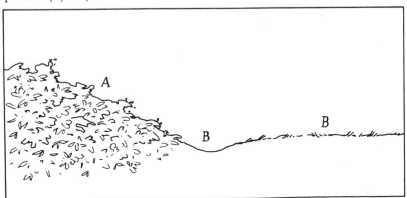

at your local garden center, but you may be able to dig some on your property or that of a friend. Club mosses, ferns, Canadian yew, and pasture juniper are often found in large masses in the wild. Garden catalogs list a great variety of ground covers, but it is best not to be too hasty in writing out a check. Try to find something you like that is growing well in your area in a location with the same sunlight, soil, and wind exposure as yours.

GROUND COVERS

AJUGA *(Ajuga)*—Sometimes called bugle, this vigorous, creeping perennial grows only a few inches high with green or bronze-colored foliage. Grows best in the sun, and competes fairly well with grass. Try to keep it out of gardens and lawns, because it will take over.

BLUEBERRY, WILD *(Vaccinium angustifolium)*—Good cover for a sheltered, sunny area of acid soil. Eight or more inches tall, with shiny foliage, tasty fruit, and good fall color.

BEARBERRY *(Arctostaphylos uvaursi)*—Rich foliage, white flowers, and red fruit make this a good bet for banks and slopes. Six inches tall. Likes poor, acid soil.

BUNCHBERRY *(Cornus canadensis)*—Five inches tall. Nice foliage, white flowers, and orange-red fruit. Sometimes difficult to get started, and is not too competitive. Likes acid soil and light shade.

CLUB MOSS *(Lycopodium)*—Several of the evergreen club mosses are natives and grow well in the North. *Ground cedar (L. complanatum)* at 2 inches, is the most dwarf; *Princess pine (L. selago)*, the tallest, reaches about 8 inches; and *Reindeer moss (L. obscurum)* is a vine. All like light shade and a sheltered location.

CROWN VETCH *(Coronilla)*—It may take a little work to get this one started in the North, but it does very well once it gets going. It has attractive pink and white flowers, and competes well with grass and weeds.

DAYLILIES *(Hemerocallis)*—In sun or light shade, daylilies are useful for holding banks and in other difficult areas. Usually the older,

more vigorous varieties are more successful than the newly introduced, large-flowering hybrids; but all are useful and attractive.
They need almost no care to look nice for years. Weed and grass
killers may be used around them to eliminate unwanted plant
growth.

EUONYMUS *(E. fortunei)*—Good vine or ground cover in sheltered
places only, in zones 3 and 4. *Coloratus* is one of the most satisfactory varieties, with a rich green color in the summer and a
beautiful red-purple color in the fall.

FERNLEAF BLEEDING HEART *(Dicentra exima)*—Useful for areas
where you'd like a somewhat fancy cover and where grass and weed
competition won't be tough. Spreads fast, and has pink, heart-
shaped blooms all summer.

FERNS—Ferns are often overlooked as ground covers, but there are
so many native varieties in the North that some are perfect for
every spot—sunlight and deep shade, wet, dry—and some even grow
in water. If you dig up wild ones, collect yours from a spot with
conditions similar to those where you plan to grow them.

GOUTWEED *(Aegopodium podagraria)*—Also called "Bishop's Weed"
and "Snow on the Mountain," it becomes a vicious weed in many
places. In spots where it can be kept under control, however, its
variegated white and green foliage looks nice.

JUNIPER *(Juniperus)*—There are many varieties of this versatile
shrub, and they range from one inch in height to sizable trees. The
creeping kinds make the best ground covers, and are hardy. *Bar
Harbor* is one of our favorites. *Wilton Blue Rug* is beautiful, but
needs a well-protected spot, and we have found *Andorra* to be
rather susceptible to disease and short-lived. Native pasture juniper
is less attractive than many of the named kinds, but more hardy
and healthy.

LILY OF THE VALLEY *(Convalaria)*—For moist, shady spots and
slightly acid soils, this fragrant beauty is a good choice. Long-lived,
needs no care, yet its shiny foliage always looks nice.

MUGHO PINE *(Pinus mugo)*—The lower-growing strains of this hardy shrub are among the best ground covers. Rich, attractive green, and long-lived, it grows well in poor soil. It is expensive, needs weed and grass control, and grows rather slowly, though a single bush can eventually cover 100 square feet.

MYRTLE *(Vinca minor)*—For partly shady spots, myrtle, with its shiny green leaves, blue flowers, and healthy appearance, is a favorite ground cover. It will grow in full sun on cool northern slopes as well as in shade. May get out of control and creep into lawns and other plantings; or winter-kill if covered with water or ice for extended periods. Don't be alarmed if some springs it appears dead. Usually it revives in a few days and looks fine. Grow only on a slope if possible, to prevent winter-kill.

PACHYSANDRA *(Pachysandra)*—This 6-inch high plant needs a most sheltered location to do well in the North. It prefers a moist, slightly acid soil and no wind.

PHLOX *(Phlox sublata)*—Dwarf, or creeping phlox, is used often for mass plantings further south, but in the North it has a difficult time competing with weeds and grass, so needs frequent weeding. It is often used for colorful rock garden plantings, however. Plants must be divided every few years to keep them looking well, and should be mulched over winter if snow cover is sparse.

PLANTAIN LILY *(Hosta)*—A tall (1 to 2 feet) large leaf plant, *Hosta* provides foliage and slender white or lavender flowers in shady areas. Its many varieties include both green and variegated foliage. Likes moist soil and is ideal for perennial borders or massed with ferns along shady paths.

QUINCE, FLOWERING *(Chaenomeles japonica)*—Further south this is a medium-sized bush, but in the North, regular winter dieback keeps it to ground-cover size. Spreads over a wide area by layering, and its orange flowers are in bloom for several weeks.

SEDUM *(Sedum)*—There are many sedums of varying heights, from those that creep low along the ground to a foot or more tall. Some of them get very weedy, so you'll want to be careful about where you plant those kinds. *S. spurium* is one of the best, but even it needs to be kept under control.

Snow-in-Summer *(Cerastium tormentosum)*—Gray-white foliage with pure white blooms. This is a nice low-growing plant in rock gardens, but not competitive enough for large plantings.

Thyme *(Thymus)*—Many of the low-growing varieties are suitable for planting in terraces, rock gardens, and along stone paths. Most need hand-weeding and some kind of grass control to keep them healthy and looking nice.

Yew *(Taxus)*—If you choose this plant, use only the low-growing, spreading varieties that can cover a large area, but it may take many years. Japanese Spreading Yew *(Taxus capitata cuspidata)* is hardiest and best for sunny places; and Canadian yew *(Taxus canadensis)* is better for the shady spots. Both must be grown out of the wind.

VINES

Northerners have a good choice of hardy vines, and in the protected shelter of a house the list of possibilities grows even larger. They may be flowering or berry producing, such as clematis, honeysuckle, or bittersweet; vigorous, such as woodbine, or massive, like Dutchman's pipe. Vines may be grown along fences as a substitute

Vines growing on fences may be substituted for hedges where space is limited or heavy snows may crush down a hedge.

for hedges, to shade porches or gazebos, or to provide privacy. Often they are merely decorative.

If a perennial vine presents too many problems with overgrowth or seems unsightly during the winter, an annual vine may be a better choice. Morning glory, flowering bean, sweet pea, or wild cucumber grow to full size even in the North's short season.

Most of the hardy vines need no special care in the North. Some of the more tender, such as rambler roses and all but the hardiest grapes, should be taken off their trellis for the winter and laid on the ground. In the coldest areas it may be wise to cover them lightly with evergreen boughs.

Perennial Vines

BITTERSWEET *(Celastrus)*—Bittersweet needs a sheltered spot in the coldest areas. Only the female plants produce the orange-red berries that are so decorative, so both males and females are needed for pollination.

CLEMATIS—These are half hardy. Where we live they die to the ground each winter, but come up and bloom on their new growth each summer. *Ernest Markham* (red), *Comtesse de Bouchard* (pink), *Jackmani* (purple), and *Ramona* (blue) are all good, reliable ones. Many other varieties are more delicate and often short-lived. Clematis vines grow best on the east side of the house, where they get only the morning sun, in a sweet soil (pH of 7.0) and with a mulch of grass clippings over the roots all summer.

DUTCHMAN'S PIPE *(Aristolochia macrophylla)*—This vine usually gets off to a slow start, but then grows rapidly and vigorously. Its huge leaves in large numbers make a dense screen that can effectively cover a porch, gazebo, or play area. The name comes from its uniquely shaped flowers that hide amongst the foliage. Plant it on the sheltered east or south side of the house, or in another protected spot.

GRAPE *(Vitex)*—Hardy varieties such as *Beta* and the wild grapes make good heavy vines for covering arbors, trellises, and bowers.

HONEYSUCKLE *(Lonicera)*—Most of the common varieties of the honeysuckle vine are not hardy in the North, but a new kind, the *Dropmore,* which originated in western Canada, is very dependable. It has showy orange-red flowers and blooms over a long season. Many nurseries now carry it.

HOPS *(Humulus lupulus)*—This long-lived perennial vine often dies to the ground each winter in the North. It can still cover a large trellis and often the side of a small house before summer is over.

IVY *(Hedera)*—Most of the ivies are not hardy in the North, and even the sturdy Boston ivy and Wilson ivy need the sheltered location of the lower elevations, where they are often used to cover brick and stone buildings.

RAMBLER ROSES—The old-fashioned rambler roses *(not* the climbing roses) are still available at some nurseries and are good for

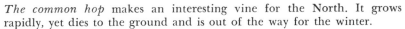

The common hop makes an interesting vine for the North. It grows rapidly, yet dies to the ground and is out of the way for the winter.

trailing over fences and walls. They are quite hardy, but it is best to lay them down on the ground for winter.

WISTERIA—This vine will grow quite well in sheltered places in the North, but seldom blooms enough to make it worth planting.

WOODBINE *(Parthenocissus quinque folia)*—Often called Virginia creeper, this is useful as a hardy, fast-growing vine, and a ground cover that will quickly cover not only the ground, but rocks, junk, and stumps. It will climb up trees, wires, and creep into lawns and gardens as well; so, although it can be a multipurpose plant in its place, use it carefully.

RECOMMENDED READING

Northern Gardening

Gardening in the Upper Midwest by Leon Snyder. University of Minnesota Press

Vegetables and Herbs

A to Z Hints for the Vegetable Gardener by the Men's Garden Clubs of America. Garden Way Publishing

Crockett's Victory Garden by James Crockett. Little, Brown and Co.

Down-to-Earth Vegetable Gardening Know-How by Dick Raymond. Garden Way Publishing

Health, Happiness and the Pursuit of Herbs by Adele Dawson. The Stephen Greene Press, Viking Penguin, Inc.

Intensive Gardening Round the Year by Paul Doscher, Timothy Fisher, and Kathleen Kolb. The Stephen Greene Press, Viking Penguin, Inc.

Putting Food By by Ruth Hertzberg, Beatrice Vaughan, and Janet Greene. The Stephen Greene Press, Viking Penguin, Inc.

The Rodale Herb Book: How to Use, Grow & Buy Nature's Miracle Plants edited by William H. Hylton. Rodale Press

Root Cellaring: The Simple No-Processing Way to Store Fruits and Vegetables by Mike and Nancy Bubel. Rodale Press

Stocking Up edited by Carol Hupping Stoner. Rodale Press

Fruits and Nuts

Fruits and Berries for the Home Garden by Lewis Hill. Garden Way Publishing

Handbook of North American Nut Trees edited by Richard A. Jaynes. (Available from the editor. Write to him at 13 Broken Arrow Road, Hampton, Ct. 06518)

Greenhouses and Solar Equipment

The Passive Solar Energy Book: A Complete Guide to Passive Solar Home, Greenhouse, and Building Design by Edward Mazria. Rodale Press
Sunspaces: How to Live With Your Attached Greenhouse by Peter Clegg and Derry Watkins. Garden Way Publishing (Available Summer 1987)

Flowers

Growing Flowering Perennials. USDA Bulletin +G91
How to Grow Annuals, Revised Edition, by Ann R. Robbins. Peter Smith

Landscaping

Landscape Plants for Vermont. Extension Service, University of Vermont, Burlington, Vt. 05405
Pruning Simplified, Updated Edition, by Lewis Hill. Garden Way Publishing
Trees and Shrubs for Northern Gardens by Leon C. Snyder. University of Minnesota Press

PUBLISHERS OF GARDEN BOOKS

BROOKLYN BOTANIC GARDEN, 1000 Washington Ave., Brooklyn, NY. 11225
DOVER Publications, Inc., 31 E. Second St., Mineola, N.Y. 11501
GARDEN WAY Publishing, Schoolhouse Road, Pownal, Vt. 05261
A. A. KNOPF, Inc., 201 E. 50th St., New York, N.Y. 10022
MACMILLAN Publishing Co. Inc., 866 Third Ave., New York, N.Y. 10022

The Stephen Greene Press, Viking Penguin, Inc., 299 Murray Hill Pkwy., East Rutherford N.J. 07073

Rodale Press, Inc., 33 E. Minor St., Emmaus, Pa. 18049

United States Department of Agriculture, Publications Division, Office of Communications, Washington, D.C. 20250

University of Minnesota Press, 2037 University Ave. S.E., Minneapolis, Minn. 55414

SEED COMPANIES

W. Atlee Burpee Co., 300 Park Ave., Warminster, Pa. 18974

DeGiorgi Co. Inc., P.O. Box 413, Council Bluffs, Iowa 51502

Johnny's Selected Seeds, P. O. Box 2580, Albion, Maine 04910

R. H. Shumway, Seedsman, P.O. Box 1, Graniteville, S.C. 29829

Stokes Seed Co., P.O. Box 548, Buffalo, N.Y. 14240

Otis Twilley Seed Co., P.O. Box 65, Trevose, Pa. 19047

Vermont Bean Seed Co., Garden Lane, Bomoseen, Vt. 05732

Vesey's Seeds Ltd., P.O. Box 9000, Charlottetown, Prince Edward Island, Canada, C1A 8K6

See also Farmer, Henry Field, Gurney, and J. W. Jung in the nurseries list.

ORIENTAL VEGETABLES FOR WINTER GARDENS

Herbst Brothers, 1000 N. Main St., Brewster, N.Y. 10509

Kitazawa Seed Co., 356 W. Taylor, San Jose, Calif., 95110

Sunrise Enterprises, P.O. Box 10058, Elmwood, Conn. 06110-0058

Thompson and Morgan, P.O. Box 1308, Jackson, N.J. 08527

NURSERIES

Alexander's Nurseries (Blueberries), 376 Wareham St., Middleboro, Mass. 02346

Farmer Seed and Nursery, P.O. Box 129, Faribault, Minn. 55021

Henry Field Seed and Nursery Co., 407 Sycamore St., Shenandoah, Iowa, 51602

Dean Foster Nurseries, P.O. Box 127, Hartford, Mich. 49057

LE JARDIN DU GOURMET (European vegetables and herbs), P.O. Box 44, West Danville, Vt. 05873

LOUIS GERARDI NURSERY (Nut trees), Rt. 1, Box 143, O'Fallon, Ill., 62269

GURNEY SEED AND NURSERY CO., 1224 Page St., Yankton, S.D. 57078

J. W. JUNG SEED CO., 335 S. High St., Randolph, Wis. 53956

S O U R C E S   O F   F R U I T   T R E E   S C I O N S
F O R   G R A F T I N G

WORCESTER COUNTY HORTICULTURAL SOCIETY, 30 Elm St., Worcester, Mass. 01608

E V E R G E E N   S E E D L I N G S   N U R S E R I E S

MUSSER FORESTS Inc., Rte. 119 North, P.O. Box 340, Indiana, Pa. 15710-0340

VAN PINES, 7550 144th Ave., West Olive, Mich. 49460

WESTERN MAINE NURSERY, Fryeburg, Maine 04037

Accelerated growth, 23–24
Acidity (pH) of soil, 30–32, 153–154,
    172–173, 221
Apples
    spring frost threat, 36
    ripening inside, 38
    varieties, 123–125, 127–128
    See also Trees and tree crops
Artichokes, 196–197
Asparagus, 15, 193–195 (ill., 194)

Barley, 212
Beans
    culture and varieties, 103–104
        (ill., 103)
    mulching, 26, 94
    thinning, 88
Beets
    culture and varieties, 106
    in raised beds, 34, 90
    mulching, 25, 93
    thinning, 88
Berries
    juice, 151–152 (ill., 152)
    mulching, 154–155
    soil conditions, 152–154
    transplanting from wild, 155–156
    See also under individual berries,
        by name
Blackberries, 31, 156–160 (ill., 157)
Blueberries, 31, 172–174 (ill., 173)
Broccoli
    culture and varieties, 112
    in raised beds, 90
    mulching, 25, 93
    starting seeds, 40
Brussels sprouts
    culture and varieties, 112
    mulching, 25, 93
    starting seeds, 40
Buckwheat, 210
Bulbs. See under Flowers: perennial
    and biennial
Butternuts, 97, 185, 187–190 (ill., 188)

Cabbage family
    culture and varieties, 112–113

    in raised beds, 90
    mulching, 25, 93
    starting seeds, 40
Canada, 4, 119
Carrots
    culture and varieties, 107
    in raised beds, 34, 90
    mulching, 25, 93
    thinning, 88
Cauliflower
    culture and varieties, 113
    in raised beds, 90
    mulching, 25, 93
    starting seeds, 40
Celery, 40, 85, 110
Chard
    culture and varieties, 110
    in raised beds, 34, 90
    mulching, 25, 93
Cherries, 126, 175
    See also Trees and tree crops
Chicory, 100, 110
Chinese vegetables, 100–101, 113
Chrysanthemums. See under Flowers:
    perennial and biennial
Climate
    benefits of cold, 15
    growing season, 5, 12, 16, 23
    microclimates, 21–22 (ill., 21)
    northern conditions, 4 (ill.), 5, 16
    planting zones, 4–5
    See also under regions, by name
Cold frames, 44–45 (ill., 44), 98–100
    (ill., 99)
Cold spells
    affect new growth, 10
    bud damage, 10–11
    dangers of, 9
    protecting grapes, 183
    protecting strawberries, 166–168
        (ill., 167)
    protecting trees, 140–143 (ill., 142)
    root damage, 10
Compost, 26–28 (ills., 27, 28), 59
Corn
    culture and varieties, 104–105
    field (grain) corn, 211–212

in raised beds, 34
mulching, 26, 93
spring frost protection, 35
thinning, 88
Cucumbers, 34, 85, 92, 94, 115
Currants, 15, 31, 151, 168–170

Eggplants, 25, 34, 40, 117–119 (*ill.*, 118)
Elderberries, 15, 38, 170–172
Endive, 100
Espaliers, 130 (*ill.*)
Evergreens
    best species, 216, 235, 240–242
    broadleaf species, 260
    cutting back, 237–240 (*ills.*, 237, 238)
    dwarf varieties, 243–245
    fertilizing, 220–221
    planting, 218–220
    salt susceptibility, 224–225
    topiary, 240
    winter protection, 236 (*ill.*)

Fall frosts
    dangers of, 8–9
    protecting against, 8, 37–38, 118
        (*ill.*), 183
Fertilizers
    berries, 152–153
    correct application, 29–30, 80–81
    grapes, 179–180
    liquid, 30, 131–132, 180
    ornamentals, 220–221
    seedlings, 67
Flowers: annual
    frost protection, 264–265
    growing conditions, 263–264
    keeping "gift" flowers, 266
    starting seeds, 262–263
Flowers: perennial and biennial
    bulbs, 272–273
    chrysanthemums, 271–272
    cutting back, 268–270 (*ill.*, 269)
    dividing plants, 270–271
    growing conditions, 268
    in landscaping, 216
    in northern climate, 15, 267 (*ill.*),
        268 (*ill.*)
    snow and ice damage, 14
    tender species, 273–274
    winter protection, 270
Frost, 36
    See also Fall frosts; Spring frosts
Fungicides, 65

Gardening
    fall planting (for spring crops), 87–88

garden location, 18–21, 77–78
    in winter, 98–102 (*ill.*, 99)
    planning, 86–87
    raised beds, 34–35, 89–91 (*ill.*, 90)
    successive planting, 87
    superstitions about, 3
    thinning, 88–89
    watering, 31, 33
Gooseberries, 15, 31, 151, 168–170
        (*ill.*, 170)
Grains. *See* individual species, by name.
Grapes
    frost protection, 183
    location of planting, 178–179 (*ill.*,
        178)
    mulching, 25
    pruning, 180–182 (*ills.*, 181, 182)
    soil conditions, 31, 179–180
    varieties, 184
    winter protection, 184
Grass (lawns)
    in northern climate, 15, 285–286
    lawn care, 288–291 (*ill.*, 289)
    pests, 291
    snow and ice damage, 14, 285
    starting a lawn, 286, 287–288
    varieties, 286–287
Greenhouses
    attached to house, 50–51
    cover materials, 53–54
    for winter gardening, 98
    heat collection and retention, 51–53
        (*ills.*, 50, 52, 53)
    heat in, 57–58
    homemade, 54–55
    orientation, 49–50 (*ill.*, 49)
    underground, 55–56 (*ill.*, 55)
Ground covers
    best species, 292, 294–297
    competition from weeds, 292–293
    growing conditions, 293 (*ill.*)
    snow and ice damage, 14
Growing season. *See under* Climate

Hazelnuts (filberts), 185, 191–192
Hedges
    deciduous species, 275, 276, 281–284
    evergreen species, 275–276, 280–281
    maintenance needs, 276, 277
    planting, 276–277
Herbicides, 86, 92
Herbs, 86, 199–204 (*ill.*, 200)
Horseradish, 195–196
Hotbeds, 45–48 (*ill.*, 46)
Hot caps (and like devices), 70–74
        (*ills.*, 71, 72, 73)

Intensive gardening. *See under* Garden-
    ing, raised beds

Juneberries, 36, 174–175

Kale, 87, 91, 100
Kohlrabi, 93, 114

Landscaping
    deciduous species, 216, 218, 221,
        224–225, 228, 234
    energy saving, 221–222 (*ill.*, 222)
    fertilizing, 220–221
    in cemeteries, 217–218
    in wet places, 234
    perennial flowers, 216
    planning, 216–217 (*ill.*, 217)
    planting, 218–220 (*ill.*, 219)
    selection of species, 215–216
    shade trees, 226–227 (*ill.*, 227)
    See also Evergreens; Hedges; Shrubs;
        Trees and tree crops
Lawns. *See* Grass
Lettuce
    culture and varieties, 111
    in indoor gardens, 101
    in raised beds, 34, 90
    location in garden, 86
    mulching, 25, 93
    starting seeds, 40
Lilacs, 216, 247–251

Manure
    dried, 29
    for berries, 152–153
    rotted vs. fresh, 29
    types of, 29
    when to apply, 80
    See also Fertilizers
Melons
    culture and varieties, 115–117 (*ills.*,
        114, 116)
    in raised beds, 34
    mulching, 25, 94
Midwest, 4
Midwinter thaws, 11–12
Millet, 210–211
Mulch
    berries, 154–155, 164–165 (*ill.*, 164),
        166
    materials, 93–94 (*ill.*, 93)
    potential danger of, 25, 33, 94
    purpose of, 25, 31
    special requirements in North,
        25–26, 93–94

trees, 134–135
    weed control with, 91, 132

New England
    northern, 4
    southern, 4
New York, 4
Nuts. *See under* Trees and tree crops

Oats, 97, 209–210
Onions, 88, 90, 107

Parsnips
    culture and varieties, 107
    in raised beds, 90
    mulching, 93
    thinning, 88
Pears, 36, 38, 126, 129
Peas
    culture and varieties, 105–106
    mulching, 25, 93
    thinning, 88
Peppers
    culture and varieties, 117–119 (*ill.*,
        118)
    in hotbeds, 45
    in raised beds, 34, 90
    mulching, 25
    starting seeds, 40
Pests and pest control, 94–96, 112,
        155, 291
    See also Trees and tree crops
Plant varieties
    deceptive descriptions of, 17
    hardy, 15
Plums, 31, 36, 38, 125–126, 129
Potatoes
    culture and varieties, 108–109
    in raised beds, 34
    mulching, 25, 93–94
    spring frost protection, 35
Prairie states and provinces, 5
Preserving, 96–98 (*ill.*, 96)
    See also under Trees and tree crops
Pumpkins
    culture and varieties, 117
    in raised beds, 34
    mulching, 25
    ripening inside, 38

Radishes
    culture and varieties, 109
    in raised beds, 34, 90
    mulching, 25
    thinning, 88
Raspberries, 15, 151, 156–160 (*ill.*, 157)

Rhubarb, 15, 197–198
Ripening vegetables inside, 38
Root cellaring. *See under* Preserving
Root-pruning, 218–219 (*ill.*, 219)
Roses, 251–252, 259
Rye, 212

Seedlings, 85–86
Seeds: saving your own, 83–85
Seeds: selecting, 81–83
Seeds: starting indoors
  diseases and pests, 64–67
  easy species, 40
  fertilizing, 67
  flats, 59, 61–62
  in windows, 40–41 (*ill.*, 41)
  over heat pads, 43–44
  setting out plants, 69–70 (*ill.*, 70)
  timing, 60
  transplanting, 67–69 (*ill.*, 68)
  under lights, 42–43 (*ill.*, 42)
  water and temperature, 62–63
Shrubs
  best species, 253–258
  bloom succession, 248
  in landscaping, 216
  in northern climate, 15, 246
  pruning against snow damage, 14
    (*ill.*)
  road salt damage, 260–261
  See also Landscaping; Lilacs; Roses
Snow and ice
  benefits of, 13
  dangers of, 13–14
  early melting, 78–80 (*ill.*, 79)
  protection from, 22
Snow traps, 278–280 (*ill.*, 279)
Soils and growing media, 58–59, 69, 78,
    91
Spinach
  culture and varieties, 111
  in raised beds, 34, 90
  in indoor garden, 101
  location in garden, 86
  mulching, 25, 93
Spring frosts
  dangers of, 7–8
  protection against, 35–37, 70–72
    (*ills.*, 71, 72), 165–166, 264–265
Squash
  culture and varieties, 117
  in raised beds, 34
  mulching, 25
  spring frost protection, 35
Strawberries
  31, 36, 161–168, (*ills.*, 163, 164, 167)

Sunscald, 10, 143–144
"Super-water," 63–64

Tomatoes
  culture and varieties, 117–118, 120
    (*ill.*)
  in hot beds, 45
  in raised beds, 34, 90
  mulching, 25
  spring frost protection, 35
  starting seeds, 40, 68 (*ill.*)
Transplanting, 67
Trees and tree crops
  cider, 146 (*ill.*)
  frost damage, 36, 140–143
  grafted trees, 121–122, 129, 227–228
  hardy varieties, 122
  in northern climate, 15
  location of orchard, 129–131 (*ill.*, 130)
  nuts, 185, 186
  pests, 135–137
  picking, 135, 145–146
  planting trees, 131–132, 142 (*ill.*)
  preserving, 147–149
  pruning, 132–134 (*ill.*, 133), 137–138
    (*ill.*, 137)
  road salt damage, 223–225 (*ill.*, 223)
  snow and ice damage, 14, 144–145
    (*ill.*, 145), 236 (*ill.*)
  sunscald, 143–144
  thinning fruit, 138–140 (*ill.*, 139)
  See also Apples; Landscaping; Pears;
    Plums; and nut species, by name
Turnips
  culture and varieties, 109
  in indoor garden, 101
  in raised beds, 90
  mulching, 25, 93
  thinning, 88

Vines, hardy
  best species, 298–300 (*ill.*, 299)
  uses, 297–298 (*ill.*, 297)

Walnuts, 185, 186, 190–191 (*ill.*, 190)
Watering. *See under* Gardening
Weeds, 33, 91–92, 132, 155, 165
Wheat, 206–208
Wind, 11
Windbreaks, 22, 222, 278–280 (*ill.*, 279)
Windburn, 11, 235–236

Zones. *See under* Climate, planting
  zones.